THE CAPITALIST U

THE CAPITALIST
UNCONSCIOUS

MARX AND LACAN

SAMO TOMŠIČ

VERSO
London • New York

First published by Verso 2015
© Samo Tomšič 2015

1 3 5 7 9 10 8 6 4 2

Verso
UK: 6 Meard Street, London W1F 0EG
US: 20 Jay Street, Suite 1010, Brooklyn, NY 11201
www.versobooks.com

Verso is the imprint of New Left Books

ISBN-13: 978-1-78478-108-8 (PB)
ISBN-13: 978-1-78478-111-8 (HC)
eISBN-13: 978-1-78478-110-1 (US)
eISBN-13: 978-1-78478-109-5 (UK)

British Library Cataloguing in Publication Data
A catalogue record for this book is available from the British Library

Library of Congress Cataloging-in-Publication Data
Tomšič, Samo.
[Kapitalisticno nezavedno. English]
The capitalist unconscious : Marx and Lacan / Samo Tomsic.
pages cm
ISBN 978-1-78478-108-8 (paperback) – ISBN 978-1-78478-111-8 (hardback)
– ISBN 978-1-78478-110-1 (US) – ISBN 978-1-78478-109-5 (UK)
1. Marx, Karl, 1818-1883. 2. Lacan, Jacques, 1901–1981. 3. Psychoanalysis. 4.
Capitalism. 5. Consciousness. I. Title.
HX39.5.T55513 2015
335.4'12–dc23
2015027998

Typeset in Minion Pro by Hewer Text UK Ltd, Edinburgh, Scotland
Printed in the UK by CPI Mackays

Contents

Acknowledgements

I would like to thank to my friends and colleagues who have contributed to the preparation of this volume with their readings, discussions and feedback: Pietro Bianchi, Chiara Bottici, Nathaniel Boyd, Andrew Cole, Jodi Dean, Katja Diefenbach, Michael Friedman, Dominiek Hoens, Sami Khatib, Gal Kirn, Peter Klepec, Boštjan Nedoh, Benjamin Noys, Ozren Pupovac, Rado Riha, Eric Santner, Aaron Schuster, Dubravka Sekulić, Jan Sieber, Olivier Surel, Jelica Šumič, Tzuchien Tho, Dorothea Walzer, Mai Wegener and Andreja Zevnik.

The work on the book began during my postdoctoral research at the Humboldt University in Berlin (2011–13) sponsored by the Alexander von Humboldt Foundation (Bonn). I am most grateful to Professor Joseph Vogl, who has welcomed me at the Institute for German Literature and supported my research in the most generous way.

The preparation of this volume is most indebted to Mladen Dolar, Alenka Zupančič and Slavoj Žižek, whose work remains a major inspiration for me.

Finally my greatest thanks go to Jenny Nachtigall for her invaluable personal and intellectual support.

Introduction:
Lacan's Second Return to Freud

Don't expect anything more subversive in my discourse than that I do not claim to have a solution.

Jacques Lacan, *The Other Side of Psychoanalysis*

Karl Marx is just one of the many theorists referred to in Jacques Lacan's teachings. Other classic thinkers seem to have left a much deeper mark on his work, notably Plato, Descartes and Hegel. Why then, among such an abundance of influences, should one privilege Marx? Is it in order to make Lacan yet another representative of the Freudo-Marxist orientation, a tradition marked by a rather failed endeavour to ground radical politics on the liberation of desire? Or is the aim simply to turn Lacan into a leftist thinker?

Such an attempt is, of course, immediately countered by a wealth of biographical trivia and more or less trustworthy anecdotes regarding Lacan's political preferences, which, it is said, inclined towards Charles de Gaulle's conservatism.[1] We should also mention his notoriously ambiguous reaction to the student and worker uprisings in the late 1960s. While figures such as Jean-Paul Sartre, Michel Foucault, Gilles Deleuze, Felix Guattari and many others of comparable stature strongly identified with the promise of a communist revolution, Lacan went against the intellectual current and labelled himself a liberal. Moreover, he portrayed the students as hysterics who demanded a new master; he reduced the political definition of revolution to its astronomical meaning of circular movement and finally argued that the student demands were merely manifesting the transformation of capitalism into a 'market of knowledge' or, to recall the formula that

---

1   The present book leaves aside the broader biographical context and explores merely the theoretical potential of Lacan's engagement with Marx's critique of political economy. The best and most exhaustive intellectual biography remains Elisabeth Roudinesco, *Jacques Lacan*, New York: Columbia University Press, 1999.

may today already sound anachronistic, 'knowledge society'.[2] All these consciously controversial statements make Lacan appear more like a prede- cessor of the *nouveaux philosophes* than a revolutionary thinker.

In addition to these episodes, the various reservations against reading Lacan as a thinker whose ideas were consonant with Marx's were best taken up by the man himself. He saw the most subversive aspect of his teaching in the fact that he did not pretend to have a solution for social antagonisms. Indeed, among Lacanian psychoanalysts, one often encoun- ters a restraint in discussing political matters, a peculiar distance that often drifts into cynicism[3] and seeks legitimacy in Lacan's ambiguous remarks on revolutionary movements. Hence the inevitable question: if psycho- analysis recurrently appears as a form of sophistry that relativises the scope of leftist political struggles and questions their resistance to capital- ist forms of exploitation, then why argue for its continued political relevance? Why associate Lacan's structural psychoanalysis with Marx's critique of political economy, which provides, and on this point at least both its supporters and opponents agree, the paradigmatic case of a discourse that claims to have a solution?

Lacan's teaching is generally associated with its famous motto of a 'return to Freud'. In the following pages I argue that in the late 1960s Lacan initiated a second return to Freud, in which the reference to structural linguistics (particularly Saussure and Jakobson) was supplemented with Marx's critique of political economy. This development inevitably led to a radicalisation of the structuralist research programme and also a rejection of the stereotypes that public opinion, on the Left as well as on the Right, formed about Marx and Freud and their methods, concepts and goals. Some leftist voices would probably claim that psychoanalysis prospers only in the capitalist universe and even that it was historically invented to be nothing more than a class-therapy, serving the mental well-being of the

---

2   See P. F. Drucker, *The Age of Discontinuity: Guidelines to Our Changing Society*, London: Heinemann, 1969, notably part four. For a critique of the capitalist commodification of knowledge, see J. Lacan, *Le Séminaire, livre XVI, D'un Autre à l'autre*, Paris: Seuil, 2006, 39, and *Seminar, Book XVII, The Other Side of Psychoanalysis*, New York: Norton, 2007, 32. Whether Lacan was aware of Drucker's work remains debatable, but his reading of the university discourse in connection with capitalism in many ways echoes the central themes of Drucker's book.

3   For a condensed but well-pointed critical account of 'psychoanalytic politics', see S. Žižek, *Less than Nothing*, London: Verso, 2012, 967–71.

bourgeoisie.⁴ Such critiques could easily find theoretical support in Foucault, Deleuze and Guattari, who, despite their philosophical differences, strived to show that several psychoanalytic currents actively contribute to the normalisation of desire and thereby openly reproduce capitalist forms of domination. Neurotisation of desire, reduction of psychic conflicts to the Oedipal triangle of Father-Mother-Child, as Deleuze and Guattari have insisted,⁵ is the paradigmatic case of an ideological operation that maintains desire in the capitalist–patriarchal order. We nevertheless have to acknowledge that Lacan insistently countered these criticisms, for instance by demonstrating the mythical status of the Oedipus complex in Freud's theories and by dethroning the infamous primacy of the phallus – which the critiques of Freud continue to reduce to its anatomical signification, thereby reproducing the vulgarised version of Freudianism, which has barely anything in common with the epistemic complexity of Freudian and Lacanian psychoanalysis.

There are also the voices of free-market ideologists, cognitive-behavioural therapists and neuroscientists, who immediately recognise in psychoanalysis a time- and money-consuming practice, incapable of providing society, that is, the demands of the market, with what it requires: an adaptable and flexible workforce. So while for the leftists all psychoanalysis does is normalise, for neoliberals it never normalises enough and should therefore be abolished. In opposition to these two options, the guideline of the present book will be that psychoanalysis remains a symptomatic point, both epistemologically and politically speaking, that offers a particular critical insight into the production of capitalist subjectivity.

As for Marx, his work is often criticized as being at once utopian and disastrous. Marx is said to have composed something equivalent to a gospel that, in its endeavour to dissolve the capitalist mode of production, also promises the abolition of *all* forms of social antagonism. One often encounters the notion that Marx called for unmediated and authentic human

---

4   The most exhaustive historical account of the ups and downs of the relations between Marxism and psychoanalysis remains H. Dahmer, *Libido und Gesellschaft*, Frankfurt am Main: Suhrkamp Verlag, 1982, in particular 241ff., where the author analyses the motives for the Marxist resistance to Freud's theories.

5   G. Deleuze and F. Guattari, *L'Anti-Oedipe*, Paris: Minuit, 1972. Of course, Deleuze and Guattari remained consistently ambiguous in their criticism of psychoanalysis. There is no doubt that their privileged target is its institutionalised version, the International Psychoanalytic Association, and its successful integration of Freudian discoveries and therapeutic goals into the free-market ideology.

relations, the association of free men mentioned in *Capital* but left unexplained, and hence for the elimination of all possible variants of subjective and social alienation. This is how both humanist Marxists and psychoanalysts (first and foremost Freud) perceived Marx's critical project.[6] That said, we could certainly claim that Marx never intended to elaborate a communist worldview and that speculation about the future social order did not belong in his mature critical work. In addition to this, *Capital* openly refutes the conventional reading of the 11th thesis on Feuerbach, the opposition of theory and practice, interpretation and revolutionary change.

Marx's critical project repeatedly shows that the passage from interpretation to political action involves a move from the production of philosophical, political and religious worldviews – which, as Freud would later mockingly claim, spend their time filling in the gaps of reality – to a materialist interpretation that, in quite the opposite fashion, uncovers the very gaps that existing worldviews strive to foreclose.[7] By detecting these structural gaps, the materialist method provides a rigorous understanding of *logical* relations that support the capitalist social link, thereby also detecting the structural disclosure that enables one to address the question of change. It is precisely at this point that Lacan intervenes in the debates regarding Marx's epistemological and political coordinates, proposing a structuralist reading that implies a much more unorthodox, albeit no less politically radical, Marx.

Psychoanalysis is neither gospel nor worldview, and the departure for Lacan's reading of Marx is that his critique of political economy should not be treated as an epic tale of the historic necessity of communism either. Nor is it a vitalist attempt to liberate living labour from the vampirism of capital. Marx's gothic metaphor of the ghostly negativity of capital versus the creative potential of living labour is misleading. Recall that the critique of political economy begins with an examination of value, containing a rigorous logic; it could even be considered the most Hegelian part of *Capital*, a condensed Marxian equivalent to the *Science of Logic*. The analysis of the value-form indicates that Marx locates the revolutionary potential not so much in a specific consciousness, that of the working class, but in a

---

6   Freud carefully touches the Marxist 'worldview' in his *New Introductory Lectures on Psychoanalysis* (1933). His reservations will be examined in the second chapter.

7   For a critical reading of Marx's *Theses on Feuerbach*, see P. Macherey, *Marx 1845. Les 'thèses' sur Feuerbach*, Paris: Éditions Amsterdam, 2008, notably 229–32.

structural negativity, labour-power, which occupies the place where the contradictions of the capitalist mode of production are brought together. At the same time, the appearance of capital is associated with a vitalist fantasy, 'money-breeding money', in which psychoanalysis helps us to discern the fictional hypothesis of a subject without negativity. Marx's mature critical project most incontestably intersects with psychoanalysis at the point when it reintroduces negativity *qua* subject into what appears as the purely vitalist and autonomous machinery of capital, expressed in its presumed power to 'bring forth living offspring' or to 'lay golden eggs'.[8] Marx thus continuously moves on two different but intimately related levels, that of the *logic of production*, which explains how the abstract and seemingly neutral relations between values support and reproduce concrete social antagonisms, and that of the *logic of fantasy*, which examines the reproduction of objective appearances, whose function is to repress, distort and mystify the existing structural contradictions. The logic of production and the logic of fantasy are the two basic components of Marx's notion of critique.

Only by reintroducing the negativity that capitalism simultaneously produces and forecloses – there is no capitalist mode of production without labour-power as a source of value, but there is also no capitalist fetishisation of social relations without the foreclosure of labour-power – can the critical project succeed in uncovering the logical paradoxes that are the necessary precondition for thinking social change and for the production of a new subjectivity that no longer depends on the abstract universality of the value-form. This means, then, that Marx's localisation of labour-power in the general structure of the capitalist mode of production unfolds a theory of the subject. For Lacan the logical, and even homological, response to this subjectivised negativity is the subject of the unconscious. The analysis of the structural deadlocks of capitalism, Marx's central effort in *Capital*, is thus necessarily accompanied by a new – de-psychologised and de-individualised – understanding of the subject. With these two features Marx, as Althusser has insisted,[9] rejected

---

8   K. Marx, *Capital*, Vol. 1, London: Penguin Books, 1992, 255.

9   L. Althusser, *Pour Marx*, Paris: Maspero, 1965, 235–6. According to Althusser, Marx abolished the category of 'man' as the main theoretical ground of (the critique of) political economy. Lacan pursued this Althusserian line by introducing the subject of the unconscious, thereby proposing a psychoanalytic version of 'theoretical anti-humanism', yet one which moved away from Althusser, who rejected the notion of the subject.

the humanist and the cognitive comprehension of the subject, distinguishing between subjectivity that is still embedded in the empiricist theories of cognition and in various, essentially idealist worldviews, on the one hand, and the subject that is implied by the autonomy of exchange-value, on the other. A materialist theory of the subject rejects both empiricism and idealism, which come together in their efforts to reduce subjectivity to consciousness.

One of the foundations of Marx's critique is precisely the autonomy of value, which operates in every 'innocent' act of exchange. When Marx departs from the gap between the use-value and the exchange-value that determines the double character of commodities – he in fact anticipates the main achievement of structuralism: the isolation of the system of differences. Furthermore, this autonomy is envisaged as the terrain where the change that would destabilise and potentially abolish capitalism needs to be thought. The change of the mode of production is in the last instance a structural displacement in the organisation of production. The notion of the subject finds its place in this precise context. Far from rejecting it as a mere bourgeois category, Marx's critique of the subject provides the necessary tools to differentiate between the (economic, political, juridical and cognitive) *fiction* of the subject and the *real* subject of politics. If the former is criticised as abstraction, the latter is revealed as negativity, so that the *tension between abstraction and negativity* is the kernel of a materialist theory of the subject. The Marxian lesson is here entirely univocal: the subject of cognition (including Lukács's notion of class-*consciousness*) cannot be the subject of politics. On the contrary, the subject of politics that a materialist critique can only be decentralised, de-individualised and de-psychologised. Lacan enters at this point by stressing the epistemologically and politically subversive potential of the critique of political economy in the claim that it was none other than Marx who invented the notion of the symptom.

That Marx was the first theoretician of the symptom implies that the proletariat *is* the subject of the unconscious. This means that the proletariat designates more than an empirical social class. It expresses the universal subjective position in capitalism. But as a symptom, that is, as a formation through which the repressed truth of the existing social order is reinscribed in the political space, the proletariat entails a rejection of the false and abstract universalism imposed by capitalism, namely the universalism of commodity form. With the shift from the proletarian seen simply as an empirical subject to the subject of the unconscious, the notion and the reality of class struggle also appears in a different light. It no longer signifies merely a conflict of actually existing social classes but the manifestation of structural contradictions in social *and* subjective reality, thereby assuming the same epistemological-political status as the unconscious. Neither class struggle nor the unconscious stands for some invariable transhistorical essences – their entire 'consistency' lies in the distortion of appearances that accompany the reproduction of the given order.

Marx and Lacan reject the simple opposition between negativity and positivity, dead and living labour, abstract structure and concrete experience, structure and genesis. The failure of Freudo-Marxism and other attempts to free the creative potential of unconscious desire and of living labour suggests the conclusion that capital *is* creative potential, that capital *is* Life, and that capitalism *is* a specific form of vitalism. Of course, this does not imply that every vitalism should be denounced as being, in the last instance, a vitalism of capital. It merely strives to problematise the simple and all too comfortable opposition of the 'bad' negativity, alienation and lack of being, on the one hand, and the 'good' positivity, creative potential and fullness of being, on the other. The dynamics and adaptability of capital – its capacity to mystify, distort and repress subjective and social antagonisms, assimilating symptomatic or subversive identities and so on – sufficiently indicates that capital should be understood as *life without negativity*, or more precisely, that the efficiency and the logic of capitalism is supported by a fantasy of such life, subjectivity and society. With regard to this vitalist fantasy, Marx's critique of fetishism turns out to be more than a mere philosophical curiosity in the entirety of *Capital*, since it targets precisely the hypothesis of the inherent creative potential of the three central capitalist abstractions: commodity, money and capital. The critique of fetishism *is* the critique of capitalist vitalism, of vitalism as a spontaneous capitalist philosophy.[10] If we recall Marx's enumeration of the four fundamental concepts of economic liberalism – freedom, equality, property and 'Bentham' (private interest) – we again encounter the fantasy of a subjectivity and society without negativity, notably without class struggle, this principal Marxian name for the negativity that traverses society and the subject.

Freudo-Marxism's most visible representatives, Wilhelm Reich and Herbert Marcuse, seem to have walked into a similar vitalist trap. In their

---

10   I rely here on Benjamin Noys's ongoing project 'Anti-Life'.

respective readings, they adopted the opposition between drives and culture that echoes in Freud's late dichotomy of Eros and Thanatos. Based on Freud's cultural writings, they declared sexuality the privileged terrain of emancipatory struggle and opposed its creative vitality, its 'polymorphous perversion' to the cultural tendencies, to normalisation and notably to the commodity form as the general agency of capitalist normalisation.[11] Freudo-Marxism thus amounted to what Michel Foucault rightly criticised as the 'repressive hypothesis',[12] a hypothesis that seduced even Deleuze and Guattari in their critique of psychoanalysis. The minimal common ground between Freudo-Marxism and schizo-analysis could be seen in the idea that the efficiency of capitalism is rooted in the repression of sexuality, the inhibition of drives and the neurotisation of desire. Social oppression is equated with psychic mechanisms of repression, the class conflict becomes an external form of psychic conflict, while libidinal energy is channelled into the restrictive mechanisms of the capitalist mode of production and subjected to alienation (castration and commodification). Here we should recall that Freudo-Marxist interpretations focused predominantly on Freud's 'second topic' (id, ego, superego), in which a problematic substantialisation of the unconscious, by means of rather speculative biological metaphors, phylogenetic fantasies, and most importantly by the energetic model of the psychic apparatus, indicate the possibility of a more vitalist version of psychoanalysis.[13]

With the failure of the Freudo-Marxist attempt to ground politics on sexual liberation in mind, it is not surprising that Lacan decidedly rejected direct translations of psychoanalytic contents into Marxist contents. He instead accentuated their logical affinity, thereby taking a necessary step back to the common epistemological ground of psychoanalysis and the critique of political economy. By placing the accent on logic, Lacan also

---

11   Marcuse's *Eros and Civilization* (Boston: Beacon Press, 1966 [1955]) remains the most accomplished document of this direction. For a critical account of Marcuse's reading of Freud, see J. Laplanche, *Le primat de l'autre en psychanalyse*, Paris: Flammarion, 1997, 59–88.

12   M. Foucault, *The Will to Knowledge*, London: Penguin Books, 1998, 17.

13   The question of Freud's biologism and vitalism is surely more complex. The introduction of the death drive, which visibly shocked the psychoanalytic community, suggests that Freud never abolished the speculative line, in which the discussion of negativity plays an important part in the theory of libido. An exhaustive critical reading of Freud's biologism can be found in J. Laplanche, *Le fourvoiement biologisant de la sexualité chez Freud*, Paris: Presses Universitaires de France, 2006.

relativised the expectation that Marxism and psychoanalysis contain a corpus of positive knowledge that could potentially lead to a new political worldview.

The dialectics of Marx's *Capital* sufficiently shows that the revolutionary character of critique is not in the promise of such a worldview but in its method, in the analysis of structural relations that sustain the apparent universality of commodity form and the fantasmatic vitalism of capitalist abstractions. And if Marx's political project indeed contains a 'communist hypothesis',[14] then the term 'hypothesis' should be read in pair with Newton's *hypothesis non fingo*. Why? Because the communist hypothesis, grounded on a materialist science of value, most certainly does not assume the same status as the pseudoscientific hypotheses of political economy: the fetishist hypothesis of the vital forces of capital, the liberal hypothesis of the homeostatic and self-regulatory nature of the market (Adam Smith's 'invisible hand') or the hypothesis of the capitalist social relation founded on abstract freedom and equality, and supplemented with property and private interest. The communist hypothesis assumes a different status and is inscribed in the epistemological horizon of scientific modernity, on which Marx strived to ground his science of value and his critical method. This inscription can be demonstrated in the way materialist dialectics approaches social reality. It uncovers the immanent breaks in existing social appearances, thereby repeating the way modern science uses the mathematical apparatus in order to grasp the real of physical appearances.[15] The dialectical materialist method, following modern epistemic ideals, discerns the structural real, which amounts to Marx's central hypothesis in *Capital*: there is no such thing as social *relation*.[16] Or to quote *The Communist Manifesto*,

---

14   A. Badiou, *The Communist Hypothesis*, London: Verso, 2010.

15   The main point is that the real explored by modern science is non-empirical and that its procedures are not centred on the 'human observer'. Alexandre Koyré, whose readings of scientific modernity were Lacan's main epistemological reference, emphasised this autonomy of mathematical formalisation throughout his work.

16   The axiom 'There is no such thing as social relation' should not mislead us in drawing the neoliberal conclusion 'There is no such thing as society' (Thatcher). Quite the contrary – there is society albeit without an underlying social relation; whereas for neoliberals there is only social relation (supported by the already mentioned freedom of the market, equality in exchange, the right to private property and the realisation of private interests) but without society.

'the history of all hitherto existing society is the history of class struggles', which means, first and foremost, that History does not exist. The
plurality of class struggles reveals the decentralisation of history in the
same way as the unconscious exposes the decentralisation of thinking.
Capital also contains a critical epistemology, which problematises the
mobilisation of scientific methods and knowledge in the historical
transformation of labour, in the genesis of capitalist social abstractions
and in the introduction of two new figures of negativity in the social
link: labour-power and surplus-value. It is in these that Lacan will
recognise his subject of the signifier and object *a*.

Freud summarised the movement of modern scientific revolution in
three major insults to human narcissism, linked with three scientific decentralisations: of the universe (Copernicus, but one should rather say
Newton), of life (Darwin/Wallace) and finally of thinking (Freud). He
thereby undoubtedly indicated that the discovery of the unconscious – a
specific manifestation of negativity, a form of knowledge without the
subject of cognition, and finally a real discursive consequence – is made
possible only in the horizon of modern science. More precisely, the Freudian
theory of the unconscious becomes possible only once the consequences of
modern scientific revolution have already been extended to the field of
human production – in short, after Marx's 'epistemological break', as
Althusser would have put it.

Scientific revolution as a process that enables us to think the function
and the place of negativity in the social link became the basis for the structuralist coupling of Marx with Freud already in Althusser, who undoubtedly
inspired Lacan's interest in the critique of political economy. Althusser was
the first one to associate Marx systematically with the structuralist program,
insisting that, by thinking negativity in history and thought, Marx and
Freud subverted the very notion of science. Althusser described psychoanalysis and the critique of political economy as 'conflictual sciences'.[17]
Their antagonistic character comes from the fact that they both depart
from the 'persistence of the negative'[18] in the social and subjective sphere,
rather than from its foreclosure. In this light, alienation also appears as
constitutive of the subject and of society, a process that no longer stands
merely for deprivation but also and above all for transformation. One of the

17   L. Althusser, *Écrits sur la psychoanalyse*, Paris: Stock/IMEC, 1993, 226.

18   B. Noys, *The Persistence of the Negative: A Critique of Contemporary Continental Theory*, Edinburgh: Edinburgh University Press, 2012.

main points in Lacan's reading of Marx lies in the attempt to overcome the opposition between vitalist positivity and dialectical negativity by reinterpreting the very concept of alienation.

To repeat, the present book starts from the assumption that the reference to Marx signifies an important development in Lacan's teaching and inaugurates a second return to Freud that displaces the accent from structural linguistics to critique of political economy, and from the representation of the subject to the production of *jouissance*. *Jouissance* (enjoyment, or what Freud called libido) thereby reappears as the central problem of psychoanalysis; this was already the case with Freud, but it was systematically neglected in the progressive subordination of psychoanalysis to the ideals and demands of economic liberalism, through which the adaptation and reintegration of individuals into the existing social order became the main goal of analytic treatment. *Jouissance* does not only offer a privileged entry into the political importance of Freudian theory, it also reveals a limit of classical structuralism: to think the subject and the object that are produced by the autonomy of the signifier.

We should recall that Freud's discovery of the unconscious places the main accent on the role of labour (*Arbeit*) in the satisfaction of the unconscious tendency (desire or drive) and that it constantly uncovers the productive dimension of the unconscious. This reference to labour should be taken literally. By placing the energetic notion of labour-power at the core of his discoveries Freud outlined a *labour theory of the unconscious*.[19] Lacan's main point of interest in the late 1960s evolves around this important aspect in Freud's theory. In the concept of *jouissance*, Lacan brings together Freudian 'psychic energy' (libido) and the notion of unconscious labour. In order to fully determine the revolutionary character of Freud's discoveries, a theory of production was needed, a theory that Saussurean structuralism could not offer. But Marx did.

---

19 This is also the main difference between his understanding of the unconscious and the philosophical notion of 'unclear representation' or the Jungian 'collective unconscious'.

CHAPTER 1

'The Unconscious Is Politics':
From Saussure to Marx

STRUCTURE AND HISTORY

1963 marks a considerable shift in Lacan's teaching. It is the year of the infamous 'excommunication' from the International Psychoanalytic Association. In response Lacan created the École freudienne de Paris, which was meant to make an important institutional and doctrinal break with the official guardians of the Freudian legacy. The school was founded with the objective of constituting an organism

> where a labour is to be accomplished – a labour, which, in the field opened up by Freud, renews its sharp razor of truth, – a labour, which accompanies the original praxis he introduced under the name of psychoanalysis in the task that it has in our world, – a labour, which, through a persistent critique, denounces the deviations and compromises that impede its progress by degrading its use.[1]

Such a foundational act does not conceal its political dimension, which consists notably in the attempt to render the subversive political, philosophical and epistemological dimension of psychoanalysis. The deviations and compromises that traverse the history of psychoanalysis concern particularly the successful combination of its practice with the free market economy, a combination that Lacan already denounced on several other occasions.[2] According to the famous anecdote, Freud supposedly said to

---

1   J. Lacan, *Autres écrits*, Paris: Seuil, 2001, 229. See also J. Lacan, *Television: A Challenge to the Psychoanalytic Establishment*, New York: Norton, 1990, 97.

2   To quote an exemplary passage where Lacan also recalls that the critical kernel of his return to Freud consists in the return to the constitution of the subject through alienation (initially addressed in the concept of the mirror stage and later in the notion of barred subject): 'I won't go back over the function of my "mirror

Jung during their visit to the United States (1909) that Americans are not aware him and Jung were bringing them the plague.[3] In turn, Freud in his enthusiasm remained ignorant for the fact that American capitalism already possessed an antidote against this continental disease. This antidote was nothing other than the ideology of economic liberalism. Freedom, equality, property and private interest, this efficient ideological junction of political universalities with private egoism, or 'human narcissism', as Freud would likely have put it, successfully neutralised the radicality of psychoanalytic insights into the nature of thinking, subjectivity and society. The price for the psychoanalytic success story in the land of opportunities was high and led to the oblivion of the critical truth that Freud revealed in his discovery of the unconscious, the interdependency of subjectivation and alienation.

According to Lacan's founding act, the main task of the school was to open up the space where labour could finally become a process, in which critique and truth would intertwine. The labour in question is not merely theoretical but even more so the labour that Freud attributed to the unconscious. This form of labour comprises an inquiry into the processes that have determined the subject's mode of existence and accompany it to the point of transformation. What matters for Lacan is 'not a long list but determined workers'.[4] He offers his return to Freud as an example of such labour, which may sound pretentious but in fact contains a rejection of any attempt that would want to ground the psychoanalytic institution on transference. The latter may hold the psychoanalytic community together but for the price of transforming it into a Church – hence Lacan's reference to the excommunication of Spinoza.

There is one crucial reason why transference must be removed from the foundations of the school (and, homologically, from the party). By

---

stage" here, the first strategic point I developed as an objection to the supposedly "autonomous ego" in favor in psychoanalytic theory, whose academic restoration justified the mistaken proposal to strengthen the ego in a type of treatment diverted thereafter towards successful adaptation – a phenomenon of mental abdication tied to the aging of the psychoanalytic group in the Diaspora owing to the war, and the reduction of an eminent practice to a *Good Housekeeping* seal of approval attesting to its suitability to the "American way of life". J. Lacan, *Écrits*, New York: Norton, 2006, 684–5.

3   The anecdote comes from an exchange between Lacan and Jung. See Lacan, *Écrits*, 336.

4   Lacan, *Autres écrits*, 233.

grounding the institution on the production of positive knowledge rather than on critical truth (the 'sharp razor'), it displaces the accent from the subject of the unconscious to the subject of cognition. As we know, Lacan's institutional experiment later failed, and various subsequent formations all restored the more orthodox type of institutional politics. In 1980, the school would be ultimately dissolved as it had regressed back to the transference relation, even if Lacan had consistently rejected identification with the position of the master:

> Fortunately, I never said I was the Freudian School . . . I do not take myself for the subject of knowledge. The proof lies in the fact . . . that I invented the subject supposed to know, so that psychoanalysts would stop believing, I mean identifying with it.[5]

The school not only strived to abolish the difference between Lacan and the analytic community, but even more so between the analysts and the analysands. When analysts are no longer identified with knowledge, they are deprived of their meta-position, which is always-already a position of domination. In this respect, the subject supposed to know is a critical invention, which offers deeper insight into the phenomenon of transference within and without the psychoanalytic context. Transference inevitably contains a moment of fetishisation, through which knowledge is projected onto the other and turned into an intrinsic and positive quality. In distinctive contrast to this scenario, Lacan maintained that, in relation to his audience and to the analytic community, he assumed the position of the analysand, where the opposite figure of knowledge and of the subject is at work: the unconscious and the subject of the signifier. Of course transference cannot be eliminated from this relation, which is why Lacan emphasised the importance of formalisation in the transmission of knowledge and truth. Only logics can successfully mediate in the opposition of two concurrent forms of transmission, the one grounded on *philia*, transference love, which would be the 'philosophical' transmission, still presupposing the figure of the master; and the other grounded on the autonomy of discourse (e.g., the formal language of mathematics), which would ideally constitute a community that does not gravitate around a master-figure. The separation of transmission from the speaker's position of enunciation prevents the analyst from identifying with the subject of

---

5   J. Lacan, 'Lumiere!', *Ornicar?*, 21–2, 1981, 8–9.

knowledge and believing to possess some substantial knowledge of the unconscious. Transmission through formalisation abolishes the idea of a dogmatic corpus that all the members of the school should uncritically adopt. It designates a labour process, in which Lacan is one among many subjects of labour, a case of the determined worker, whose aim is not to produce knowledge but to support the 'transfer of labour'.[6] Transmission enables determined workers to overcome the frames of their singular case and pass over to universality (community). A case becomes the point from which a universal can be *constructed*. Such a constructible universal is no pregiven abstraction that subsumes particular cases but a singular universal. It demands labour – hence the 'transfer of labour', the intimate connection between labour, formalisation and transmission. We can observe more generally here the importance of what Freud already called *Durcharbeiten*, working through, in the analytic context.

After the excommunication we can also speak of Lacan's second return to Freud. This return is marked by the change of theoretical alliances and, consequently, by a significant reinterpretation of previous teaching. The first return famously read Freud with structural linguistics and culminated in the claim that Freud's theories anticipated the Saussurean and Jakobsonian theory of language. Metonymy and metaphor, the two central operations in language, are discovered in the way the unconscious processes manipulate the conscious and the preconscious material. The two linguistic operations translate into condensation and displacement, the main achievements of unconscious labour. The linguistic return to Freud became a synonym for Lacan's structural psychoanalysis, and the most condensed formula of this early development, 'The unconscious is structured like a language', has since turned into a common doxa.

After the excommunication, Lacan progressively elaborated an alternative reading of the Freudian discovery that found its new privileged alliance in Marx's critique of political economy. The move away from the linguistic paradigm was accomplished immediately after May '68, though these political events were not the only circumstance that contributed to the reorientation of the return to Freud. The move towards the critical paradigm was not unrelated to the limits of structuralism, notably in respect to the theorisation of unconscious production and the growing weight given to the problem of *jouissance* in Lacan's teaching.

6   Lacan, *Autres écrits*, 236.

Nevertheless, Lacan's second return to Freud did not simply deny the importance of the structuralist isolation of the signifier:

> With Saussure and the Prague linguistic circle linguistics is constituted on a cut, which is the bar placed between the signifier and the signified in order to expose the difference, on which the signifier is constituted in an absolute way, and through which it effectively obtains its autonomy.[7]

Linguistic structuralism begins with the recognition of the autonomy of the signifier and with the minimalism of structure. Saussure starts from the bar between the signifier and the signified that enables him to isolate both constitutive components of the linguistic sign and expose the arbitrary nature of their relation. We can recall that the bar in question does not aim at the external relation between words and things but at the internal consistency of linguistic signs. It thus designates the absence of any substantial, essential or immanent link between the two components, which implies that the relation between the signifier (the series of sounds) and the signified (the associated mental representation) is actually a non-relation: an instable, shifting and groundless link. Saussure thereby exposes the structuring function of the bar and conceives the autonomy of the signifier, independent from its association to the signified and even more so from its relation to the referent, the element of external reality. The underlying thesis of this structural minimalism can also be formulated as follows: *the structure is a cut*. This reformulation takes into account one of the most famous Saussurean metaphors, where the process of structuration is interpreted as an intervention, which orders the undifferentiated and chaotic flux of sounds and mental images. What is crucial here is that the cut can be considered both a case of difference and something that lies in the very foundation of differentiation.[8]

The Saussurean signifier is thus constituted in an absolute and autonomous way *as* a difference to another signifier, and hence as difference in itself. The signifying chain, this most general and formal representation of linguistic structure, contains a repetition of the cut, thereby forming a chain of pure differences or negativities. The revolutionary character of structural linguistics lies in the fact that it no longer theorises language

---

7   Ibid., 403–4.
8   See F. de Saussure, *Course in General Linguistics*, New York: The Philosophical Library, 1959, 112. For the general introduction of the bar, see ibid., 66–7.

on the assumption of stable and univocal referentiality, be it external or internal, but rather through the cut, pointing towards a non-relation and instability between the two components of the sign. If an encounter between words and things, on the one hand, and between sounds and meanings, on the other, nevertheless takes place, it is inevitably contingent, in the sense that such an encounter always contains a failure and displacement, a distortion of referentiality. To repeat, the implicit thesis of structural linguistics is that *language is a non-relation rather than relation*, and Lacan's accent on the autonomy of the signifier pushes this premise in the foreground.

The bar between the signifier and the signified initiated an epistemological revolution in human sciences, because the structuralist paradigm disrupted the historical predominance of 'Aristotelianism' in linguistics and in philosophy of language. Before the emergence of structuralism, language was almost exclusively conceived in reference to Aristotle's notion of *organon*, which enabled the definition of language as a tool and an organ of communication and of social relation, an abstract convention between autonomous, rational and conscious subjects. Through the lenses of structural linguistics, language turns out to be a far more paradoxical and complex object, a system of differences that resists totalisation, and because it is untotalisable, it is both autonomous and inexistent – hence the Lacanian use of the very same bar that in Saussure separates the signifier from the signified, in order to designate the inexistence of the Other and the split of the subject.

The psychoanalytic discovery of the unconscious stands in immediate continuity with the autonomy of the signifier. One can speak of the unconscious only under the condition that language constitutes an autonomous register serving more than mere communication and having material consequences that cannot be reduced to cognitive and neurobiological processes. The necessary predisposition for the discovery of the unconscious is thus the rejection of the linguistic Aristotelianism that nowadays lives on in the analytic philosophy of language, Chomsky's linguistics and normative theories of communication such as Habermas's.

In psychoanalysis, the autonomy of the signifier obtains a different expression. From the manifestations of the unconscious, which is precisely a concretisation of linguistic autonomy, one cannot eliminate the presence of the body, the site of discursive production that contains two aspects: the production of subjectivity and the production of *jouissance*. This association of language with production renews the old philosophical problematic of causality, which led Lacan to rank the signifier among material causes – an anti-Aristotelian move within an Aristotelian vocabulary. One crucial aspect of this structural causality was thematised already in the first return to Freud, which defined the subject of the unconscious as an inevitable effect of the signifier. But only the development of the theory of discourses in the late 1960s provided the framework for the whole nexus of problems that had preoccupied psychoanalysis since its beginnings, the issues of the autonomy of the signifier, the subject of the unconscious and *jouissance*. By recognising the causality of the signifier, Lacan decisively counteracted the pragmatic tradition, which saw in language an unproblematic *immaterial and ineffective existence*. For psychoanalysis, on the contrary, language is a *material and effective inexistence*.[9]

Here the main feature of psychoanalytic materialism can be detected. Language has real consequences only as a disclosed system of negativities (signifiers as pure differences) concretised in speech through which these negativities are inscribed in the living body. Lacan's second return to Freud will designate this disclosed structure of language with the notion of *non-all*, thereby proposing yet another translation of the Saussurean bar. And, as already mentioned, in the context of structural psychoanalysis the same bar designates the alienation of the subject and the inexistence of the Other. The barred subject that the signifier represents to another signifier and the barred Other, the open system of differences, both explicate the significance of the autonomy of the signifier. But this is also the point where the limit of classical structuralism begins to show.

Lacan's second return to Freud is not unrelated to the shift that Jakobson introduced in relation to Saussure by extending the autonomy of the signifier to poetic language. In this way, Jakobson showed that the poetisation of the signifier (linguistic equivocity) should be thought in parallel with its formalisation and as an expression of its autonomy. Unlike Heidegger, for whom poetic language unveils the original 'sense of being', Jakobson accentuates in poetry the productive dimension of language, which needs to be situated beyond the relation between the signifier and the signified, in the relations between the signifiers. In this sense, Jakobson's poetics echoes Freud's discovery of the libidinal investment of the signifier. Inspired by Jakobson's developments, Lacan defines the signifier as an

---

9   See, for instance, the following riddle from *Seminar XVII*: 'What has a body and does not exist? Answer – the big Other' (Lacan, *The Other Side of Psychoanalysis*, 66).

apparatus of *jouissance*,[10] although Jakobson's linguistics does not entirely support this definition, as it restricts discursive production to the equivocity of meaning.

In his second return to Freud, Lacan did not produce any axiom that could match 'The unconscious is structured as a language', but its most fundamental point is nevertheless well encapsulated in an apparently enigmatic statement: 'The unconscious is politics'.[11] The formulation leaves no doubt that it should be read in pair with the first one. How to understand the shift from the structure of language to politics? Does Lacan simply oppose abstract structure and concrete experience? Not really. The second axiom strives to overcome the opposition of structure and politics, to which their opponents had pushed the representatives of structuralism. This abolition is most unambiguously expressed in Lacan's notorious intervention after Foucault's lecture, 'What Is an Author?' (1969). In his response, Lacan firmly rejects the claims that May '68 negated structuralism, or at least his own notion of structure, which, at this point, significantly differed from the Saussurean system of differences:

> Structuralist or not, I would like to remark that the field, which is unclearly marked by this move, does not seem to express the negation of the subject. What is addressed is the subject's dependency, which is something completely different; and notably, at the level of the return to Freud, the subject's dependency in relation to something truly elementary, what we tried to isolate with the expression 'the signifier' . . . I do not think that it is in any way legitimate to write that structures do not descend into the street, for if the May events demonstrate anything, then [they demonstrate] precisely the descent of structures in the street. The fact that this was written at the very site where this descent took place, simply shows us something that is very often, and even most often immanent to what we call the act, namely that it misrecognises itself.[12]

---

10   See notably the second lecture of *Seminar XX*, meaningfully entitled 'To Jakobson'. J. Lacan, *The Seminar, Book XX, Encore*, New York: Norton, 1999, 14.

11   To be found in the introductory lecture of the unpublished *Seminar XIV*. Lacan's statement resonates in Frederic Jameson's classic *The Political Unconscious* (London: Routledge, 1983), which inspired the title of the present book.

12   Lacan's intervention in: M. Foucault, *Dits et écrits*, Vol 1, Paris: Gallimard, 2001, 848–9. The context of Lacan's polemic was the public tension between the structuralist and the existentialist interpretation of May '68. For a detailed discussion see F. Dosse, *Histoire du structuralisme*, Vol 2, Paris: La Découverte, 1992, 147–9.

The idea of structures in the street shows that this key structuralist notion neither stands for an unproblematic and invariable system of differences nor designates the transcendentalism of the symbolic order. The descent of structure to the street is marked by an immanent break, contradiction and instability, which place the autonomy of the signifier in a different light. Lacan thus suggests that the possibility of a social change should be thought on this level because only rigorous structural analysis can explain why the revolutionary potential of the social movement, grounded on the alliance of students and workers, ended with a failure and instead contributed to the establishment of a 'new spirit of capitalism'.[13] The core of Lacan's polemic against the post-'68 critiques of structuralism concerns the notion of the subject. Various forms of subjectivity can certainly be thought, but there is one form that the social structures build on, and that is the subject that is caused by the autonomy of the discursive relations. It is on this basis that the given order determines the thinking and action, and it is also here that the subject comes to think and act against the established regime. The subject's dependency can be exposed in the way the agents of May '68 conceived their act, namely through a misunderstanding that is best seen in the graffiti: 'Structures do not march on the streets'. The agents and the supporters of May '68 opposed structure and the event, or structure and politics, and herein lay one of their key failures. Instead of thinking the events as an outburst of the structural real, they were guided by the fantasy of a pure real outside structure, thereby overlooking the fact that the demanded liberalisation, for instance of education, initiated a more direct commodification of knowledge.[14]

For Lacan, the political events demonstrated the action of structure within the concrete actions of students; on the one hand, the antagonism between the determination of the subject through structural relations; on the other, the subject's resistance to the impositions of the system. In this respect, May '68 was indeed an act. This was the case not only because a political subject manifested itself, but also because it contained a minimal shift between the place where the acting subjects – the revolutionary

---

13   L. Boltanski and E. Chiapello, *The New Spirit of Capitalism*, London: Verso, 2007.

14   De Gaulle's Ministry of Education created an experimental university in Vincennes and introduced the credit-point system, in which Lacan detected a new stage in the evolution of capitalism. The topic will be further discussed in the final chapter of this book.

students – saw themselves and the place of their actions in the general transformation of the capitalist system. The descent of structure to the street thus formulates an unambiguous thesis on the link between politics, structure and the unconscious: structural paradoxes highlighted by the logic of the signifier are directly linked to the antagonisms that traverse the established social order. And if the unconscious can be associated with politics, i.e., if political acts contain the subject of the signifier as their internal negativity, then the Freudian concept does not signify a detached and private experience but, on the contrary, provides insight into the same structural dynamic that eventually led to the destabilisation of social links. In short, political events are realisations of structural contradictions and logical formations.

'The unconscious is politics' contains a change in the notion of structure and suggests a specific understanding of the link between psychoanalysis and politics. It insists that the discovery of the unconscious entails a transformation of politics, although not in the sense that it reduces politics to unconscious complexes. Lacan leaves no doubt that 'the unconscious is politics' does not mean 'politics is unconscious'. The latter would indeed imply a psychologisation of politics, its reduction to the content of unconscious complexes. The 'is' between unconscious and politics is not reflexive. It rather concerns the formal inclusion of the subject of the unconscious in the field of politics, which, notably after Marx's critique, thinks the constitution of social links through alienation and negativity. It is therefore not surprising that Lacan's second return to Freud was guided by the effort to elaborate a theory of discourses that demonstrated the logical dependence of unconscious mechanisms on the predominant social link. Consequently, the second return to Freud did not simply equate the unconscious with the structure of language but with the structural real, the intertwining of representation and production, the two faces of the causality of the signifier. Thereby Lacan problematises the transcendentalism of the symbolic order that had marked his earlier teaching as well as the entirety of classical structuralism.

The new materialist orientation, which emphasises the real status of the unconscious, implies two seemingly opposite claims, that the structure of language is the condition of the unconscious and that the unconscious is not entirely reducible to the symbolic structure. Instead, it testifies to an ontological scandal that concerns the autonomy of the signifier as such, an autonomy that turns most real in the breakdown of structural consistency (e.g., traumatism in Freud). The more language withdraws from its relational aspect, the more its real effects become manifest. With this move, Lacan avoids the direct ontologisation and substantialisation of the unconscious, as well as its simple reduction to a single discursive structure, in the given case the capitalist discourse.

The limits of linguistic structuralism are addressed in yet another reformulation of Lacan's classical axiom:

> People make a false opposition between structure, which would be synchronic and therefore outside of history, and dialectic, which would be diachronic, sunken in time. But this is inaccurate. Take, in my book, the text entitled *The Rome Discourse* and you will be able to estimate the importance I ascribe to history, to the point that it appears to me coextensive with the register of the unconscious. The unconscious is history. The experienced [*le vécu*] is marked by a first historicity. All this is written, black on white, in my book.[15]

'Unconscious is history' rejects two false oppositions: between structure and dialectics, and between unconscious and history. These oppositions are merely variations of a more fundamental opposition, which marked postwar continental philosophy, between structure and genesis. As mentioned earlier, this opposition needs to be substituted with a specific intertwining of structure and historicity, one that does not hide its dialectical pretensions. We can understand why this opposition makes little sense for psychoanalysis. The unconscious is situated in the intersection of synchronicity and diachronicity, which means that it constantly demonstrates transformations and instabilities, on the one hand, and temporary fixations, on the other. In this way the dichotomy of structure and history becomes entirely inoperative and meaningless. For Freud, every mental structure contains movement, in which a 'psychic conflict' can be isolated. Consequently, his idea of structure comes down to this immanent dynamic and not to some ahistorical constellation of rigid relations. The minimum of structural stability can be

---

15   J. Lacan, interview in *Figaro littéraire*, 29 December 1966. Lacan's connection of the unconscious with history has as a clear target: the existentialist, and notably Sartre's critique of structuralism as a current that presumably rejects history and substitutes the dialectical movement with the non-dialectical (synchronic) structural permutations. Looking at all the actually existing structuralisms, we can notice that only Lévi-Strauss and Saussure could potentially fall under such criticism, and even in their case such criticism would be possible solely under the condition that the instabilities of their epistemic objects be omitted.

located in the processes of condensation and displacement, which find their linguistic equivalent in metaphor and metonymy. But to repeat again, these two operations are unthinkable without their diachronic dimension, which introduces temporality in the picture. Diachrony is the necessary condition, which allows Freud to theorise condensation and displacement as specific achievements of unconscious labour.

Freud provided probably the most passionate, although not unproblematic, vision of the intertwining of structure and history when he compared the unconscious with Rome. In *Civilisation and Its Discontents* we read that, unlike the actual Rome, whose history is present in the form of ruins and fragments that are impossible to reconstruct, the unconscious Eternal City is comparable to a hologram, in which everything remains intact: all buildings are preserved in all their historic stages, and all of the city's past is constantly present.[16] The unconscious seems to know no time, as far as the essential part of temporality is corruption, change and forgetting, while from another perspective it is nothing but time: history pressing on the present and manifesting in disruptions of discourse, in lapses, dreams and jokes, in interruptions of the 'eternal present', in which Marx and Engels recognised the most elementary operation of ideology. The main ideological achievement thus lies in the rejection of temporality, in declaring the end of history, in the false eternalisation of the dominating discourse.

Freud was naturally aware of the limits of his metaphor, which more betrays his personal fascination with Rome than correctly determines the relation between structure and the temporality of the unconscious. There is another, more suitable discussion of their relation in an early writing on screen memories. There, Freud claims that human memory is not simply an archive of unchangeable data but a collection that is subjected to constant modifications. Far from being neutral, these changes express an irreducible conflict between heterogeneous psychic instances and their particular tendencies. What matters here is the conclusion that Freud draws from the way screen memories interpret other, presumably historically more accurate memories:

> The falsified memory is the first that we become aware of: the raw material
> of memory-traces out of which it was forged remains unknown to us in its
> original form. The recognition of this fact must diminish the distinction we

16   See *The Standard Edition of the Complete Psychological Works of Sigmund Freud*, Vol. 21, London: Vintage, 2001, 70.

have drawn between screen memories and other memories derived from our childhood. It may indeed be questioned whether we have any memories at all *from* our childhood: memories *relating to* our childhood may be all that we possess. Our childhood memories show us our earliest years not as they were but as they appeared at the later periods when the memories were aroused. In these periods of arousal, the childhood memories did not, as people are accustomed to say, *emerge*; they were *formed* at that time. And a number of motives, with no concern for historical accuracy, had a part in forming them, as well as in the selection of the memories themselves.[17]

The immediate lesson of this passage leaves no doubt: history does not exist, or, put differently, history is not an objective history of events, just as memory is no archive of neutral facts. Instead, Freud proposes to see it as a series of deformations, displacements, rewritings and, most importantly, conflicts, which nevertheless contain a minimum of structural relations that support the entire movement or simply are a structure in movement. History is structured as a language, and just like language it does not exist but nevertheless has material consequences for the subject.

What Freud encountered in this representation of history is the retroactive causality, which will mark his subsequent conception of the historicity of the unconscious. Retroaction does more than merely modify the meaning of historical events from the viewpoint of the present. In a certain sense, this very retroactive modification constitutes the history and memories of the past. Retroactivity is envisaged as a form of causality and not as a distortion of objective facts. The formation of memories of early childhood, of the years in which a series of events that determined the subject's subsequent development took place, plays the main role in the retroactive constitution and transformation of the subject's history.

We can recall here the most famous example of this retroaction, the traumatic event that triggered illness in the case of the Wolf Man. The event did not simply take place 'objectively' somewhere in the patient's early childhood and repeat itself later in life. It was a real effect of retroactive structural causality, which associated a contingent occurrence or observation from the past with an anxiety dream, in which the patient saw wolves sitting on the tree in front of the family house and immovably staring at him through the bedroom window. Freud's interpretation of the dream content is not crucial here; what matters is the fact that he himself

17   Freud, *Standard Edition*, Vol. 3, 322.

openly acknowledges that it is unimportant what actual event in the past triggered the illness – the retroactive causal link already provides the sufficient formal interpretation of the event that has an equally traumatic effect to that which a concrete occurrence in reality could possibly have. Trauma is thus not a singular transcendental event, which stretches into the present, but a real effect of the temporal relation, through which the present retroactively alters the past, which, in turn, determines the present. For Freud, structure and history are inseparable, even the same, and the concept that overcomes their simple opposition is nothing other than retroactivity (*Nachträglichkeit*).

In his interview for *Le Figaro litteraire*, Lacan evokes the following crucial passage from his Rome discourse, which addresses the relation between the unconscious and history: 'The unconscious is the chapter of my history that is marked by a blank or occupied by a lie: it is the censored chapter. But the truth can be refound; most often it has already been written elsewhere.'[18] First, the truth is written on the subject's body, as the materiality of alienation and of discursive production. The unconscious is marked by an antagonism and contradiction, whose witnesses are censorship and lie, these specific features of the Freudian unconscious, in comparison to others, which contain no structural conflict but most often merely a mental archive of unclear representations and archetypes. The entire originality of the Freudian method depends on the discovery of this conflictual reality in the unconscious:

> For if the originality of the method derives from the means it foregoes, it is because the means that it reserves for itself suffice to constitute a domain whose limits define the relativity of its operations. Its means are those of speech, insofar as speech confers a meaning on the functions of the individual; its domain is that of concrete discourse qua field of the subject's transindividual reality; and its operations are those of history, insofar as *history constitutes the emergence of truth in the real.*[19]

Freud establishes the link between truth, history and contradiction, thereby proposing, just as Marx and Hegel had before him, a conception of history in terms of the movement of contradiction that constitutes the subject in the discrepancy with consciousness. Freud attributes to this contradiction

18   Lacan, *Écrits*, 215.
19   Ibid., 214 (my emphasis). Translation modified.

a real status, indicating that history not only contains a difference between reality (in the sense of factuality) and the real but also manifests the impossibility of their integral overlapping. The truth that emerges in the real is clearly not the relational and adequate truth of cognition but the conflictual truth of social relations, and therefore a political truth. The evocation of truth is crucial, as the significance of Marx's critique for psychoanalysis will be associated with his invention of the social symptom as a specific truth-formation. It also indicates a notion of structure that is no longer Saussure's neutral system of differences without a subject.

SAUSSURE AND POLITICAL ECONOMY

In his *Course in General Linguistics*, Saussure draws a strong analogy between linguistics and political economy. He justifies it by reminding the reader that both disciplines can be considered sciences of value. And though linguistic value is not the same as economic value, Saussure suggests that they share a common logical background. Value can only emerge from the difference between two signs. Where there is difference, there is value; the latter therefore can neither be grounded in the relation to the signified nor in the qualitative aspect of a commodity, its use-value. This isolation of value already reflects the absolute autonomy of the system of differences. With it, Saussure provided a strong foundation for the later structuralist readings of Marx. The signifier and exchange-value become indistinguishable.

Yet an important complication emerges here, since for Marx commodity is not a simple notion. The first volume of *Capital* begins precisely by focusing on its complexity, which reveals an equivocity that has widereaching structural and social implications. The close examination of the commodity form shows that commodity, a seemingly unproblematic empirical object, is divided on use-value and exchange-value. This split within the commodity on the qualitative and the quantitative aspect is reflected in the split between qualities and form, or as Jean-Claude Milner rephrased it, between *qualities without matter* and *matter without qualities*.[20] Milner's specification is intimately linked with the new conceptualisation of materiality in the universe of modern science, where matter no longer designates a positive substance, defined by a collection of

---

20   J. C. Milner, *Le triple du plaisir*, Paris: Verdier, 1997, 76.

empirical qualities (such as solidity, extension, consistency) but becomes a geometrised and subsequently mathematised abstraction. An element of matter is an abstract theoretical object isolated from empirical observation. The dematerialisation of matter, its progressive detachment from positive qualities, which still imply a relation of the object to the human observer, reaches its peak in quantum mechanics. But this is no place to go in a detailed account of this historical development.[21] What is important here is that the scientific distinction between matter and empirical qualities leads directly to the non-empirical materiality of commodities and of the relations between commodities that Marx isolates in his analysis of commodity form.

Let us continue with the split of the commodity that Saussure actually excludes from the linguistic science of values. Use-value and the empirical qualities of the products of labour may be of lesser importance, but this notion significantly supports Marx's account of the equivocity of commodities and the necessary illusions that result from their double character. Use-value makes every commodity appear as an object that can satisfy a need precisely through its qualities. This need does not necessarily precede a commodity but can also be fabricated together with the product.[22] Consequently, every commodity is an articulation of use-value and exchange-value, no matter how abstract the produced object (services, websites, smartphone apps and so on). Commodity has to be tied at least to a fantasy of quality, which represents the minimal ground for the production of a corresponding need. The immediate conclusion is that the need is not some quasi-natural and non-symbolic tendency but already comprises symbolic mediation. Even if commodities are not produced with the aim of satisfying human needs but first and foremost to support exchange and stimulate consumption, one of the cornerstones of production of value, they have to maintain the fiction of usefulness and need, no matter how abstract, futile and fantasmatic. It is precisely the

---

21   For a brief but well-pointed account, see J. M. Lévi-Leblond, 'La matière dans la physique moderne', in: *Qu'est-ce que la matière?*, Paris: Éditions Le Pommier, 2005, 61–120.

22   Marx explicitly claims that the production of commodities always-already comprises the production of needs. For example, in the famous lines: 'Production not only supplies a material to the need, but it also supplies a need for the material . . . Production thus not only creates an object for the subject, but also a subject for the object. Thus production produces consumption.' K. Marx, *Grundrisse: Foundations of the Critique of Political Economy*, London: Penguin Books, 1993, 92.

fantasy that supports the union of use-value and exchange-value, matter without qualities and qualities without matter, two heterogeneous and unrelated levels. The dimension of exchange and the circulation of commodities immediately imply that commodities lose the exclusive and seemingly univocal feature of addressing human needs (adequate relation between products and needs) and that another aspect of production steps into the foreground, the production of value, through which one finally enters the autonomy of the system of differences. Simultaneously, both exchange and the market turn commodity from a unique object into a mass product, thereby exposing a repetition, that cannot be associated with the dimension of use-value or, more precisely, that complicates the relation between the usefulness and the exchange.[23]

A commodity thus contains a double and not a single difference. Besides the split between use-value and exchange-value, there is also the difference that is exchange-value as such. Use-value manifests in the relation between commodity and consumption, making of the former both the sign of a need and the sign of a psychological subject, to whom the need can be attributed. Exchange-value, however, concerns the relation between commodities themselves and is apparently without a subject. Marx then shows that this is not the case because in the world of commodities there is one commodity that forms an exception: labour-power, the only commodity-producing commodity. This exception means that exchange-value is *not* without any subject whatsoever but only without a subject of need (psychological or empirical subject). The labour theory of value that Marx adopts from his predecessors (Smith and Ricardo) now determines the subject of value and can be read as Marx's theory of the subject.

The first lesson of Marx's science of value is thus already doubled: the difference between use-value and exchange-value uncovers the autonomy of value and defines value as difference to another value. At this point, Marx's critique of political economy seems to overlap with Saussure. Although this lesson implies an immediate corollary: exchange-value is not without a subject, but this subject is not the same as the subject of use-value (need). Exchange-value is not merely a vertical relation between

---

23   See, for instance, the condensed summary of the problems implied by the structure of commodities, in G. Duménil and D. Lévy, *Économie marxiste du capitalisme*, Paris: La Découverte, 2003, 8. The problematic aspects of the relation between use-value and exchange-value are discussed at length in W. Pohrt, *Theorie des Gebrauchswerts*, Berlin: Edition Tiamat, 2001.

value-signifier and commodity-signified but also a representation of the subject of exchange, which can be presupposed in all commodities and which Marx associates with labour-power. Saussure does not draw this conclusion, and in this respect Lacan's deduction of the subject from the logic of the signifier already in the first return to Freud exceeded the strict epistemological frames of structural linguistics.

The science of value thus begins already at the level of the non-symbolic use-value that seemingly precedes exchange. Marx's critique starts from the political-economic idea of *Warenkunde*, expertise-knowledge of commodities, and the science of values is supposed to form a subset of this discipline. 'In bourgeois society', Marx writes in a footnote, 'the legal fiction prevails that each person, as a buyer, has an encyclopaedic knowledge of commodities'.[24] Everyone enters the market with a presupposed knowledge, precisely as *homo oeconomicus*, who presumably possesses spontaneous knowledge of his/her private interests, and above all as a value-scientist. For Marx, this presupposition is built on shaky ground, because it treats everyone as subjects of cognition. The presupposed knowledge of economic subjects is first tested in the way people relate to commodities, in commodity fetishism, where Marx again shows that the difference between use-value and exchange-value implies two incompatible and heterogeneous subjects, of which one is the centralised subject of need, interest and positive knowledge, and the other the decentralised and non-psychological subject of value. But what matters for now is that, whether we speak of linguistic or economic values, linguistic exchange or economic exchange, knowledge is already presupposed for the subject. This knowledge is not necessarily reflected but is most certainly at work in the way commodities and values relate to one other, and also in the way everyone relates to commodities, in the action of structure as well as in the actions of men.

Linguistics and political economy enter these relations between values and commodities, between signifiers and signified, where they first encounter the double character of their values. An additional factor complicates the matter for both sciences of values. Saussure notes that linguistics and political economy are internally doubled, not because the notion of value contains a qualitative and a quantitative dimension but because the quantitative dimension marks their scientific object with temporality. History re-enters the structure. The field of value is stained with constant change that makes values vary over time. The oscillation of

---

value reveals 'inflation' in the Other, a structural dynamic and instability in the system. In order to illustrate this point, Saussure first gives examples of sciences in which time does not cause particular complications in the structure of their field and of their object. Such is the case with astronomy, which investigates changes in the composition of stars, whereby the temporality of these changes does not call for an inner differentiation of astronomy as such; the same goes for geology, which explores different geological epochs but can easily switch to the description of unchangeable states. The temporal shift does not alter the object of research and the laws behind the changes are considered stable.

All these conditions of scientificity change in the framework of linguistics and political economy, where the object transforms depending on whether we think it within or without temporality, meaning also within or without the relation to the subject. Political economy and economic history form two separate disciplines within one science, and the same goes for static linguistics and evolutionary linguistics. This already indicates that linguistic and economic models do not have universal validity. They are always-already historically and geographically limited, something that critical economists will willingly admit.[25] This limitation of economic models is closely related to the instability of the market, the same structural instability that marks the field of language, a feature on which Lacan will build his theory of the barred Other.

As previously mentioned, the immanent split in both sciences of value is caused by the temporal factor that is associated with the social dimension of exchange: 'Both sciences are concerned with a *system for equating things of different orders* – labour and wages in one and a signified and signifier in the other.'[26] The parallelism does not stop here. Just as political economy handles the difference between exchange-value and use-value, Saussure introduces an analogical difference between linguistic value and meaning. Meaning still presupposes a relation between speakers, whereas linguistic value implies an autonomous relation between signifiers themselves. Value relations go unbeknownst to the speaker and to the production of meaning, and in order to attain this level of language linguistics needs to abstract

---

25   The lack of universality, which is intimately linked with the lack of stability and of predictability, follows directly from the impossibility of the integral mathematisation of the market. See notably P. N. Giraud, *Le commerce des promesses*, Paris: Seuil, 2009, 324.

26   Saussure, *Course in General Linguistics*, 79.

language from speech. Saussure summarises this gesture in the famous thesis that the object of linguistics, *la langue*, is *le langage* (language) minus *la parole* (speech). Only once this operation has been made can language appear as an abstract system of differences. To say that in language there are only differences means that what we normally experience as language contains two heterogeneous aspects and even two different languages, the language of values and the language of meaning. When humans communicate among themselves they unknowingly speak the language of values, a language that does not communicate meaning, and the question is whether it communicates at all. The autonomy of the signifier stands for a non-communicative kernel of linguistic communication.

Let us return to Saussure's example, which serves to illustrate the coincidence of linguistic and economic value. Saussure claims that from the perspective of value the relation of labour to wage is homological to the relation between the signified and the signifier. At this point, we can already note that Saussure was not exactly fortunate in his choice of example. He overlooked the problematic character of this comparison, as he did not refer to just any economic relation but to the most problematic commodity exchange that puts the entirety of political economy into question. He thus chose an example that, for Marx, reveals the symptomatic status of labour-power in the commodity universe and in economic exchange. Saussure's analogy repeats the same mistake that Marx criticised in classical political economy: what is bought and sold on the market is not a process (labour) but a specific commodity (labour-power). But let us take a few steps back here.

Because temporality cannot be entirely eliminated from the field of value, the system of equivalences can take two directions. The equation can concern things here and now, as well as things in temporal succession. If it concerns the present state of things, it pictures the market as a static constellation of actually existing commodities; we are, then, dealing with political economy as the grammar of market relations. If, however, the equation relates to the temporal succession of things, it comprises not only exchange but also production and relations of production. Or, to link it back to Saussure's formula, temporality reintroduces speech into language. Here, the split produced by the notion of value finally receives its full weight. Saussure illustrates it with the intersection of two axes: the axis of simultaneity, which designates the relations between coexisting things and from which the dimension of time is excluded; and the axis of succession, 'on which only one thing can be considered at a time but upon which all the things on the first axis together with their changes are located'.[27] In linguistics, this distinction is absolute and imperative, for 'language is a system of pure values, which are determined by nothing except the momentary arrangement of its terms'.[28] This distinction is therefore necessary in a field that has no external determination or from which it is impossible to extricate oneself. Language and the market are two fields that know no Outside. Because of this absoluteness, discussion of them is only possible by splitting them into their temporal and atemporal aspects. Value can become a scientific object only if language and market are separated from their temporality, for this temporality reveals that their structure is more paradoxical than it may appear. Because they have no exteriority, they are not whole. Because they are not whole, they are internally barred. And, consequently, because they are barred, they do not know positive existence. The Other (Language, Market) does not exist. For linguistics, it is necessary to construct its object, language, by separating it from temporality, but, simultaneously, this separation excludes the problematic existence of language that follows directly from the negativity of the signifier. Similarly, political economy has to construct the field of its object, the market, which is presupposed in its positive existence, that is, as a fully constituted and homeostatic order that follows stable laws and whose functioning is more or less predictable and translatable into mathematical language. Adam Smith's 'invisible hand of the market' brings together both features, whereby the persistence of this originary metaphor in contemporary economic debates testifies that the hypothesis of the Other's existence is alive and well. To the economic Other we send positive signals, in the form of reforms and austerity measures that should calm its instable and capricious character. For linguistics and for political economy, the Other *does* exist, at least as the idea of a logically predictable and self-regulating system of values.[29]

The structural and logical overlapping of commodity exchange and language, value and signifier, also stands at the very unfolding of the critique of political economy. In the section on commodity fetishism, which

---

27   Saussure, *Course in General Linguistics*, 80.

28   *Ibid.*

29   It is no surprise that not only Saussure but also Chomsky's linguistics comes suspiciously close to the fetishist traps and ideological reductionisms contained in economic liberalism (and neoliberalism). See the excellent critical account in J. J. Lecercle, *Une philosophie marxiste du langage*, Paris: Presses Universitaires de France, 2004, 22–45.

concludes the first chapter of *Capital,* Marx addresses the cognitive consequences of the autonomy of exchange-value through the idea of commodity
language.[30] He demonstrates this language at work in the well-known
prosopopoeia of commodities:

> If commodities could speak, they would say this: our use-value may interest
> men, but does not belong to us as objects. What does belong to us as objects,
> however, is our value. Our own intercourse as commodities proves it. We
> relate to each other merely as exchange-values.[31]

From the double character of commodities it seemingly follows that language
is situated in exchange-value, while use-value stands outside language. The
critical axis of the idea of commodity language, by contrast, consists in the
fact that it places the couple of use-value and exchange-value in language,
thereby determining the relation between two linguistic levels, human
language and commodity language, communication and autonomous difference, or, to put it with Saussure, meaning and value. Besides structurally
linking exchange and language, Marx also situates the specific structural
effect of the commodity split, which immediately follows from the primacy
of exchange-value over use-value: the seemingly intrinsic character of value.
After commodities have said their piece, Marx leaves the word to political
economists, where it turns out that economists are actually not the ones who
speak but, rather, it is commodities, which continue their *parole* through the
mouths of political economists and the theories of political economy:

> Now listen how those commodities speak through the mouth of the econo-
> mist. 'Value' (i.e., exchange-value) is a property of things, riches (i.e.,
> use-value) of man. Value, in this sense, necessarily implies exchanges, riches
> do not'. 'Riches (use-value) are the attribute of men, value is the attribute of
> commodities. A man or a community is rich, a pearl or a diamond is
> valuable . . . A pearl or a diamond is valuable as a pearl or a diamond'.[32]

---

30   For a broader discussion of commodity language and the doubling of
human language, see notably W. Hamacher, 'Lingua Amissa: The Messianism of
Commodity-Language and Derrida's *Specters of Marx*', in: M. Sprinker (Ed.), *Ghostly
Demarcations*, London: Verso, 2008, and most recently S. Khatib, '*Teleologie ohne
Endzweck'. Walter Benjamins Ent-stellung des Messianischen*, Marburg: Tectum
Verlag, 2013, 583–98.
31   Marx, *Capital*, Vol. 1, 176–7.
32   Ibid., 177.

A strange ventriloquism is at stake in political economy. Marx unveils that there is an immediate continuity, equivocity, inseparability between commodity language and human language. He quotes the British utilitarian philosopher and economist Samuel Bailey, whose words demonstrate that the commodity language is not to be taken as a metaphor; the prosopopoeia of commodities does not assume the status of a rhetorical fiction but simply *is* language in action. *Ça parle*: it, the commodity, speaks. Commodity language turns out to be a pleonasm, for the economists simply repeat the appearance that is produced by the autonomy of exchange. The appearance of value being intrinsic to commodities is thus a logical consequence of the autonomy of exchange-value and demonstrates the structural overlapping of commodity language, the way commodities communicate among themselves through values, and human language, the way signifiers relate to one another behind human communication. When Marx speaks of commodity fetishism, he does not envisage some 'generalised perversion' but a minimal shift between the appearance and the logical autonomy of value.

The inseparability of human language and commodity language anticipates an important Lacanian axiom, 'There is no such thing as a metalanguage', or, put differently, there is no criterion that would delimit the autonomy of the system of differences, which implies the primacy of the relation between signifiers over their relation to the signified, and thereby over the communicative and referential dimension of language. Language is not univocity but equivocity, not a relation but the paradigmatic example of non-relation. And because there is no such thing as metalanguage, there is no language either. The linguistic and the economic system form an open set. Consequently, the inexistence of a metalanguage (the Other of the Other) and the inexistence of the Other are one and the same.

From the equivocity and the inseparability of human language and commodity language and from the structural overlapping of economic and linguistic value, which is the signifier as difference or relation to another signifier, Marx deduces the constitution of subjectivity that is coded under the expression 'commodity fetishism', a subjectivity that is marked by a structurally determined misunderstanding. Thus, Marx accentuates the difference between the speaker and the subject, between the subject implied by use-value (the psychological and empirical subject of cognition) and the subject of exchange-value, whose place is in the autonomy of the system of differences and which is therefore decentralised and metonymic. Marx's analysis of commodity fetishism thus contains two elements, the signifier-as-cause and the alienated subject, the material consequence of the autonomy of value. To reiterate, the idea of a commodity language implies that commodity exchange is structured like a language. This openly linguistic meaning of Marx's critique of fetishism was apparent for Lacan, who detected the affinity of the critique of political economy with structuralism already in his early teaching, anticipating Althusser's structural Marxism:

> It is enough to open the first volume of *Capital* in order to become aware that the first step of Marx's analysis of the fetish character of commodity consists precisely in the fact that he addresses the problem on the level of the signifier as such, even if the term itself remains unpronounced.[33]

Marx starts from the autonomy of exchange in order to deduce the specific form of subjectivity that this autonomy inevitably produces. This deduction demonstrates the dependency of the subject on the signifier: the system of differences, commodity exchange, the way in which commodities communicate among themselves, shapes the subject independently from every reference to the consumer. This hidden aspect of subjectivation is then exemplified in commodity fetishism, the political-economic mystification of the source of value, which strives to hold apart both flip sides of structural causality: production of (surplus) value and production of (alienated) subjectivity. According to the fetishist position commodities are endowed with intrinsic value, although this misunderstanding is objective and not subjective. The autonomy of the system of differences necessarily produces the appearance that value is a positive quality of things and that it is without a subject, or, better, that it is its own subject. Commodity fetishism consequently evolves into the fetishisation of capital, in which financial abstractions seemingly engender each other independently from any negative subject of value. Capital becomes the privileged description for a spectral life without negativity. The case of Samuel Bailey is merely an exemplification of how each individual spontaneously relates to commodities. In each consumer there is a political economist, the presupposed subject of cognition, for which one assumes an encyclopaedic knowledge of commodities – *homo oeconomicus*, this ideal subject of the economic science of value. In the end, the hypothesis of this ideal subjectivity makes political economy blind for the structurally generated fetishisations – and the task of critique, as Marx repeatedly demonstrates, is precisely to think

---

33   J. Lacan, *Le Séminaire, livre VI, Le désir et son interprétation*, Paris: Éditions de La Martinière, 2013, 371.

the production of value together with the production of fantasies of production of value. Differently put, political economy still engages in the quest for the origin of value, in relation to which it can only produce more or less scientific myths. Critique of political economy, in contrast, abolishes this quest and focuses instead on the interdependency of exploitation and fetishisation.

The speech of commodities comes suspiciously close to the way Saussure treats the signs that compose language, without the reference to temporality. This does not mean that Saussure's relation to language is fetishist, but it does mean that by (unknowingly) repeating the political-economic lapsus, he restricts linguistics to the register of exchange, leaving the connection between linguistic representation and linguistic production unthematised. By failing to envisage the difference between labour-process and labour-power, as well as between labour-power and other commodities, Saussure situates production outside the science of language. For him, language knows no surplus and the use of language remains throughout communicative and meaningful. This will eventually become the central point of Lacan's critique of Saussure:

> Communication implies reference. But one thing is clear – language is merely what scientific discourse elaborates to account for what I call *lalangue*. Language serves purposes that are altogether different from that of communication . . . If communication approaches what is effectively at work in the *jouissance* of lalanguage, it is because communication implies a reply, in other words, dialogue. But does lalanguage serve, first and foremost, to dialogue? As I have said before, nothing is less certain.[34]

Saussure is affirmed and negated in one and the same gesture. The autonomy of the signifier as such implies a restriction of the communicative dimension of language, and hence of the linguistic use-value (meaning, relation to the signified). What Lacan here describes as lalanguage is already the result of a shift from Saussure to Marx. The distinction between language and lalanguage now covers the difference between linguistic meaning and the autonomy of the signifier. *Lalangue* stands entirely on the side of this autonomy, negating the primacy of communication and relationality (dialogue). The signifier appears here first and foremost an apparatus of *jouissance*. The autonomy in question, the kernel of Saussure's discovery,

---

34 Lacan, *Encore*, 126. Translation modified.

provides the necessary ground for the passage from language to lalanguage, but this cannot take place without introducing the subject and the surplus-object. Lacan's second return to Freud thus ends up extending the autonomy of the signifier to the Marxist problematic of the mode of production.

In Saussure, the introduction of synchronicity and diachronicity artic-ulated the split within linguistics (static linguistics and evolutionary linguistics) and within its object. Language is both state *and* movement. Linguistics confronts here an impossible dilemma: if it aims at the static, atemporal aspect of language, it loses an important aspect of its object, the production of linguistic value; and if it focuses on temporality, it has to admit that language does not exist, meaning that it deals with an unstable and paradoxical object. In the first case, linguistics becomes a 'pondering of knowledge on lalanguage',[35] whereby language turns out to be a scientific fiction, a construct of linguistic knowledge; in the second case, linguistics cannot fully account for communication since the unity of language (*la langue*) dissolves in the multiplicity of 'private' languages (*lalangue*). This dichotomy of language and speech is what Lacan criticised in Saussurean linguistics and instead strived to construct a linguistics, renamed *linguiste-rie*, that would take language 'more seriously', considering the 'life' of language, its temporal as well as causal dimension. Lacan here seems to be in accord with Deleuze's later remark that 'linguistics has done a lot of harm',[36] notably when it separated language from production, not seeing that it was an essential aspect of the autonomy of the signifier. One cannot have language without its inherent instability. The same critical position directs Marx's relation to political economy.

Political economy, too, reveals its insufficiency because it cannot account for the production of value without the implicit fetishisation of commodities, money and capital – another pondering of knowledge, which ascribes value to commodities, to money and, at the most abstract level, to the immediate productivity of fictitious capital. *Geld heckendes Geld*, money-breeding money, as Marx writes, is the main fetishist fantasy that emerges from the autonomy of value, and it is therefore not a surprise that this fantasy of self-engendering stands in the core of all capitalist fetishisms and becomes a driving force of financialisation. This financial vitalism can

---

35   Ibid., 125. Translation modified.
36   Deleuze quoted in J. J. Lecercle, *Deleuze and Language*, New York: Palgrave Macmillan, 2002, 64. See also Lacan, *Autres écrits*, 313–14.

only be supported on the basis of the foreclosure of negativity, of the split that marks the subject of value and through it the entire commodity universe. However, the critical point is not simply to reintroduce production into language but to expose its double aspect, the mutual dependency of production of the negative subject and the primitive surplus-object.

Saussure nevertheless tried to theorise the temporal and the atemporal aspect of language when he compared the inscription of language in the intersection of synchronicity and diachronicity with a chess game. This comparison combines the static and the dynamic dimension of language, showing that the value of particular elements depends on their position on the chessboard. It illustrates the link between value and difference, and with it Saussure rejects something that we might call linguistic fetishism, an attempt to conceive language as a 'language of being' (Heidegger) or, put differently, an endeavour to establish a relation and continuity between linguistic value and meaning.

In the history of philosophy, we find two prominent versions of such fetishism, which oriented the philosophical relation to language. First in *Cratylus,* in which Plato strived to illustrate the mimetic relation between words and things, and thus to theorise linguistic value in correspondence to the natural connection between the signifier and the reference:

> Then, as to names, ought not our legislator also to know how to put the true natural name of each thing into sounds and syllables, and to make and give all names with a view to the ideal name, if he is to be a namer in any true sense?[37]

The mythic figure of the namer translates *physis* into language without any loss. The development of the entire dialogue amounts to the idea that language stands in a harmonious mimetic relation to nature, so that even in its basic components, the phonemes, we encounter an imitation of natural sounds, qualities and states. Plato tries to provide a mythical proof that the relation between the signifier and the signified is as such rooted in nature (*physis,* being), and that signifiers always-already mean something *in* and *from* themselves, that they are necessarily referential and that language is essentially communication, language of being, in which every letter follows from a natural sound, state or quality. Plato hereby formulated a mythical

---

37   *Crat.* 389d. See Plato, *The Collected Dialogues*, Princeton, NJ: Princeton University Press, 2005, 428.

version of what would later become the doctrine of *adaequatio,* adequate relation between words and things.

Another case of linguistic fetishism, and even another founding myth of linguistics, emerges with the pragmatic tradition stretching from Aristotle to Habermas. Although this pragmatism does not postulate any natural or substantial link between *logos* and *physis,* the signifier and being, it nevertheless continues to presuppose that the nature of language consists in stable referentiality and a normative form of communication. Language is defined as *organon* (tool, organ), and even if this conception seems to reduce language to its communicational use-value, we again come across the same hypothesis as in Plato's mythical rootedness of the signifier in the ideal name: the signifier, in itself, supports a relation between the words and the things, the symbolic and the real. There is no surplus in language; the former comes from elsewhere, for Aristotle from the sophistic misuse of language, for Wittgenstein from false philosophical problems.[38]

For both Plato and Aristotle, there is more at stake here than the problem of language. The same dilemma is encountered in economy through chrematistics and usury, where money becomes its own telos and enrichment for enrichment's sake the only economic imperative. The true issue concerns the denaturalisation of social links through the autonomy of the signifier and value, and the rejection of the idea that the human community is grounded on a stable social relation. How do we delimit the good and the bad use of language and money? How do we guarantee the overlapping of value and meaning and simultaneously prevent another possible overlapping, the one between value and *jouissance,* which negates the former and threatens to dissolve the social link? For Plato and Aristotle, the paradigmatic case of the good use of language is not simply communication but even more so philosophy, the language of ontology, spoken by philosophers and moreover by being as such. In a certain sense ontology understands itself as one immense prosopopoeia of being. The ideal functioning of language consequently takes place in the highest form of *philia,* the love of wisdom, which is also a form of friendship, a social link. The ontological language of being is rooted on the axiom professed by the Parmenidian Goddess: being is, non-being is not, which makes of *language without negativity* one of the main philosophical ideals. Precisely this negativity, however,

---

38   'Most philosophical questions and statements are based on the fact that we do not understand our linguistic logic.' L. Wittgenstein, *Tractatus logico-philosophicus,* Frankfurt: Suhrkamp, 1984, 26.

is what Marx and Freud encounter at the other end of metaphysics in the fetishist disavowal of alienation and of castration.

In contradistinction to the language of being and to the ideal of a language without negativity stands the language of the sophists and poets, where enjoyment, seduction and equivocity question the primacy of communication and external referentiality. If the language of ontology is a prosopopoeia of being, then the language of sophistry is a prosopopoeia of *jouissance*. The signifier is no longer the bearer of meaning but an apparatus of *jouissance* and a tool of deception. It remains an *organon* but serves other purposes. The supposedly natural link between the signifier and the signified is suspended, and *jouissance* invades their intermediate space, uncovering the autonomy of the signifier and production in language. In the extreme case, this *jouissance* dissolves the dialogue and the social link, leading to a discursive self-abolition, as in the case of Cratylus, who is said to have abandoned all language and merely moved his index finger. The denaturation of language into an apparatus of *jouissance* makes of sophists 'human plants',[39] but it also makes them speak only for the pleasure in speaking. In the figure of the sophist two extremes coincide, pure babbling, on the one hand, and pure silence, on the other, the life and the death of language, Joyce and Cratylus.

What sophistry is in relation to language, chrematistics is in relation to money. It detaches money from its social function, turning it into an obscene self-reproducing entity.[40] Exchange turns from the metaphor of social relation into a means of *jouissance*. Buying and selling should reflect and realise the idea of social relation. But the sophist and the usurer do not reflect or imitate anything; at the background of their actions there is neither eternal idea nor normative structure. The delimitation of the normal and the pathological functioning of linguistic and economic apparatus is an impossible task that calls for a fantasmatic foundation of the presupposed relation. Plato and Aristotle's attempt rejects the topological problem, according to which the

---

39   'But if all are alike both right and wrong, one who believes this can neither speak nor say anything intelligible; for he says at the same time both "yes" and "no". And if he makes no judgment but thinks and does not think, indifferently, what difference will there be between him and the plants?' *Met.* 1008b. See *The Complete Works of Aristotle*, Vol. 2, Princeton, NJ: Princeton University Press, 1995, 1592.

40   For the discussion of money and value in Plato and Aristotle, see M. Hénaff, *Le prix de la vérité*, Paris: Seuil 2002. The sophistic 'perversion' of language as negativity that haunts the constitution of philosophy in Aristotle is examined in B. Cassin and M. Narcy, *La décision du sens*, Paris: Vrin, 1992.

border between the signifier and *jouissance* is both nowhere and everywhere in the system of differences. From the philosophical condemnation of chrematistics and sophistry, it follows that the main point of philosophical repression is the intimate connection between communication and production in language. In order to ground the homeostatic vision of language (language as a language of being), Plato and Aristotle produce the fantasy of a 'subject supposed to enjoy'.[41] Psychoanalysis and the critique of political economy, however, reveal that the autonomy of the signifier and of value should not be exaggerated – the presumed autism of *jouissance* in language and the autism of fictitious capital are the privileged targets of both the Lacanian and Marxian critiques. A sensationalist dramatisation of the problem misinterprets the autonomy of the signifier and of value and walks straight into their immediate fetishisation. The key problem remains the discrepancy between communication and *jouissance*. If communication implies a response, this does not suggest that this response in turn implies an ideal communicative model, on which the pragmatic tradition strives to ground the fantasy of a consistently regulated and stable social relation.

By comparing language with chess, Saussure strived to show that the system of differences is merely temporary and depends on the formal rules of the game, which remain unaltered. The passage from one synchronicity to another takes place with each move, establishing a new distribution of figures and new relations, thereby changing their values. However, Saussure expresses the following reservation:

> At only one point is the comparison weak: the chess player *intends* to bring about a shift and thereby to exert an action on the system, whereas language premeditates nothing. The pieces of language are shifted – or rather modified – spontaneously and fortuitously . . . In order to make the game of chess seem at every point like the functioning of language, we would have to presuppose an unconscious or unintelligent player.[42]

For Saussure, there is no unconscious intention; intentions can only be associated to consciousness, hence to the subject of cognition. The border that would support the integral overlapping of chess and language is nothing other than the unconscious, but then another figure of

---

41   M. Dolar, 'Introduction: The Subject Supposed to Enjoy', in: A. Grosrichard, *The Sultan's Court*, London: Verso, 1998, xviii.

42   Saussure, *Course in General Linguistics*, 80. Translation modified.

subjectivity would have to be introduced. Here Freud's discoveries receive their full weight. Returning to Freud through Saussure is possible only under the condition that the *Interpretation of Dreams* drew a strict equivalence, in all points, between chess and language, thereby making the move that radicalised the implications of the autonomy of the signifier. Yet, in presupposing an unconscious player, Freud also checkmated Saussure, as the unconscious introduces a serious complication in the conception of structure: it names the instability of structural relations, by connecting both aspects of the autonomy of the signifier, representation and production. The issue is additionally complicated by the fact that the unconscious is split between unconscious desire and the dream work. The latter comprises all the mechanisms that manipulate the conscious and preconscious material and are homologous to linguistic operations. But these mechanisms serve to produce the object of satisfaction. The Freudian unconscious player turns out to be marked by a conflict, which makes the presupposed intention appear in its inconsistency. In order to illustrate this split, Freud will refer to nothing other than political economy:

> A daytime thought may very well play the part of *entrepreneur* for a dream; but the *entrepreneur,* who, as people say, has the idea and the initiative to carry it out, can do nothing without the capital; he needs a *capitalist* who can afford the outlay, and the capitalist who provides the psychical outlay for the dream is invariably and indisputably, whatever may be the thoughts of the previous day, *a wish from the unconscious.*[43]

In this excerpt, Freud focuses on the relation between unconscious desire and the day's remains, the dream work being excluded from the comparison. But, given the substantial role of the dream work in *Interpretation of Dreams*, we can tentatively claim that what Freud encounters in the unconscious appears to be homologous to the capitalist social link; it is the same contradiction as that between the capitalist and the labourer. With this distinction, Freud separates the intention from the subject. Unconscious desire and dream work are intentions *without* a subject – and we can recall at this point that Freud defines dream work as a process that neither thinks, calculates, nor judges, in short as pure intention. The

---

43   Freud, *Standard Edition,* Vol. 5, 560–1 (Freud's emphasis). For a more extensive comment on this passage, see part 2 of the present book.

subject of the unconscious, however, is a subject *without* intention, a decentralised and metonymic subject that is represented in the relation between linguistic and economic values. To anticipate later discussions, the subject without intention is produced in the difference between the repressed signifier of unconscious tendency (S_1) and all other signifiers among which the operations of the dream work take place (S_2). The problem of subjective transformation in analysis calls for a short circuit between the subject without intention and the intention without subject, between the decentralised subject of unconscious and the no less decentralised unconscious labour.

It is here that another crucial aspect of Lacan's later critique of Saussure enters the picture, this time regarding the arbitrariness of the sign. By defining the relation between the signifier and the signified as arbitrary, Saussure moved beyond the linguistic fetishism of his predecessors. The idea of arbitrariness implies that nothing within the signified unites it to the series of sounds that constitute the signifier. Lacan's first return to Freud radicalised Saussure by isolating the signifier from the Saussurean sign and thereby exposed the kernel of linguistic autonomy. The second return to Freud took a step further by isolating in arbitrariness its true logical modality, which Saussure did not accentuate sufficiently, namely contingency:

> For no signifier is produced as eternal. That is no doubt what, rather than qualifying it as arbitrary, Saussure could have formulated – it would have been better to qualify the signifier with the category of contingency. The signifier repudiates the category of the eternal and, nevertheless, oddly enough, it is intrinsically. Isn't it clear to you that it participates, to employ a Platonic approach, in that nothing on the basis of which something entirely original was made *ex nihilo*, as creationism tells us?[44]

Contingent is what participates in nothing. We can immediately note the scandal this subversion of participation has not only for Platonism but also for Christianity, the religion of the *creatio ex nihilo*. Participation in nothing introduces a strange hybrid of Plato and creationism. On the one hand, it evokes Plato's doctrine of the participation of appearances in eternal ideas. But the weakness of this doctrine consists in the conclusion that these ideas again participate in the highest Good. Plato thereby mystified

---

44 Lacan, *Encore*, 40.

the 'impenetrable void',[45] the negativity of the cut, in which every signifier participates. On the other hand, the proposed definition of contingency corrects Plato's doctrine of participation with the idea of creation of the world out of nothing. Of course, this does not suggest that Lacan simply accepts the creationist model, since creationism still understands God, not simply as the Other but as the Other of the Other (the Other of Creation). For this reason, creationism is incapable of really thinking the radical contingency of the act of creation, which would in itself have to undermine the religious hypothesis of the Other of the Other and make creation appear as non-whole, or not thoroughly constituted ontologically. From the viewpoint of contingency, God cannot be the eternal Creator but falls on the side of the effects of the created: 'God is unconscious' (*Seminar XI*), 'God comprises the integrity of the effects of language' (*Seminar XXII*), and finally the neologism *dieure* introduced in *Seminar XX*, which brings together God (*dieu*) and saying (*dire*). Both atheism and materialism are situated between Plato and creationism.

The introduction of contingency as a participation in nothing is a corollary to the autonomy of the signifier and indicates a double move beyond Saussurean epistemic coordinates:

> To say that the signifier is arbitrary does not have the same range as to simply say that it bears no relation to its effect of the signified, for the former involves slipping into another reference. The word 'reference', in this case, can only be situated on the basis of what discourse constitutes by way of a link. The signifier as such refers to nothing if not to a discourse, in other words, a mode of functioning or a utilisation of language qua link.[46]

Situating the signifier as difference already provides the minimal definition of the social link, under the condition that this definition includes the subject: 'The signifier is what represents a subject to another signifier'. The contingency of the signifier demonstrates that the mode in which language functions is in no way grounded on a necessary background that would guarantee its immanent stability and relation to an external reference. No invisible hand, no relation to nature, and finally no eternal creator, to whom we could ascribe *creatio ex nihilo*. Historically it makes sense that Plato tried to explain the creation of signifiers out of *physis*, since for Greeks

---

45   J. Lacan, *Le Séminaire, livre VIII, Le transfert*, Paris: Éditions du Seuil, 2001, 13.
46   Lacan, *Encore*, 30. Translation modified.

creatio ex nihilo was unthinkable. Moreover, the radicality of *creatio ex nihilo* is not entirely thinkable for Christianity either, insofar as religion still ascribes the act of creation to a presupposed Other of the Other, which supports and guarantees the consistency of the created Other (language, reality). *Creatio ex nihilo*, contingency in the entirety of its rigour, only becomes thinkable in the universe of modern science, where the autonomy of the signifier is not only discovered but also formalised.

The creation of the signifier out of nothing contains a twofold thesis on language and on social reality, for we are speaking of the use of language as a link. If the signifier bears no relation to the signified, then the social link, too, is not grounded on a stable background but is internally broken: there is no social relation. Or, to retranslate this axiom into Marx's language, all history is history of class struggles, whereby the plurality of class struggles specifies that the class struggle is not a transhistoric essence that would unify the historic movement and make of History a secularised Other of the Other.

With the introduction of arbitrariness, Saussure only partially uncovered the immanent instability of language. It is precisely for this reason too that the axioms of Lacan's second return to Freud, 'The unconscious is history' and 'The unconscious is politics', cannot be associated to Saussurean structuralism without modifying the very notion of structure. The imperative of structural linguistics consists in thinking language through the opposition of structure and life, without reference to the subject, while its object is constructed through the subtraction of language from speech. With this operation, Saussure grounded linguistics on an operation that Lacan will elsewhere describe as 'repression of the subject': the science of language treats the latter as if no subject would speak it. For linguistics, negativity does not speak, and its object is more like a language of immaterial beings, language without a body. On the contrary, the move from the signifier to the social link necessarily implies a theory of the subject:

> We must still indicate here what this link means. The link . . . is a link between those who speak. You can immediately see where we are headed – it's not just anyone who speaks, of course; it's beings, beings we are used to qualifying as 'living', and it would, perhaps, be rather difficult to exclude the dimension of life from those who speak. But we immediately realise that this dimension simultaneously brings in that of death, and that a radical signifying ambiguity results from this.[47]

---

47   Ibid.

Discourse does not only presuppose living bodies, it also introduces death, and hence negativity. By returning to this discursive intertwining of life and negativity, of the speaking body and the barred subject, psychoanalysis and the critique of political economy encounter the logical nexus of the autonomy of the signifier – the representation of the subject and the production of surplus.

REPRESENTATION AND PRODUCTION

Before 1968, Marx is not a major reference in Lacan's teaching. His name appears only sporadically, and mainly in relation to the subject of the signifier. All this changes in the seminar following the May '68 events, in which Lacan elaborates the homology between the object of *Capital* and the object of psychoanalysis. The title of the corresponding seminar resumes the underlying orientation of Lacan's second return to Freud, *D'un Autre à l'autre*: from the big Other, the field of language and the absolute autonomy of the signifier, to the small other, object *a*, the object of *jouissance*, but also the object that is logically associated with surplus-value. As the seminar's title already indicates, the accent is displaced from representation to production, introducing another level to the theory of the signifier. The emphasis on representation only approaches the signifier through the transcendentalism of the symbolic, where the signifier seems to be separated from *jouissance* and to entail its prohibition.[48] Subsequent orientation progressively abolishes this position and moves towards a conception of the signifier that is not simply invested with *jouissance* but becomes its privileged cause and apparatus. However, the causal relation presupposes a specific labour within language. Lacan thereby returns to the revolutionary kernel of Freud's theories, his labour theory of the unconscious, which explains the satisfaction of the unconscious tendency by the consumption of 'psychic energy' (labour-power) in the mental process.

---

48   Recall Lacan's position in *Seminar VII*, in which, in a Hegelian manner, the word is understood as a murder of the Thing, and the signifier a mortification of *jouissance*. The topic is there developed in reference to the Freudian theme of the murder of the primordial father in *Totem and Taboo* and then the murder of the Great Man in *Moses and Monotheism*. See J. Lacan, *Seminar*, Book VII, *The Ethics of Psychoanalysis*, New York: Norton, 1992, 81, 174.

The move from the Other of language to the other of *jouissance* overlaps with the shift from Saussure, the privileged theoretician of representation, to Marx, the key theoretician of production. The linguistic Other is now envisaged through the parallax of the subjective lack and the objective surplus, the two faces of discursive production. It is more than indicative that from this point on Lacan will repeat the well-known slogan 'The Other does not exist'. The claim should not be taken too lightly, notably not in the sense of vulgar atheism, which declares God an illusion that the progress of science necessarily abolishes. Lacan chooses a more sobering direction. Not only was the postmodern marked by an increase in religious belief, from institutionalised religions to various new-age obscurantisms, but the logic of capital, too, successfully imposes its religious component that Marx envisaged through the notion of fetishism. Lacan's prognosis of a triumph of religion over revolutionary science and emancipatory politics meanwhile became reality.

'The Other does not exist' also contains a materialist lesson, which links inexistence of the Other and causality of the signifier, while distinguishing the linguistic Other (language, discourse) from the theological and metaphysical God (the 'Other of the Other').[49] While inexistence (disclosure, incompleteness) does not prevent the Other from having real consequences, the persistence of religion consists in the idealist counter-offensive, which strives to attribute the consequences in question to a positive being: 'as long as things are said, the God hypothesis will persist'.[50] In the context of fetishism, this means that the inexistence of the Market (the global market as an instable and antagonistic space of values) goes hand in hand with the hypothesis of the vital forces of capitalist abstractions.[51] It is no coincidence

---

49   We can again recall the riddle from *Seminar XVII*. The point can be related to Marx's critique of commodity fetishism, in which the reconstruction of its logical mechanisms does not simply abolish the fetishisation of capitalist abstractions but rather shows that the efficiency of commodity fetishism is grounded on a discrepancy between thinking and action. Marx will say: 'They do not know it, nevertheless they do it'. Alfred Sohn-Rethel used this statement in order to introduce the notion of real abstraction, for which one can immediately notice that it comes rather close to Lacan's notion of discourse. See A. Sohn-Rethel, *Warenform und Denkform*, Frankfurt: Suhrkamp, 1978, 103–33. For the psychoanalytic contextualisation of his work, see S. Žižek, *The Sublime Object of Ideology*, London: Verso, 1989, 16–21.

50   Lacan, *Encore*, 45.

51   Lacan's remark could also be translated: 'As long as things are exchanged, the hypothesis of money-breeding money will persist'. Clearly, the hypothesis dates further back than capitalism.

that Lacan speaks of the triumph of religion at the dawn of financialisation, only a couple of years after the American abolition of the Breton-Woods system that terminated the gold standard and inaugurated the era of 'free-floating' currencies. The triumph of religion has a concrete name in political economy, neoliberalism, with its wild hypothesis that the deregulation of capital liberates its 'creative potentials' and immanent teleology, the spontaneous tendency of the market towards equilibrium.[52]

In its theory of the Other, psychoanalysis cannot but assume the position of atheism and materialism. The move to the small other extends this positioning in a logical alliance with the critique of political economy: 'I will proceed with a homological outlook based on Marx in order to introduce today the place where we need to situate the essential function of object *a*'.[53] The choice of terms contains an implicit criticism of Freudo-Marxism for remaining in a metaphorical or analogical framework, without exhaustively thematising the *logical, epistemological* and finally *political continuity* of Marx's critique of economic discourse and Freud's elaboration of libidinal economy. The thesis is that the unconscious production of *jouissance* and the social production of value follow the same logic and display the same structural contradictions, tensions and deadlocks: not repression of productive potentials of sexuality, drives and desires but the insatiable demand for production, 'production for the sake of production' (Marx), from which the repressed unconscious tendencies cannot be excepted.

The homology in question is supposed to situate the object of psychoanalysis, now translated as surplus-*jouissance*, in the discursive structure. This translation is coined according to Marx's surplus-value, *Mehrwert*, and Lacan even proposes a German term, *Mehrlust*. The coupling of *jouissance* and surplus, however, is not Lacan's invention but is already present in Freud, who, in his book on jokes, centred his analysis of unconscious satisfaction on what he called *Lustgewinn*, pleasure gain.[54] Freud thus already used the notion of the surplus-object but did not situate it logically and

---

52   For the function of theodicy in classical liberalism and contemporary neoliberalism, see J. Vogl, *The Specter of Capital*, Stanford, CA: Stanford University Press, 2014.

53   Lacan, *D'un Autre à l'autre*, 16.

54   See the second chapter of the present book, in which Freud's introduction of *Lustgewinn* is extensively examined. In the unpublished seminar from 20 November 1973, Lacan openly acknowledges the continuity between *Lustgewinn* and *plus-de-jouir*.

topologically. Subsequent development in psychoanalysis abolished the revolutionary consequences of the Freudian insight, so that Lacan's intervention aims at the same critical status as Marx with regard to the political-economic debates regarding surplus-value:

> This object *a*, in a certain sense I invented it, just as one can say that Marx's discourse invented something. What does this mean? Marx's discovery is surplus-value. It is not that object *a* was not approached before my discourse, of course, but it was approached in an insufficient way, as insufficient as the definition of surplus-value was before Marx's discourse made it appear in all its rigour.[55]

Inventions and not discoveries, then; and what is invented is not objects, which were already known before Marx and Lacan, but a method that exposes the hidden logic of their production. Here we again come across the inseparability of materialism and logic, as both inventions contain a turn in the understanding of discourse. At the root of this logical and materialist orientation stand the aforementioned quarrel regarding discursive consequences and the notion of material cause, now associated with the signifier.

Lacan leaves no doubt that his concern is solely the logical and not the analogical relation between Marx and Freud: 'To say homology means that their relation is not analogical. It is the same thing and the same stuff, as far as it is the discursive scissor cut (*trait de ciseau du discours*).'[56] The French phrasing alludes directly to the first chapter of *Capital*, where the commodity exchange and the double character of labour are repeatedly exemplified through tailoring. What matters is the inversion of the relation between concrete labour and abstract labour, since only through this inversion can the place and the function of surplus-value in the capitalist mode of production be unveiled. One of Marx's corrections of political economy resides in acknowledging the structural function of the gap between abstract and concrete labour, which depends on the double character of commodity. Through the social implementation of the commodity form, the absolute autonomy of exchange introduces a set of consequences in the subjective and the social reality. No cut is merely concrete labour; rather, it is part of a broader discursive logic that supports the capitalist organisation of labour. The action contains the central abstraction next to capital, the commodity-producing commodity that is

---

bought and sold on the market. In this way, every concrete labour is stamped by the contradiction that leads back to the double character of commodity. But let us here take a few steps back.

Without any logical gap that would separate the object of psychoanalysis from the object of the Marxist critique, both endeavours are joined by material implication:

> Only my theory of language as structure of the unconscious can be said to be implied by Marxism, if, that is, you are not more demanding than the material implication . . . that is, that my theory of language is true whatever be the adequacy of Marxism, and that it is needed by it, whatever be the defect that it leaves Marxism with. So much for the theory of language implied logically by Marxism.[57]

A material implication is false only when truth implies something false. Then there are only a few options left: either Marx's theory is true, which implies Lacan's theory of language as something true; or Marx's theory is false, which nevertheless implies that Lacan's theory of language is true; or, finally, both Marx's and Lacan's theories are false, but even in this case the homology remains valid and the material implication conserves its truth value. In any case, the critique of political economy precedes and conditions psychoanalysis not merely historically but above all logically, epistemologically and politically.

To say 'Marxism' naturally does not mean the same as to say 'Marx'. The quote contains more than it seems, for Lacan later alludes to the theory of language that Marxism implied historically. In the background stands Stalin's intervention into the Soviet linguistic debates, in which he negated the scientific status of Marrism, the theories of the Soviet linguist Nikolay Yakovlevich Marr, who defined language as a superstructure. Marr's theory implied that every major change in the base should lead to a major change in the superstructure. This would then mean that the Soviet revolution should have introduced a new language, or produced radical changes in the actually existing multiplicity of languages in the Soviet Union. Empirically this was naturally false and practically impossible. The development of language takes place independently from social revolutions, and Stalin's intervention into the debate consisted in declaring Marr's theory of language anti-Marxist, ending the debate with the order that 'language is *not* a

---

57 Lacan, *Television*, 111–12.

superstructure'.[58] Saussure claimed something similar in his lectures: the impossibility of a linguistic revolution comes from the fact that each subject participates in language individually. This individual participation prevents social revolutions from introducing major changes into the functioning of language. However, for Saussure, the same individual participation implies that language is subject to constant change. To repeat, language is not a state but a movement: it cannot be revolutionised, but there is nevertheless a permanent revolution, or better, a constant development and non-teleological becoming in language. This permanent revolution is located opposite individual participation, and does not mean that it is the subjects who consciously or intentionally change language.[59]

Lacan additionally specifies the characteristics of his theory of language: 'The least you can accord me concerning my theory of language is, should it interest you, that it is materialist. The signifier is matter transcending itself into language.'[60] The critical value of this materialism is contained in the description of the signifier as matter transcending itself into language. An unusual matter, of course, since it violates the spontaneous understanding of materiality, but, then again, the modern scientific understanding of matter is consistently counterintuitive and counter-empirical. The signifier, and consequently language as such, appears as transcendence within immanence, *torsion* within materiality. The causality of the signifier then does not consist in the simple scenario, where the signifier intervenes from some presupposed Outside but in the act of self-transcending, through which an autonomous system of differences emerges from materiality.

Lacan thereby rejects two seemingly opposite but nonetheless anti-materialist readings: conventionalism, for which language is a cultural

---

58   Stalin's text also refrained from declaring language simply a base, since this would merely repeat the dilemma regarding the relation between language and revolution, linguistic transformation and social transformation. For a detailed contextualisation of Stalin's axiom in Lacan's teaching, see J. C. Milner, *L'oeuvre claire*, Paris: Seuil, 1995, 85–8. For a broader discussion of Marrism, see R. L'Hermitte, Réne, *Marr, marrisme, marristes. Science et perversion idéologique*, Paris: Institut d'Études Slaves, 1987. Lacan remained politically realistic: the basic structural relations isolated by the logic of the signifier are the same as what he later calls the master's discourse, the structure of domination. Consequently, politics would contain a permanent struggle against relations of domination and a structural tension between the tendencies of domination and liberation.

59   See Saussure, *Course in General Linguistics*, 73–4.

60   Lacan, *Television*, 112.

product (human convention with the exclusive aim of communication), and neurolinguistics, which places language in the broader context of cerebral evolution (and for which language is no less an organ of communication). Neither a convention nor a biological product of evolution, since both reductions exclude the autonomy of the signifier, a contingent but no less real consequence that accompanies the emergence of language and without which language is unthinkable. This autonomy denaturalises the apparently natural or conventional tool of cerebral or cultural evolution. Language is therefore an internal exteriority, a foreign body in the biological body.[61] Its 'atom', the signifier, becomes a cause by loosening its ties both to cerebral materiality and to communication. At this point, the relation between use-value and exchange-value re-enters the picture and Lacan's materialist definition of the signifier echoes Marx's description of commodity as a *sinnlich übersinnliches Ding*,[62] sensual suprasensual thing, where the same act of transcendence, articulation of materiality (commodities) into (commodity) language, is at stake. And just as the transcendence of the signifier produces a metonymic subject and an ungraspable object of *jouissance*, the transcendence of commodities transforms labour into labour-power and situates surplus-value as the privileged object-cause in the capitalist social link.

The materialist definition of the signifier pursues the quarrel regarding alienation. An idealist would necessarily claim that the subject is constitutively unalienated and that alienation is secondary. At the same time, as soon as one starts from the primacy of the signifier, alienation turns out to be constitutive of the subject. The articulation of the signifier into an open system of differences can only produce a decentralised subjectivity, and Marx's critical move in the first chapter of *Capital* consists in differentiating constituted alienation, fetishism, which still concerns the 'cognitive' misperception of commodities, from constitutive alienation, production of capitalist subjectivity *qua* labour-power. Labour-power designates the capitalist appropriation of the subject of the signifier, its transformation in accordance with the commodity form. In other words:

---

61   Commenting on a case of psychosis, which articulated the symptom of 'imposed words', Lacan compared language with cancer: 'How come that everyone does not feel that the words, on which we rely, are, in a way, imposed on us? In this way those usually called patients sometimes go much further than a healthy person. The question is, rather, why a so-called normal person does not perceive that speech is a parasite, a plague, a form of cancer that affects the human being?' J. Lacan, *Le Séminaire, livre XXIII, Le sinthome*, Paris: Éditions du Seuil, 2005, 95.

62   K. Marx, *Das Kapital*, Berlin: Dietz Verlag, 1962, 85.

Value represents what of labour-power is contained in each object that carries value, but it can only represent it in commodity exchange, that is, for another value. But labour-power is simply the subject. It is Marx's name for the subject.[63]

According to Marx, his materialist predecessors, notably Feuerbach, failed to theorise the logical connection between alienation and structure. It is not materialist enough to simply reverse the relations between God and Man, or to proclaim that God is a projection of Man's desires, something that Freud formulated in his critique of religion. Marx founded materialism on the detachment of alienation from imaginary projection, associating it instead with structure and logics, the paradigmatic example here being the equivocity of commodity language and human language. The materialist orientation consequently substituted the reference to Man and to its transcendental essence with the reference to the subject, understood not as an autonomous consciousness but as a real consequence of the autonomous signifier. This is the essential point of Marx's *Theses on Feuerbach*, which is actualised in *Capital*:

> The chief defect of all hitherto existing materialism (that of Feuerbach included) is that the thing, reality, sensuousness, is conceived only in the form of the *object or of contemplation*, but not as *sensuous human activity, practice*, not subjectively. Hence, in contradistinction to materialism, the *active* side was developed abstractly by idealism – which, of course, does not know real, sensuous activity as such . . . Feuerbach resolves the religious essence into the *human* essence. But the human essence is no abstraction inherent in each single individual. In its reality it is the ensemble of the social relations.[64]

Pre-critical theories of the subject continue to use the idealist vocabulary of cognition (contemplation, consciousness), keeping as their ultimate reference transcendental and centralised subjectivity, while the critique of political economy departs from the repressed flip side of this idealist subject, the alienated subject *at work* in every discursive action. This is the *logical* subject of politics. In order to achieve this, discourse, too, needs to be envisaged as more than mere *organon*. The aim of Marx's analysis of

---

63   J. C. Milner, *Clartés de tout*, Paris: Verdier, 2011, 90.
64   K. Marx, *Early Writings*, London: Penguin Books, 1992, 422–3.

labour therefore cannot be the simple liberation of living labour from blood-sucking capital but a rigorous determination of the actual subject of capitalism, labour-power, whose abolition would initiate a structural transformation of the entire mode of production and a transformation of the subject, since the logical subject of the autonomous system of differences would thereby be separated from the commodified form imposed by capitalism. Marx did envisage a liberation of the subject, not from alienation, as the humanist Marxists continue to claim, but from the false universalism of commodity form and from its abstract representation in the regime of values. Political economy, and the capitalist vision of politics that is grounded on its concepts, sees in the subject a mere commodity, hence an object, while enthroning the tendencies of capital and the private interests of the capitalist class as the privileged subject of politics.

Milner proposed to call the materialist orientation that Lacan elaborated in his reference to Marx 'discursive materialism'. The expression risks falsely suggesting that Lacan was attempting to construct some sort of postmodern materialism, a combination of vulgar materialism and the linguistic performative. Yet it all comes down to how we understand Lacan's claim that discourse has consequences.[65] If we interpret them within the framework of performative theory, then they remain within the symbolic, confirm the autonomy of the signifier and address merely the permanent modifications of linguistically constructed reality. Lacan's recurrent appeal to formal logic and mathematics goes beyond these narrow frameworks of performativism and exposes another kind of production in language from the mere proliferation of language games and metonymic meaning. The issue is most evidently at stake when it comes to the subject of representation (labour-power, the subject of the unconscious) and the object of production (surplus-value, surplus-*jouissance*): they are not simply performative effects of the capitalist discourse but real consequences of the structural causality in social reality and in the living body.

Lacan often uses the example of the moon landing in his attempts to theorise discursive consequences. This event was not so much a 'giant leap for mankind' but rather an event in perfect accordance with what Foucault described as the 'death of Man'. The true event is not the actual moon landing

---

65   The significance of this formulation for the understanding of Lacan's materialist orientation was extensively analysed by Alenka Zupančič (*Seksualno in ontologija,* Ljubljana: Analecta, 2011), on whose readings I rely on for my own developments.

but the fact that it lies within the realm of discursive possibilities alone: 'scientific discourse was able to bring about the moon landing, where thought becomes witness to an eruption of the real, and with mathematics using nothing other than a linguistic apparatus.'[66] The moon landing is thus a discursively generated event, which does not make it in any way less real. Only that the materiality of the real demonstrated by the moon landing, as an event that has its mathematical foundations, goes much further than the reality of the moon landing, the empirical presence of Man on the moon. The appearance of the moon landing being an achievement of Man conceals the capacity of scientific discourse to produce an event by means of the linguistic apparatus, without Man as its central agent but not without a subject as its effect. Behind the 'giant leap for Mankind' there lies the final erasure of the idealist human essence; the event once again demonstrated Man's actual status in the capitalist universe as a quantifiable subject (labour-power) mobilised by a successful cooperation between science and capitalism, meaning that Man was again confirmed in his status of waste material rather than a sublime generic essence.

When Lacan points out the discrepancy between the historical and the logical deployments of the Marxist theory of language, he indicates that Marxism failed to recognise that Marx's idea of commodity language and the inversion of the relation between use-value and exchange-value (exchange as an abstract but nonetheless productive action) already made it further than the Saussurean determination of the double character of linguistic signs. Lacan's correction of structural linguistics – the isolation of the signifier from the sign and the introduction of the subject – provides the materialist theory of language indicated in Marx's critique (in the earlier-quoted excerpts Lacan writes twice: '*my* theory of language'). In turn, Marx's theory makes the same correction in relation to the political-economic labour theory of value. A critical and materialist theory of value can be elaborated only under the condition that the abstract political-economic subject of private interest is replaced with the alienated subject *qua* labour-power. In this case as well, Marxism regressed back to the idealist framework that Marx criticised in his *Theses on Feuerbach*. The Marxist variant of idealist subjectivity is proletarian class-consciousness, yet another version of the transcendental subject of History.[67] A significant part of

---

66   Lacan, *Television*, 36. Translation modified.

67   Žižek describes Lukács's introduction of class-consciousness as an idealist misreading of Hegel: 'This is why Lukács also remains all too idealist when he proposes simply replacing Hegelian Spirit with the proletariat as the Subject-Object

Marxism (one but surely not the only exception being Althusser's theoretical anti-humanism) inverted Marx's logic, which begins with the autonomy of value in order to arrive at the production of decentralised subjectivity. That *Capital* is about structural and not empirical or cognitive reality is made explicit in the very preface, where Marx writes:

> To prevent possible misunderstanding, let me say this. I do not by any means depict the capitalist and the landowner in rosy colours. But individuals are dealt with here only in so far as they are the personifications of economic categories, the bearers of particular class-relations and interests. My standpoint, from which the development of the economic formation of society is viewed as a process of natural history, can less than any other make the individual responsible for relations whose creature he remains, socially speaking, however much he may subjectively raise himself above them.[68]

Again, Marx does not aim to ground politics on the cognition of the capitalist relations of production, whose efficiency is independent from consciousness, but on a materialist theory of the subject, which is supposed to give ground to an actual universalism while also demonstrating the root at which the false universality of commodity form grabs each individual and society as a whole. The rejection of the primacy of cognition is further expressed in the following well-known reversal, where Marx's implicit understanding of the signifier already surpasses Saussure:

> Men do not therefore bring the products of their labour into relation with each other as values because they see these objects merely as the material integuments of homogeneous human labour. The reverse is true: by equating their different products to each other in exchange as values, they equate their different kinds of labour as human labour. They do not know it, nevertheless they do it. Value, therefore, does not have its description branded on its forehead; it rather transforms every product into a social hieroglyphic. Later on, men try to decipher the hieroglyphic, to get behind the secret of their own social product: for the characteristic which objects of utility have of being values is as much men's social product as is their language.[69]

---

of History: Lukács is here not really Hegelian, but a pre-Hegelian idealist.' S. Žižek, *Living in the End Times*, London: Verso, 2011, 226.

68   Marx, *Capital*, Vol. 1, 92.

69   Ibid., 166–7. Translation modified.

Because there is exchange, different kinds of labour are condensed into an abstraction, which is nonetheless material. The system of differences transforms labour, which does not leave the subject unaffected. Hence the question is not in deciphering the hidden meaning of social hieroglyphs but in situating the subject they signal in their autonomy. For whether in civilisation or in the desert, a hieroglyph always implies another hieroglyph and the subject of the relation independently of consciousness. A hieroglyph is always-already social because of this implication and not because of its use by concrete and conscious individuals.

When it comes to social hieroglyphs, fetishism is already an attempt at their interpretation, which leaves the structure of the commodity universe unknown and the logic of production mystified. By ascribing to commodities, money and capital, the value of having a positive and intrinsic quality, fetishisation comes rather close to hermeneutic interpretation (just as for Plato and Heidegger being was an immanent feature of language and not its effect). On the contrary, a materialist interpretation highlights the autonomy of structural relations and traces the fetishist interpretation back to the equivocity of commodity form. Slavoj Žižek has suggested on several occasions that 'they do not know it, nevertheless they do it' should be supplemented with 'they know it, nevertheless they do it'. The efficiency of structural relations being immune to consciousness, Marx's critical method cannot envisage an overall abolition of fetishisation but the detachment of politics from the reign of economic abstractions, which has been intensified by decades of neoliberalism. The liberation of politics consequently means the same as the abolition of the rootedness of social links in the commodity form as their unique formal envelope.

The statement 'they do not know it, nevertheless they do it' seems to contain the division between conscious knowledge and unconscious action, but the actual and more fundamental division exists in the regime of knowledge: between reflected knowledge, on the one hand, and unknown knowledge, contained in both thinking and action, on the other. Marx is here even more Freud's predecessor, showing that the necessary precondition for abolishing the political reign of capitalist abstractions resides in a systematic reintroduction of negativity into politics. Class struggle is not the sole politically charged signifier – the unconscious is one as well. To demonstrate the logical inscription of the unconscious into politics was the central effort of Lacan's homology.

When introducing the homology between both surpluses, Lacan expresses his regret that he did not introduce Marx earlier into 'the field in which he is, after all, entirely at home', or on another occasion, '*Mehrwert* is *Marxlust*, Marx's surplus-*jouissance*'.[70] As evident as this affinity may appear in the late 1960s, this introduction could not have happened before the invention of object *a*. In 1968, the object *a* is already the central Lacanian concept, and Marx can now become the privileged reference, which helps to uncover 'the place where we need to situate the essential function of object *a*': the homology immediately extends into homotopy.[71] The logical identity of both surpluses strives to situate the specific mode of existence of the unconscious in the social link while also accounting for the unconscious effects of the capitalist discourse; the capitalist colonisation of the mental apparatus. In homology there is no place for the opposition of the subjective and the social. Freud already tried to place psychoanalysis on this border, and Lacan's notion of discourse pursues this direction, describing both the structure articulated in individual speech and the structure of the social link. But Lacan differs from Freud in one important respect. While Freud's theories amounted to the myth of the primordial father, the originary subject of *jouissance*, the fundamental Lacanian lesson is that there is no such thing as a subject of *jouissance*, just as for Marx there is no subject of surplus-value, unless one fetishises the *appearance* of capital as the vital subject of valorisation, as is the case in the developed forms of capitalist abstractions such as financial capital (but also on the more 'immediate' level of commodities and money).

Lacan introduces his reading of Marx by recalling the most evident feature of his critical break with political economy:

> Marx departs from the function of the market. His novelty is the place where he situates labour. It is not that labour is something new but that it is bought, that there is a market of labour. This is what allows Marx to demonstrate what is inaugural in his discourse and what is called surplus-value.[72]

The departure is not the market of political economists, where all commodities and values seem to occupy the same level and are abolished

---

70 See Lacan, *D'un Autre à l'autre*, 16, and *Autres écrits*, 434.

71 Lacan, *D'un Autre à l'autre*, 16. The overlapping of homology and homotopy will direct Lacan's teaching to a progressive identification of topology and structure: 'Topology is not "made to guide us" in the structure. Topology is this structure – as a retroaction of the chain order of which language consists' (Lacan, *Autres écrits*, 483).

72 Lacan, *D'un Autre à l'autre*, 17.

in equivalence, but a 'market of labour', where labour-power is the negative metonymic constant that value represents in every commodity and that exposes the paradoxes of commodity form and of the market as such. To repeat, the main inconsistency resides in the double character of commodity, which grounds the difference between commodities and commodity-producing commodity, and more generally the gap between representation of labour-power in terms of exchange-value and production of surplus-value in the consumption of labour-power. The political economists see the market as an 'immense collection of commodities' (Marx), a closed system, whose dynamic does not necessarily contradict the immanent tendencies to self-regulation and homeostasis. The market appears homogeneous and structured on stable and predictable relations, similarly as in the previously discussed Saussurean analogy, in which there are only values that relate to commodities in an arbitrary but nevertheless stable and adequate way. In the sharpest possible contrast to this idyllic scenario, the consequent interpretation of the market as being first and foremost a market of labour exposes that this political-economic Other is traversed by contradictions and is therefore inconsistent. At the very heart of the capitalist transformation of labour stands the strikingly banal and yet wide-reaching fact that labour is bought and sold on the market, where it appears as a commodity among others. To say that Marx's novelty lies in the correct situation of labour – and not simply in the labour theory of value, to which his critical interventions could mistakenly be reduced – again argues that a materialist science of value is not possible without a theory of the subject that the political-economic labour theory failed to articulate.

Lacan grounds the homology between surplus-value and surplus-*jouissance* on a reformulation of his definition of the signifier: 'the signifier is what represents a subject to another signifier'. Saying that Marx's version would be 'value represents labour-power for another value' would not be entirely correct because it would bypass the double character of the commodity form. Lacan therefore draws a different conclusion. His old definition is 'copied from the fact that, in what Marx deciphered, namely the economic reality, the subject of exchange-value is represented next to the use-value'.[73] The extension of the double character of commodity to the logic of the signifier additionally exposes the ambiguous status of use-value, whose abstract face becomes apparent in the consumption of labour-power.

73   Ibid., 21.

Its usefulness indeed consists in the production of other commodities, but from the perspective of capital its consumption aims at the extraction of surplus-value.[74]

The gap between representation and production cannot be localised because it is everywhere and nowhere in the labour process. No quantification can draw a limit, where the production of use-values ceases and the production of surplus-value begins, and correspondingly, where labour is paid and where unpaid surplus labour begins. The problem clearly does not lie in the fact that the value of labour-power would be inadequate or that a more accurate representation of labour-power should be sought, but that labour-power is already produced as structurally inadequate and non-identical. Consequently, the articulation of representation with production, exchange-value with use-value, presupposes a different topology from the univocal division of inside and outside. The space, in which representation and production intertwine, is simultaneously continuous and discontinuous, displaying the main feature of the Möbius strip. This is the homotopy that the homology leads to.

The crucial factor that complicates the topological but also the temporal relations is the tendency of capital towards self-valorisation, which makes the production of use-values indistinguishable from the production of surplus-value. Marx writes:

> The capitalist has bought the labour-power at its daily value. The use-value of the labour-power belongs to him throughout one working day. He has thus acquired the right to make the worker work for him during one day. But, what is a working day? At all events, it is less than a natural day. How much less? The capitalist has his own views of this point of no return, the necessary limit of the working day. As a capitalist, he is only capital personified. His soul is the soul of capital. But capital has one sole driving force, the drive to valorize itself, to create surplus-value, to make its constant part, the means of production, absorb the greatest possible amount of surplus labour.[75]

---

74   The same conclusion is applicable to the distribution, circulation and consumption of commodities. Marx's moderate analyses of use-value in *Capital* nevertheless leave no doubt that even the most remote and private act of consumption is not exempt from the extraction of surplus-value and from the imperatives of capital.

75   Marx, *Capital*, Vol. 1, 341–2.

The structural tendencies and imperatives of capital push the entirety of production towards purposelessness and compulsive automatism. Through this *automaton* the main feature of *jouissance* emerges in the capitalist organisation of labour, the fact that the surplus-object 'serves no purpose'.[76] It does not satisfy another tendency except the drive for self-valorisation, so that the ultimate aim of labour consists in producing more labour.

Lacan's translation of the signifier into economic reality recapitulates the contradiction of the two circulations that Marx formalises in the introductory chapters of *Capital*. The structure of the capitalist mode of production is internally doubled on the circulation 'commodity – money – commodity' (C – M – C) and 'money – commodity – money' (M – C – M). This internal doubling is not without the appearance that we are dealing with two different and independent circulations, which can be read historically or logically, and Marx seems to propose both readings. According to the historic one, the (C – M – C) circulation (exchange, selling and buying) would be the oldest form that historically and logi-cally precedes capitalism and that, more importantly, does not contain the perversion that grounds the capitalist mode of production, whose aim is exclusively the production of surplus-value, the constant growth of profit and absolute autonomy of capital (M – M'), the formula of fictitious capital that abolishes the mediation of production through commodity labour-power. The genesis of capitalism thus implies a structural shift that is both historical and logical, and the difference between the first and the second circulation seems to recapitulate the historical passage from feudalism to capitalism. Marx formalises this development in the circula-tion (M – C – M), which he immediately corrects into (M – C – M'), where (M' = M + ∆M, increase of value) and thereby finally situates surplus-value in the social link. Lacan's definition of the signifier can be situated in both circulations but has entirely different consequences in the virtually infinite circulation (M – C – M').

The historical reading of the first circulation inevitably falls into the trap of its idealisation: the nostalgia for those good old days when commod-ity exchange was still immediate and when social reality was not corrupted by the merciless drive for profit. Placing (C – M – C) before the circulation of capital thus produces a fantasy of economic exchange as the paradig-matic case of social relation and the illusion that this exchange was once homeostatic and regulated but was thrown out of joint by the instabilities of

---

76 Lacan, *Encore*, 3.

capital; an illusion of the past, in which money still fulfilled its social function, its use-value, which consisted in supporting economic exchange and
thereby the social relation. Marx certainly does not promote this oversim-
plifying nostalgic vision, since he recalls that the paradoxes of the general
equivalent already troubled Aristotle. At the same time, both circulations
address the inner inconsistency of the capitalist social link. Their logical
reading shows that Marx in fact analyses the gap between appearance and
structure. (C – M – C) is not more immediate, not an authentic exchange
that is later corrupted by profit-oriented (M – C – M′) but an *inner fiction*
of the circulation (M – C – M′). Of course, we cannot simply claim that in
capitalism commodity exchange is inoperative. It is operative precisely as
far as it masks the circulation of capital and neutralises its immediate
obscenity and exploitative tendencies. According to the logical reading, the
first circulation, selling and buying, concerns the worker, and the second,
apparently symmetrical one, buying and selling, the capitalist. Of course,
the whole critical point of Marx's formalisation is to prove that both circulations are asymmetrical: that what the worker is selling is not the same
thing as what the capitalist is buying, or put differently, that the value for
which the labour is sold is not the same as the value for which it is bought.
When the capitalist buys labour-power he gets in one and the same package
surplus-value:

> We pay labour with money, because we are on the market. We pay it accord-
> ing to its true price, as it is defined on the market by the function of
> exchange-value. But there is unpaid value in what appears as the fruit of
> labour, because the true price of this fruit is in its use-value. This unpaid
> labour, which is nevertheless paid in a just way in relation to the consistency
> of the market in the functioning of capitalist discourse, is surplus-value.[77]

The apparently banal remark that we pay labour with money demonstrates
its point if we remember the most basic Marxian lesson regarding money.
Since we are dealing with two different circulations, money, just like any
other commodity, appears in its double character: once as use-value, a
material support of exchange, a concrete embodiment of that sameness that
is expressed by all exchanged commodities, and once as capital, the embodiment of the autonomy of exchange-value and of the surplus-object. Money
finally reveals the fantasmatic status of use-value, which is nevertheless

---

77   Lacan, *D'un Autre à l'autre*, 37.

necessary for the functioning of the capitalist machinery. Money has no use-value except that it supports exchange and embodies the autonomy of value. For this reason it becomes the fetishist object *par excellence*. But social inequality again reveals the immanent doubling of exchange, since the labourer only deals with money as means of exchange, that is, labour-power can only be represented through exchange-value, and according to the law of exchange the labourer receives a 'just' payment. The capitalist, however, deals with money as capital, and from this perspective the use-value of labour-power does not consist in producing commodities but in producing more value. For this reason, the capitalist as the personification of capital and as a social administrator of its 'private interest' tends to extend the working day and to reduce the time needed for the production of use-values. The labourer gets paid 'justly', yet the truth of labour is not in the presumed adequacy of representation but in the structural gap that both separates and links it to production.

THE LOGIC OF SURPLUS AND LOSS

The gap between representation and production certainly reflects an inner break in the social link, but it also has a structuring function that amounts to the well-known result that drives capitalist social relations: 'It is in this gap that what is called surplus-value is produced and falls. Non-identical to itself, the subject no longer enjoys. Something called surplus-*jouissance* is lost'.[78] The double production of the subject of loss and the surplus-object is accompanied by the appearance that the object originally belonged to the subject and was only lost at a later stage. This appearance is the negative correlate to the fetishisation of capitalist abstractions and motivates a misinterpretation of the worker's position. The psychoanalytic supplement to the Marxist critique of fetishism is contained in the very homophony of *plus* in *plus-de-jouir*, which means both 'more *jouissance*' and 'no more *jouissance*'. The formulation resumes the central Freudian thesis that *jouissance* knows no right measure and that its production entirely undermines the homeostatic model, on which, for instance, Aristotelian ethics as well as economic liberalism built their economic and political theories. Behind the subjective pursuit of egoistic private interest, the multiplicity of small human narcissisms, from which, for Adam Smith and other liberal

---

78   Ibid., 21.

economists, somewhat miraculously grows a stable social relation, there is a structural loss, which in advance corrupts the capitalist pursuit of happiness and its fantastic success stories. In opposition to political economy, Freud grounded his metapsychological account of libidinal economy on the rejection of the homeostatic model. The homeostatic vision of the mental apparatus is definitively abolished in *Beyond the Pleasure Principle* (1920), where the notion of the death drive, the emblem of the constitutive instabilities of libidinal economy, enters the picture.

The two aspects of fetishism are addressed in Lacan's formula of fantasy ($ \lozenge a$), according to which the fetishisation varies depending on whether the given conditions are observed from the position of the subject or of the object. In the first case, the structurally generated appearance suggests that the subject and the object form two compatible halves that could be fused together in a non-problematic totality. In the second, the subject of valorisation appears to be capital itself, as the fetishisation of capitalist abstractions suggests. In any case, the subject's non-identity is perceived as secondary and as something that could be abolished simply by 'correcting' the structural relations that brought the subject into existence. The standard social-democratic scenario moves in this direction: including the workers in a more just distribution of profit, collective ownership of the means of production, regulating financial speculation and bringing the economy down to the solid ground of the real sector. More radical political experiments were equally unsuccessful in abolishing alienation: 'It's not because one nationalises the means of production at the level of socialism in one country that one has thereby done away with surplus-value, if one doesn't know what it is'.[79] Nationalisation does not produce the necessary global structural change, which would abolish the market of labour and thereby the structural contradiction that transforms the subject into a commodity-producing commodity. The non-relation between labour-power and surplus-value remains operative, and nationalisation in the last instance evolves into a form of state capitalism. Marx, however, did not claim that the appropriation of surplus-value would abolish the capitalist forms of alienation and fetishisation. This would suggest that the abolition of capitalists, these social fanatics of the valorisation of value and personifications of capital, would already solve the problem. Marx's point is rather that capitalism *can* exist without capitalists because the capitalist drive to self-valorisation is

---

79 Ibid., 108.

structural, systemic and autonomous – but there cannot be any capitalism without the proletariat.[80]

The critical and materialist signification of alienation departs from the autonomy of the signifier and leads to the conclusion that alienation *is* structure. No identity or *jouissance* precedes non-identity and loss, and, consequently, no subjective wholeness is abolished and no immediate access to *jouissance* is made impossible by the intervention of the signifier. Such a position would indeed place psychoanalysis in the symmetrical understanding of alienation, which echoes in Freud's earlier accounts of the relation between sexuality and culture and eventually in Freudo-Marxism.[81] Identity assumes the same status as the idealist notion of human essence that Marx criticised in his predecessors. The equivalence between aliena-tion and structure, by contrast, leaves no doubt that the flip side of the production of surplus is the reproduction of lack – the true 'matter' by which the subject is constituted.

The equivocity of the *plus* in surplus-value and surplus-*jouissance* allows Lacan to conclude that the discursive structure of capitalism imposes the renunciation of *jouissance* rather than its prohibition. This renunciation is what makes of the capitalist a modern master. The point is not necessarily self-evident, notably if we recall the conclusion of Marx's critique of primitive accumulation, the founding myth of political econ-omy, according to which the capitalist historically accumulated the first wealth through saving, while the proletarian enjoyed beyond his limits, until he was left solely with his labour-power. In this process, his entire existence was reduced to a labour without qualities, which stained his being with having. Marx mobilises this main feature of alienation to his own advantage, under the abolition of the political-economic myth of

---

80   '*Both* the proletariat and the capitalist class are bound to capital, but the former is more so: capital conceivably could exist without capitalists, but it could not exist without value-creating labor.' M. Postone, *Time, Labor, and Social Domination*, Cambridge: Cambridge University Press, 2003, 357.

81   See notably Freud's early writing 'Civilized Sexual Morality and Modern Nervous Illness', which in many ways continues to determine the perception of his later accounts in *Civilisation and Its Discontents*. The introduction of the primordial father makes an interesting about-turn, since the structure of the Freudian myth demonstrates the fantasmatic status of 'full' *jouissance*. The sons think that by killing the father they will gain access to non-castrated *jouissance*, while what they actually get after the killing is universal castration, the return of the dead father in the form of symbolic prohibition that constitutes and traverses all social relations.

primitive accumulation. In the capitalist universe, commodity is not simply yet another private property but the privileged form of being. The ontological question of being is thus necessarily preceded and conditioned by the pre-ontological question of having, whereby the asymmetry between the subjective lack and objective surplus highlights the modern coordinates of the ontological problematic. This effort implicitly traverses Marx's critique of materialism in his *Theses on Feuerbach* and determines its future orientation. There is no critique of political economy without an implicit materialist ontology.

But let us return here to the link between labour and the renunciation of *jouissance*. According to Lacan, this is not the actual novelty of Marx and Freud's concept of labour. Their critical contribution is in explaining this renunciation as something that is structurally imposed on the subject by the relations of domination:

> From the very start, contrary to what Hegel claims or seems to claim, it is precisely this renunciation that constitutes the master, who knows very well how to make it the principle of his power. What is new here is that there is a discourse that articulates this renunciation and makes it appear within something that I will call the function of surplus-*jouissance*.[82]

The correction of the political-economic idea of renunciation becomes more evident here. The master does not renounce some substantial *jouissance* but instead structurally imposes the renunciation on every subject. The equivocity of *plus* in surplus-*jouissance* again turns out to be crucial. Surplus-*jouissance* is not some *jouissance* that would reach beyond another *jouissance*, in the sense that there would be a certain quantity of *jouissance* to which something more is added. The actual correlate to the surplus-*jouissance*, produced by the same discursive cut, is the lack of *jouissance*. The renunciation of *jouissance* therefore contains more than the battle for pure prestige through which Hegel seems to approach the master-slave dialectic. The capitalist relations of domination build on this double face of the surplus. Production goes hand in hand with renunciation, the 'more' with the 'no more'. The double structural imperative – production of surplus and production of lack through renunciation – initiates a negative spiral, in which no produced surplus is surplus enough. The capitalist master constantly demands more, the famous *encore* that Lacan placed in the title

---

82   Lacan, *D'un Autre à l'autre*, 21.

of one of his seminars. Marx in his turn exemplified this imperative in the so-called abstinence theory of the capitalist:

> But, in so far as he is capital personified, his motivating force is not the acquisition of enjoyment of use-values, but the acquisition and augmentation of exchange-values. He is fanatically intent on the valorisation of value; consequently he ruthlessly forces the human race to produce for production's sake . . . Only as personification of capital is the capitalist respectable. As such, he shares with the miser an absolute drive toward self-enrichment [*Bereicherungstrieb*]. But what appears in the miser as the mania of an individual is in the capitalist the effect of a social mechanism in which he is merely a cog.[83]

The master's renunciation of *jouissance* lies in the difference between the miser and the capitalist, which entails several traps, the main one being that the miser can appear, in comparison to the capitalist, as a subject supposed to enjoy. The quoted passage contains the best description of the difference between enjoyment in the vulgar sense and what Lacan's concept of *jouissance* aims at. In everyday understanding, enjoyment is linked to consumption, which still presupposes positive qualities and concrete consumption (use-value). The miser, by contrast, displays, not some other or perverse enjoyment but that which should be properly called *jouissance*. Instead of wasting his wealth on private consumption, he accumulates, jealously protecting his treasure from the rest of the world, first and foremost from his own temptation to waste it. In his abstinence, the miser does much more than simply renounce some immediate enjoyment in consumption. His drive for enrichment can reach satisfaction only in detaching the privileged embodiments of wealth (gold and money) from their social circulation. His entire persona thereby becomes a hostage of the object.[84]

Two things are worth noticing in the difference between the miser and the capitalist, which also reveal why the capitalist is a figure of the master, while the miser is merely its comical caricature. Despite being a consequence of the social mechanism, the miser's drive is still actualised in the form of his subjective fixation and obsession, while in the capitalist the same drive is *the* structuring element of the social link, a

---

83   Marx, *Capital*, Vol. 1, 739.
84   I rely here on M. Dolar, *O skoposti*, Ljubljana: Analecta, 2002, 49–54.

systemic imperative that is interested solely in values and *jouissance* in the production process. The capitalist actualises the truth of the miser and can become what the miser cannot: the personification of the systemic imperative of accumulation of wealth, now transformed into capital, that is, into an externalised social link that no longer includes merely accumulation but also production, circulation and individual consumption. The capitalist stands for a *globalisation of the drive*, its sole function is to support and preserve the social implementation of the fanaticism of the demand, to which the drive for enrichment is reducible: the constant expansion of value, the imperative of growth, accompanied by the permanent revolution of the means of production and the forcing of populations into precarity. All this demands renunciation, indebting and production of lack, which finally makes of the capitalist an *inversion* of the miser, the social transformation of the 'spirit of the miser'. The miser so to speak renounced social relations for the sake of the illusion that the immediate access to *jouissance* is possible only in the form of treasure. For this reason, usury has been morally condemned throughout history, and the miser fetishised as an obscene subject of *jouissance*. The miser illustrates Marx's remark that 'capitalism is already essentially abolished once we assume that it is enjoyment that is the driving motive and not enrichment itself.'[85] To rephrase, the miser does not entirely follow through on his attempt to detach the treasure from personal enjoyment. He detaches it from everyone, including himself, but he does not make the *jouissance* produced through this very detachment appear as the *jouissance* of the system. For the miser, *jouissance* assumes the finite and empirical form, while for the capitalist treasure is the more endless the more it is abstract: from gold to paper money, from paper money to fictitious capital, electronic money and so on. The miser counts objects: his treasure is embodied. The capitalist merely counts: his treasure is the number. Consequently, fetishisation is displaced from concrete materiality to the ghostly materiality of financial abstractions. The more surplus is turned into an abstraction, the more it pertains to the system, and the less the systemic obscenity is visible. The enrichment itself becomes a socially acceptable and admirable abstraction.

But this enrichment contains its inevitable flip side, the production of surplus populations, the true signification of 'human capital'. The

---

85   K. Marx, *Capital*, Vol. 2, London: Penguin, 1992, 199.

equivocity between 'more' and 'no more' envisages this negative social production: 'Surplus-value is the cause of desire, which a certain economy has made its principle: that of the extensive and therefore insatiable production of a lack-of-*jouissance*'; or another variation: 'I think I have sufficiently announced from the beginning of this year that surplus-*jouissance* is something other than *jouissance*. Surplus-*jouissance* responds, not to *jouissance*, but to the loss of *jouissance*'.[86] The epistemological tool that provides an insight into the structure of the libidinal and the social economy is the second law of thermodynamics, which explains the flow of energy from regions with higher temperature to regions with lower temperature, thereby introducing the notion of entropy. The notion already supported Marx's analysis of the extraction of surplus-value from the consumption of labour-power.[87] The same asymmetry is reflected in the broader social context: the accumulation of wealth accompanied by the accumulation of misery, the revolution of the means of production combined with the production of a surplus population. The capitalist social link is structured like entropy.

Lacan approaches energetics through the autonomy of the signifier and envisages in entropy a real structure, which provides privileged insight into social contradictions. In this epistemological reading, energy is desubstantialised and ontologically problematised:

> Energy is not a substance, which, for example, improves or goes sour with age; it's a numerical constant that a physicist has to find in his calculations, so as to be able to work . . . Without this constant, which is merely a combination of calculations . . . you have no more physics . . . the condition that the system be mathematically closed prevails even over the assumption that it is physically isolated.[88]

Lacan in fact criticises Freud's energetic theory of the unconscious, which, under the pretention to provide positive scientific foundations for psychoanalytic concepts, ended up in a substantialist reading both of the objects of natural sciences and of his own inquiries. In Freud's mature work, the unconscious and the drive indeed obtained a

---

86 Lacan, *Autres écrits*, 435, and *D'un Autre à l'autre*, 116.

87 See A. Rabinbach, *The Human Motor: Energy, Fatigue, and the Origins of Modernity*, Los Angeles: University of California Press, 1992, 72–81.

88 Lacan, *Television*, 118.

problematic status, beginning to designate positive ontological entities that Freud no longer strived to explain through discursive causality but rather through the speculative phylogenetic development stretching from protozoa to the human libido. When Lacan took Freud's early insight on the linguistic nature of the unconscious seriously, he directed psychoanalysis away from positivism and biologism. In the above quote, Lacan extends the same critical move to the natural sciences, claiming that their discoveries do not simply relate to an unproblematic empirical reality but instead question the solidity and univocity of its ontological foundations. Such an interrogation is possible only under the condition that the relation between discourse and the real is no longer subsumed under the ideal of *adaequatio*, in which discourse, as Lacan occasionally remarks, is considered to have no consequences whatsoever. The Lacanian distinction between reality and the real, moreover, results from this extension of the structural reading of psychoanalysis to the entire scientific modernity. In short, the difference between the two orders consists in the fact that reality designates merely the way the real appears to the human observer – reality as a 'grimace of the real'[89] – while the real, to put it paradoxically, stands for the way the real 'appears' to the autonomy of the discourse, e.g., to mathematical language:

> When the signifier is introduced as an apparatus of *jouissance*, we should thus not be surprised to see something related to entropy appear, since entropy is defined precisely once one has started to lay this apparatus of signifiers over the physical world.[90]

We can hear the echo of Alexandre Koyré's thesis that modern science no longer explains the empirical world, in opposition to the Aristotelian and medieval science, which uses mathematics in order to 'save the appearances'.[91] Of course, the real cannot be the same in physics, psychoanalysis or critique of political economy, which deal with different

---

89   *Ibid.*, 6.

90   Lacan, *The Other Side of Psychoanalysis*, 49. For further discussion of entropy, see A. Zupančič, 'When Surplus Enjoyment Meets Surplus Value', in J. Clemens and R. Grigg (Eds), *Jacques Lacan and the Other Side of Psychoanalysis*, Durham, NC: Duke University Press, 2006, 159ff.

91   A. Koyré, *Études d'histoire de la pensée scientifique*, Paris: Gallimard, 1973, 89.

orders of reality (physical, subjective, social) but also with different versions of discursive autonomy (formal language, the signifier, value). What does unite them, however, is the logical procedure, according to which all these discourses encounter and formalise the respective *structure of the real*, in which objects like energy, *jouissance* and surplus-value can be theorised. Another way to situate the difference between reality and the real would be that in reality the process of montage or construction is at stake, while the real demands decomposition and dissolution of appearances. In scientific discourse, the real is what remains for formalisation to grasp once this decomposition has reached its bottom line, or as Lacan puts it:

> The real is what makes a hole in this articulated semblant that is the scientific discourse. Scientific discourse progresses, without being preoccupied with the question of whether it is a semblant or not. What is important is that its network, its web, its *lattice*, as we say, makes the right holes appear in the right place. Its sole reference is the impossible, to which its deductions amount. This impossible is the real. We can reach something real in physics precisely through the discursive apparatus, as far as it, in its rigour, encounters the limits of its consistency.[92]

In this respect natural sciences contain a much more dialectical-speculative and anti-empiricist kernel than the positivist epistemologies are willing to acknowledge. The encounter of the real takes place when the discourse faces its own inconsistency and not some absolute and substantial empirical Outside. The actual site of the encounter is not in experimentation but in formalisation and in the deadlocks that accompany the scientific discourse on the path that leads to the resolution, abolition or reduction of an epistemological deadlock. Verification of a hypothesis is already a step towards normalisation, a moment of stabilisation and reconstruction of reality. As Lacan often repeats, reality is what functions – and the functioning is what the 'master' constantly demands – whereas the real is what does not function, something that violates or distorts the automatic repetition

92   J. Lacan, *Le Séminaire, livre XVIII, D'un discours qui ne serait pas du semblant*, Paris: Éditions du Seuil, 2007, 28. See also A. Zupančič, 'Realism in Psychoanalysis', in: L. Chiesa (Ed.), *Lacan and Philosophy*, Melbourne: re.press, 2014, 28.

and flawless circulation of a discursive mechanism.[93] This is one of the main lessons that can be drawn from Koyré's interpretation of modern scientific revolution.[94] The scientific encounter of the real therefore rejects the all too simple distinction between extra-linguistic and intra-linguistic reality. It takes place within discourse but throws it out of joint. Pushing discursivity to its limits, where the real is inscribed into the symbolic, science exposes a dimension of language that is freed of its communicative, meaningful and pragmatic function. In the same move, it rejects the substantialisation of the real and the transcendentalism of the symbolic, showing that the real is neither an unattainable 'thing in itself' nor an unproblematic exteriority; and language is no prison without walls, from which it is impossible to escape.

Psychoanalysis and the critique of political economy are conditioned by this epistemological paradigm. The unconscious and class struggle, two real cracks in the social and the subjective reality, can be encountered by pushing the discursive consistency to its limits. Lacan's comments thus combine the epistemological and the political problematic that correlates the scientific discovery of labour-power to the economic mathematisation of surplus-value, which abolished its premodern mystification. In the background we can perceive an outline of another homology, this time between science and capitalism. It may appear that Lacan thereby came close to Heidegger's pessimistic vision, in which science is reduced to its instrumental and technological 'essence'.[95] This reduction, culminating in the controversial Heideggerian remark that science does not think, bears the mark of fetishisation. According to Heidegger, the realisation of modern science in technology accomplishes the historical process of the oblivion of being that determined Western metaphysics. With the globalisation of abstract calculation, the paradigmatic case of non-thinking, which unites the scientific and the economic thoughtless and therefore empty reason, the oblivion of being itself fell into oblivion: this is what Heidegger calls 'the

93 The symptom, in Marx and in Freud, assumes the status of the materialisation of this disfunctioning and of the real deadlock. See J. Lacan, 'La troisième', in: *La cause freudienne*, 2011, Vol. 79, 17.

94 Koyré was, so to speak, Lacan's subject supposed to know in the matters of science. This theoretical influence is extensively examined in Milner, *L'oeuvre claire*, 37–69.

95 M. Heidegger, *Vorträge und Aufsätze*, Stuttgart: Klett-Cotta, 2004, 9–10, 127.

danger'.[96] In this dark scenario, only poetic thinking can render the authentic, originary sense of being and overcome the domination of scientific calculus and capitalist abstractions. The negative fetishisation of science is supplemented by the positive fetishisation of poetry, which is for Heidegger *the* language of being.

Yet Lacan never adopted Heidegger's antagonistic reading of mathematical language versus poetic language. What he did seem to endorse is the idea that modern science contains an ontological scandal that does not stand so much for the oblivion of the question of being but instead reveals an unbridgeable gap between thinking and being, as well as between being and the real. Formalisation is an exemplification of a concurrent 'sameness' concerning thinking and the real, but the price for this sameness is the separation of thinking from being and consequently the decentralisation, or alienation, of thinking. The radicalisation of the structuralist project replaces the question of being with the examination of the ways in which the autonomy of the signifier enables thinking to encounter within being *more than being*, something that is neither being nor non-being but 'non-realised'.[97] It is no coincidence that Heidegger never thematised the philosophical importance of Freud's discovery of the unconscious, this paradigmatic example of a paradoxical entity that neither is nor is not but insists in the state of repression, as the persistence of the non-realised in thinking. It is also not surprising that Lacan found in mathematics the privileged correspondent in rethinking the ontological status of the unconscious and other real consequences linked to science, thereby making an anti-Heideggerian move *par excellence*.

The epistemological and political orientation of the return to Freud thus displaces the accent from 'Does science think?' to 'What form of thinking does modern science ground in?' For Lacan there is no dilemma; science thinks and its thinking challenges the classical philosophical ideal of the thinking of thinking, as well as the foundation of ontology on the postulate of the sameness of thinking and being:

> As a language that fits the scientific discourse best mathematics is science
> without consciousness, the one that our good old Rabelais promised us and
> in face of which a philosopher can only remain stupid: gay science is

---

96   Ibid., 30.

97   J. Lacan, *The Seminar, Book XI, The Four Fundamental Concepts of Psychoanalysis*, New York: Norton, 1998, 22.

thrilled when it observes in this the ruin of the soul. But of course neurosis survived it.[98]

The modern foundation of science on the autonomous signifier abolished the hypothesis of a centralised thinking that philosophy nevertheless renewed through the subject of cognition. As science without consciousness (without the subject of cognition as its central instance) mathematics detaches language from communication, the real from being, and thinking from itself. Marx and Freud repeat these moves in their analyses of the commodity form and unconscious formations, two concrete examples of decentralised thought. The abolition of the soul was the necessary epistemological condition for Freud's aetiology of neuroses, a theory of causality that departs from the signifier as the material cause of *jouissance* and a materialisation of the gap between thinking and being. Yet the subversive potential of mathematical language encounters its limit precisely in the commodity form, which builds on the same discursive autonomy and through which the capitalist fetishisation of economic abstractions reintroduces the hypothesis of the soul through the backdoor: the commodity soul and the spectrality of capital that vitalises the modern universe (the global market) becomes the general formal envelope of thinking, thereby necessarily channelling all the subversive potential of modern science into the permanent revolution of the means of production.

At a later point, Lacan distinguished between thinking science and objectified science, which immediately addresses its ambiguity in the capitalist framework.[99] The distinction does not necessarily suggest that we are dealing with a good revolutionary science, which unmasks the illusory character of traditional and modern worldviews, as Freud claimed, and the bad commodified science that supports the perpetuation and reproduction of capitalism. Rather, the distinction insists that the decentralisation of thinking, the revolutionary dimension of science without consciousness, is inseparable from the historic genesis of a specific form of this

---

98 Lacan, *Autres écrits*, 453.

99 'In a world in which there has emerged, in a way that actually does exist, that is a presence in the world, not the thought of science, but science objectified in some way, I mean these things entirely forged by science, simply these little things, gadgets and things, which at the moment occupy the same space as us – in a world in which this emergence has taken place, can know-how at the level of manual labor carry enough weight to be a subversive factor? This is how, for me, the question arises' (Lacan, *The Other Side of Psychoanalysis*, 149).

decentralisation: the commodity form. But it does situate science as one of the central terrains of struggle against capitalism. Together with the episte-mological conditions of the commodity form and the fetishisation tied to capitalist abstractions, modern science provides the necessary conditions for the invention of critical and conflictual sciences such as psychoanalysis and the critique of political economy.

In his analysis of the capitalist transformation of labour, Marx already encountered an essential scientific operation that Lacan named *réduction de materiel*, material reduction. The condensation of labour into labour-power, which stands at the origin of the absolutisation of the market, is a productive abstraction that seemingly reduces different forms of concrete labour but in fact amounts to a new materiality of the subject.[100] Material reduction is at work in every placement of the network of signifiers over a given reality, be it physical, social or subjective, but it also concerns the entire history of logic, in which the autonomy and the materiality of the signifier is progressively isolated:

> The material reduction means that logic begins at a precise date in history when someone who had an understanding of this substituted certain elements of language that function in their natural syntax with a simple letter. And this is what inaugurates logic.[101]

Introducing A and B instead of saying 'if this then that' does not seem to have any dramatic consequences. However, Aristotelian logic is merely the first step towards the autonomy of the signifier, the subordination of the signifier to the letter, which is still consistent with Aristotle's 'organonic' notion of language. The actual subversion takes place in modernity, when the new foundation of science brings about a different result, the

---

100 Marx thematises this material reduction in another crucial excerpt of *Capital*: 'If then we disregard the use-value of commodities, only one property remains, that of being products of labour. But even the product of labour has already been transformed in our hands. If we make abstraction from its use-value, we abstract also from the material constituents and forms which make it a use-value . . . With the disappearance of the useful character of the products of labour, the useful character of the kinds of labour embodied in them also disappears; this in turn entails the disappearance of the different concrete forms of labour. They can no longer be distinguished, but are all together reduced to the same kind of labour, human labour in the abstract' (Marx, *Capital*, Vol. 1, 128).

101 Lacan, *D'un Autre à l'autre*, 34.

mathematisation of the signifier, uncovering the distinction between reality and the real. A concrete case of this development is again offered by the historical transformation of the market, which, besides the condensation of labour, consisted in the quantification of surplus-object:

> Something changed in the master's discourse at a certain point in history. We are not going to break our backs finding out if it was because of Luther, or Calvin, or some unknown traffic of ships around Genoa, or in the Mediterranean Sea, or anywhere else, for the important point is that on a certain day surplus-jouissance became calculable, could be counted, totalised. This is where what is called the accumulation of capital begins.[102]

The extension of mathematisation to economic reality, the capture of surplus-value and the isolation of labour-power, initiated a ground-breaking change in the master's discourse, the discursive structure that comprises both the logic of the signifier and the relations of domination. What matters in approaching the origins of capitalism is that concrete transformations in trade centres like Genoa and Venice were already embedded in a broader movement of scientific revolution, which found its ultimate expression in the implementation of formalisation in the sphere of social production. We could paraphrase Marx here: the merchants did not know what they were doing, nevertheless they were doing it. The revolution was initiated before any attempt in writing a capitalist manifesto was undertaken: the subjective and the social surplus that antiquity and Christianity treated as a deviation from a presupposed normative model of social relations was integrated into the constitution of social reality.

Marx's *Capital* provides the first rigorous thought of this epistemo-political revolution, which implies a strictly determined notion of structure: 'Structure is therefore the real. This is in general determined by its convergence towards the impossible. Precisely in this the structure is real.'[103] Within the Saussurean paradigm, such a conception could not have been formulated, yet it is inevitable once structuralism is coupled to Marx's materialist dialectics.[104] Lacan's Marx is a structuralist *avant la lettre*,

---

102   Lacan, *The Other Side of Psychoanalysis*, 177.

103   Lacan, *D'un Autre à l'autre*, 30.

104   This is what Lacan adopted from Althusser's reading of *Capital*: 'Whether his commentators are structuralist or not, they seem to have demonstrated that Marx himself is one, namely a structuralist. For it is properly by being at the point . . . that

someone who enabled structuralism to 'walk on its feet again' by departing from the problem of discursive production. With the reinforced materialist orientation, material reduction, too, becomes more than an operation of scientific formalisation and of capitalist commodification. It becomes the privileged tool of critique for exposing the deadlocks and contradictions in the given regime of production. By grasping discourse at the root where it most effectively determines the constitution of the subject, the critique of political economy effectively demonstrates that 'mathematical logic is highly essential for your existence in the real, whether you know it or not'.[105] Evidently it is essential for pointing out the terrain, where politics needs to intervene in order to bring about the double transformation of the subject and of the social link. It is at this point that the Freudian notion of the unconscious most decisively continues the epistemo-political orientation of Marx's critique.

---

is determined by the predomination of the labour market, that the function of surplus-value is revealed as the cause of Marx's thought' (Ibid., 17).

105   Ibid., 35.

CHAPTER 2

The Capitalist Unconscious:
A Return to Freud

WELTANSCHAUUNG

When it comes to Freud's relation to politics, notably to Marxism, we cannot ignore his self-proclaimed indifference in political matters. However, as soon we go through his writings on culture and religion, we notice that this indifference is expressed in a rather unusual way. Freud never simply avoids political issues. Instead, he proposes a new form of addressing them, through distortions and displacements, a form that corresponds to the psychoanalytic method and to the nature of its object. It would therefore be wrong to see in the unconscious a retreat from the social into a sphere of strictly private life that has absolutely no connection to social reality. Yet it would be equally false to presuppose the existence of a collective unconscious, a container of universal cultural artefacts and archetypes. The Freudian unconscious is clearly more sophisticated. It abolishes the division of the subjective and the social, the private and the public, albeit not in the sense of the slogan 'the personal is the political' but in the sense that the existence and the formal mechanisms of the unconscious depend on the same structures, which determine the functioning of social links.

Both Lacan's axiom 'the unconscious is structured like a language' and his later claims that the unconscious 'ex-sists' only in discourse, address this singular status of the unconscious within social structures. This implies that the subject of the unconscious – the subject in its dependency on the signifier, and not the subject of cognition – is the subject of politics. Psychoanalysis isolates the political subject from its ideological fictions, be it *homo legalis*, the abstract subject of right, *homo economicus*, the no less abstract subject of political economy, *citoyen*, etc. With this distinction, the flip side to the constitution of the social is brought to light: the discursive ex-sistence of the unconscious, its *insistence* as an *extimate* discursive consequence uncovers the point, in which the given social order determines the production of subjectivity, and names the instability of the given order, the point from which emancipatory or revolutionary politics inevitably needs to depart in order to produce social change. This is, as we shall see in the following section, the main point of Marx's determination of the proletariat as a social symptom, this concrete social embodiment of the universal subjective position in capitalism and the only possible point from which the abolition of the capitalist mode of production can be brought about. The motto shared between Marx and Freud would therefore be: the impersonal is the political – namely the impersonal core of the personal.

The difference between Freud and Lacan in these matters is nevertheless striking. While Lacan never avoids polemical confrontation with the logic of capital, Freud barely addresses capitalism under its proper name. Instead, he prefers to speak about culture, thereby giving the discussion an apparently neutral, scientific and sociological tone. Another example is ideology. In his works, Freud undoubtedly develops a critique of ideology but under the screen-notion of *Weltanschauung* (worldview), an expression that covers everything from philosophy and politics to art and religion, designating a specific tendency in the constitution of reality, its totalisation and meaningful framing. Freud's discussion of Marxism will take place within this perspective and within the broader epistemological framework of the distinction between the worldview knowledge and the scientific knowledge. Freud's entire published work contains one single reflection on Marxism, and even this turns out rather disappointing, as he approaches it with the highest possible reserve. Freud expresses his lack of competence in discussing the variety of Marxist orientations and focuses merely on the so-called worldview Marxism, which enables him to envisage a logical similarity between Marxism and religion. Of course, most Marxists will be horrified by this idea. But before passing any judgment it is worth looking at the broader context of Freud's take on the general worldview mechanisms.

We find these developments in the closing chapter of Freud's *New Introductory Lectures on Psychoanalysis*. The collection was published at a dramatic historical moment, 1933, four years after the economic crash and the same year in which Hitler was elected German chancellor; it was also a time when no one could ignore the dramatic failure of the Soviet revolution with the dominance of Stalinism. The lectures address a fictional audience and revise Freud's metapsychological theories. The chapter on *Weltanschauung* forms an exception, both epistemologically and critically, since behind the discussion of the antagonisms between science and religion Freud simultaneously delivers his critical responses to the already widespread Freudo-Marxism, whose *enfant terrible* at the time was none other than Wilhelm Reich.

When Freud insists that all efforts should be made to inscribe psychoanalysis in the modern scientific paradigm, he implicitly condemns the efforts in his broader circle to shape psychoanalysis in accordance with an actually existing political worldview. Certainly one could argue that the political readings of psychoanalysis are not unrelated to Freud's discussions of social mechanisms, which already produced some sort of spontaneous political philosophy. In the face of works such as *Group Psychology and the Analysis of the Ego*, on which the Frankfurt school later grounded its critique of totalitarian personality, or *Civilisation and Its Discontents*, which guided Marcuse's critique of social repression, it is all the more surprising that Freud concludes not only that there is no such thing as a psychoanalytic worldview but even that every immediate application of psychoanalysis to politics should be avoided. Where does this reserve come from?

The answer lies in the logic of worldviews, as the lecture in question outlines it. Freud begins his critique by enumerating and discussing the general features of every worldview. His definition sounds classical from the outset:

> In my opinion, then, a *Weltanschauung* is an intellectual construction, which solves all the problems of our existence uniformly on the basis of one overriding hypothesis, which, accordingly, leaves no question unanswered and in which everything that interests us finds its fixed place. It will easily be understood that the possession of a *Weltanschauung* of this kind is among the ideal wishes of human beings.[1]

The main achievement of a worldview thus consists in totalising reality and thereby providing its meaningful interpretation. It does not leave any questions open and situates the variety of human interests under one general hypothesis (*Annahme*, presupposition). At first glance, the definition does not seem to bring any novelties to the understanding of worldview mechanisms. Yet such novelty lies in the conclusion. A unifying worldview stands in a specific relation to unconscious desire, whose reality manifests itself through the construction of a given worldview. A worldview, then, appears

---

1   Freud, *Standard Edition*, Vol. 22, 158.

as a neutral interpretation of the world, a construction of reality, but behind this interpretation Freud reveals a mechanism that establishes the conditions for the satisfaction of desire, a *dispositif* that supports its undisturbed fulfilment.

In this respect, the critique of worldview mechanisms reaches back to the earliest psychoanalytic discoveries regarding the mechanisms that satisfy an unconscious tendency through the production of symbolic formations. Freud aims here notably at dreams, which are nothing less than intellectual formations that codify a demand for satisfaction, so that he extends his early wish-fulfilment theory to the way discursive mechanisms construct intersubjective reality. More precisely, through his worldview critique, Freud points out the place where the unconscious should be situated. Desire is not simply a psychological formation but the name of a specific structural dynamic that needs to be placed on the very line that joins subjective and social reality. Desire is the border beyond which there is strictly speaking no other reality: the same structure and the same formal mechanisms work in the unconscious and in the social link. Freud's worldview critique is therefore not to be rejected as yet another psychologism.

Worldviews thus raise a logical problem that Freud approaches through the work of interpretation, which amounts to the totalisation of reality. He thereby evokes the famous lines from Heine, in which the poet mocks philosophy:

> Life and the world's too fragmented for me!
> A German professor can give me the key.
> He puts life in order with skill magisterial,
> Builds a rational system for better or worse;
> With nightcap and dressing-gown scraps for material
> He chinks up the holes in the universe.[2]

Freud already used the very same reference in the *Interpretation of Dreams* to illustrate one of the main achievements of the dream work, secondary elaboration, through which unconscious labour combines the loosely linked dream material in a whole and narrated structure. The philosopher is thus comparable to the unconscious labourer, whose main task is to

---

2   *The Complete Poems of Heinrich Heine: A Modern English Version*, Boston: Suhrkamp/Insel, 1982, 99.

create the conditions for the fulfilment of unconscious desire, to interpret reality so that it will support satisfaction (clearly this is not a very flattering vision of philosophy). The more an interpretation is totalising and the more meaning it produces, the more the constituted reality successfully masks unconscious demand. The connection of desire with worldview means that unconscious fantasy is implemented in reality, that it supports the constitution of reality as a consistent and framed totality. What Freud criticises in philosophical ontologies and theories of cognition is that they remain blind to the structuring function of fantasy: there is no reality without a fantasmatic support, and, consequently, there is no discourse without the unconscious. With the same move, Freud dismisses the Freudo-Marxist hypothesis of the exclusively oppressive character of social mechanisms: social reality does not simply repress or suppress the creative potentials of desire, drive and sexuality; on the contrary, it serves as its privileged articulation and consistency. Desire is not the producer – it is itself produced, while the producer is situated elsewhere. How exactly Freud approaches the relation between desire and productive unconscious labour will be examined further below; what matters for now is that for Freud no reality is consistently objective and every worldview, every ideological construction, contains a 'wish-fulfilment'.

This logical connection between desire and interpretation that Freud encounters in worldviews explains why he categorically rejects every attempt to construct a psychoanalytic worldview. Psychoanalysis intervenes on a different level. Its function is not to provide the conditions for satisfaction but to uncover the mechanisms that articulate unconscious desire in a specific *dispositif* of satisfaction, thereby revealing that behind the apparent conflict between this desire and social reality there is a certain complicity between desire and interpretation. For this reason, psychoanalysis does not 'liberate desires'. It rather transforms, through interpretation, the formal mechanism of satisfaction, directing the subject towards the problematic kernel of the unconscious mode of production. This is the main point of the famous Freudian *Wo Es war soll Ich werden*: where there seems to have been an automatic regime of production, the unconscious mode of *jouissance*, there the place of the subject should be revealed, a place where a subjectivation can take place. And this subjectivation entails a transformation of the overall mechanism. The task of psychoanalysis is thus in clear opposition to worldviews. It does not interpret reality by feeding it with more meaning – it creates the conditions under which the subject will be able to produce a transformative act.

This change appears to be impossible due to repression, which is actually the case, although the Freudian notion of repression differs significantly from suppression or oppression. For Freud, the mechanisms of repression are constitutive of the unconscious tendency, and if we want to attribute to the unconscious 'productive potential', then it does not pertain to the repressed desire but to repression itself, in which Freud recognises productive unconscious labour.

Freud's response to the attempts to construct a psychoanalytic world-view is highly enigmatic: 'As a specialist science, a branch of psychology – a depth psychology or psychology of the unconscious – [psychoanalysis] is entirely unsuitable to construct a *Weltanschauung* of its own: it must assume the scientific one.'[3] Psychoanalysts should refrain from inventing a world-view because there is an underlying incompatibility between psychoanalysis and worldview-tendencies, which makes psychoanalysis appear as a sabo-teur. Consequently, an analyst cannot unveil the underlying mechanisms that support the satisfaction of unconscious tendencies *and* provide condi-tions for their perpetuated satisfaction. The contradiction between psychoanalysis and ideological tendencies could not be sharper. But the conclusion Freud draws from this contrast is that not even the analysts can do entirely without a worldview, so they should simply follow the example of the father of psychoanalysis, who adopted the scientific one. Freud's persistent claim to a scientific status of psychoanalysis is only seemingly neutral. It actually contains a scientistic worldview, a fulfilment of Freud's 'epistemological' desire.

Behind the apparent unsuitability of forming a consistent worldview there is a more fundamental impossibility. Psychoanalysis cannot totalise reality, nor can it predict future events in mental life, and, finally, it reveals that even the past is subjected to retroactive modifications. The past is not a state but a movement. These restrictions differentiate psychoanalysis from other positive sciences, notably from physics, medicine and biology, on which Freud wanted to construct the scientificity of his invention and which are all orientated towards the future and can presumably predict events based on the already acquired knowledge. The limits of psychoanal-ysis logically follow from the status of the unconscious, which is by far neither an ontological substance nor a positive entity. It entirely depends on contingent and unpredictable traumatic events and on the dynamic of linguistic structures, so that no particular case is universal enough to

---

3   Freud, *Standard Edition*, Vol. 22, 158. Translation modified.

support the prediction of future developments, which is, in the end, an important part of the achievement of worldviews: the exclusion of contingency from reality, life and thinking. The unconscious may be marked by the absence of time, and even by the absence of contradiction, as Freud occasionally claimed, but this absence is misleading. It does not automatically imply that the unconscious is unchangeable; it rather demonstrates its dependency on the actually existing social condition and hence on the 'eternity' of ruling ideologies. As Althusser argued, the absence of time and the deformation of social antagonisms represent two central features of ideology, which consequently appears as neutral and coextensive with reality. But while Althusser declared every subject to be an imaginary effect of ideology, Lacan recognised in the subject of the signifier the central discursive consequence on which the difference of psychoanalysis from sciences and worldviews rested. If psychoanalysis wants to join positive sciences, it must abandon the hypothesis of the subject of the unconscious: herein lies the risk of Freud's attempts to ground psychoanalysis on energetics, neurology and biology. If, however, it wishes to produce a consistent worldview, it has to recentralise the subject: the ego should dominate the id, as many of Freud's successors interpreted *Wo Es war soll Ich werden*. Ego-psychology and various forms of psychotherapy remain within the capitalist ideological framework and even openly adopt the centralised subjectivity of economic liberalism – namely a subjectivity, which is consolidated around the egoistic pursuit of private interest, just as in the context of cognition the subject is consolidated around the self-transparent consciousness or intentionality.

A more general problem concerns the idea of a scientific worldview. Does it make sense to speak of such a worldview at all? What does it designate? The personal convictions of scientists, their 'spontaneous philosophies'?[4] To stick to Freud's definition, a scientific worldview should not be an exception. In order to seriously compete with philosophy or religion, it would have to solve *all* problems of human existence, provide a meaningful interpretation of reality and finally articulate guiding principles for social life. In short, it would have to produce knowledge, belief and ethics. Modern science fulfils merely the first condition. What might come close to a scientific worldview are the ideals of enlightenment. Let us recall their Kantian summary:

4   L. Althusser, *Philosophy and the Spontaneous Philosophy of Scientists*, London: Verso, 1990.

Enlightenment is man's emergence from his self-incurred immaturity. Imma-
turity is the inability to use one's own understanding without the guidance
of another. This immaturity is *self-incurred* if its cause is not lack of understanding, but lack of resolution and courage to use it without the guidance
of another. The motto of enlightenment is therefore: *Sapere aude!* Have
courage to use your *own* understanding![5]

Would a scientific worldview entail universalisation of the courage to know,
the social implementation of a presumably epistemological desire that
would awaken the subject from its ignorance? *Acheronta movebo,* the Virgil
quote that Freud placed to the head of *Interpretation of Dreams,* announc-
ing that his publication shall shift the underground regions, repeating the
Copernican revolution in psychic life, can be read together with the Kantian
Sapere aude. Freud had his most evident moment of enthusiasm for the
enlightenment in *The Future of an Illusion,* his most explicit confrontation
with religion, predicting the triumph of scientific knowledge over 'religious
illusions'. Along the same lines, the *New Introductory Lectures* express a
hope that 'the intellect – the scientific spirit, reason – may in process of
time establish a dictatorship in the mental life of man'.[6] Thus for Freud a
scientifically supported dictatorship of reason in mental life is the political
ideal of psychoanalysis. Except that this reason, this psychoanalytic *cogito,*
is unconscious, so that the dictatorship of reason would be an impossible
dictatorship of the decentralised subject of the signifier that would replace
the current capitalist dictatorship of the 'strong ego' (what Lacan called
Je-cratie, I-cracy). Is the dictatorship of reason a psychoanalytic response to
the dictatorship of the proletariat, maybe even just an extravagant name for
it? Freud would then be only one step away from Lacan's identification of
the proletarian with the subject of the unconscious.

On other occasions, Freud claims that modern science harms human
narcissism, thereby leaving no doubt that scientific knowledge satisfies no
desire whatsoever. The main condition for the formation of a scientific
worldview falls away. To recall again, Freud mentions three scientific
insults: the decentralisation of the universe in physics, which abolished
the ancient idea of the finite, centralised and harmonious cosmic order
with the infinite and contingent universe; then the decentralisation of life
in biology, which abolished the hierarchy of beings with man as its

---

5   I. Kant, *Political Writings,* Cambridge: Cambridge University Press, 1991, 54.
6   Freud, *Standard Edition,* Vol. 22, 171.

privileged metaphysical crown; and finally the decentralisation of thinking in psychoanalysis, which questioned the primacy of consciousness and most definitely rejected the hypothesis of a metaphysical soul. The modern scientific paradigm has exactly the opposite effect of worldview mechanisms. Instead of totalising and stabilising both the external and the internal reality, it deprives them of their centre; instead of grounding them on necessity and order, it exposes their contingency and instability; and finally, instead of producing their meaningful interpretation, it reduces them to nonsensical formal mechanisms. A scientific worldview consequently follows an entirely different logic: production of falsifiable (uncertain, provisory) knowledge, de-totalisation and foreclosure of meaning.

Freud determines the psychoanalytic relation to the scientific worldview by using the ambiguous expression *annehmen*. This can either mean that the scientific worldview already exists and psychoanalysis merely has to reach out and adopt it; or it can also suggest that such a worldview is simply presupposed, which would imply that positive sciences as such assume the position of a 'subject supposed to know', and indeed Freud often treats positive sciences in such a way. Finally, the *Annahme*, the assumption Freud talks about in relation to the scientific worldview, can also be understood in a formal sense, as the announcement of a concurrent regime of interpretation that will undermine the established worldview-form. This is what the Freudian idea of revolutionary sciences seems to address. While the existing worldviews satisfy 'human narcissism', scientific decentralisations inflict wounds because a concurrent, essentially materialist worldview announces itself at least on the logical level. The struggle between science and religion is first and foremost a conflict between two concurrent forms of thinking. The scientific worldview does not depart from the tendency of providing definite answers to human questions but reformulates the questions themselves. It also does not satisfy desire but alters the subject's relation to it. The break with the worldview interpretation is a matter of formalisation because it is only here that a concurrent regime of interpretation can be approached.

This Freudian epistemological optimism is nevertheless marked by a significant shift. The pessimistic turn that accompanies writings such as *Beyond the Pleasure Principle* and *Civilisation and Its Discontents* encounters a new problem. Instead of discussing the historic conflict between science and religion, it turns to modern culture, precisely to capitalism, where the political potential of modern scientific revolution met a more challenging limit that again concerns a specific form of thinking, the commodity form. The modern worldview operates within these formal constrictions, and in this respect the main failure of the scientific revolution consists in the incapacity to detach thinking from universal commodification; and even more so in its complicity with capitalism, the embedding of scientific knowledge in the permanent capitalist revolution. Freud's pessimist turn is closely related to the fact that the universality of commodity form successfully integrated scientific knowledge into the capitalist mode of production and into its articulation of desire. What Marx described as commodity fetishism stands above all for a specific transformation of desire within and through the implementation of the capitalist worldview in social and subjective reality. The four cornerstones of this worldview (freedom, equality, property and private interest) form an abstract coordinate system, in which the sharpness of revolutionary sciences is neutralised in advance.

At this point we can move to Freud's engagement with the Marxist worldview in his lecture on *Weltanschauung*. After expressing his lack of competence in discussing Marxism, he sums up his reservations in the following passage:

> Theoretical Marxism, as realised in Russian Bolshevism, has acquired the energy and the self-contained and exclusive character of a *Weltanschauung*, but at the same time an uncanny likeness to what it is fighting against. Though originally a portion of science and built up, in its implementation, upon science and technology, it has created a prohibition of thought which is just as ruthless as was that of religion in the past.[7]

Freud then continues with how the critical confrontation with Marxism is forbidden and how the Soviet regime produced a fetishisation of Marx's works that is comparable to that of religious texts, and so on. Freud's critique of the worldview Marxism resembles a typical right-wing moralisation, yet there is something symptomatic in his discontent, something that goes beyond the moralistic tone of his remarks and concerns the very outcome of the Soviet revolution: the epistemic transformation of Marx's critique into dogmatism and the recentralisation of his theory of the subject. Freud does not talk about Marx but about scientific socialism; and the outcome of the revolution is not so much Lenin but Stalin, the bureaucrat and not the revolutionary.

---

7   Ibid., 179–80.

Lenin nevertheless announced the worldview tendency of Marxism, when he wrote: 'Marx's theory is omnipotent because it is true. It is comprehensive and harmonious, it gives men a unified worldview'.[8] Lacan returned to this passage on several occasions in order to claim the same link between omnipotence and truth for Freud's invention of psychoanalysis, and it is rather symptomatic that the citations of this passage often omit Lenin's specification of this omnipotence and truth. Worldview Marxism is the necessary step to dogmatism, where the dialectical materialist method that oriented the critique of political economy is replaced by the three non-dialectical worldview achievements. Lacan, too, envisaged this inversion when he expressed his astonishment that the majority of Marxists depart from the primacy of a specific figure of subjectivity, which is only subsequently alienated in the commodity form, in the process of production and in the movement of History, while Marx's critical project openly departs from the autonomy of value, which consequently helps him discover the decentralised subject of politics, labour-power, and its privileged social embodiment, the proletariat.[9] The foundation of Marxism as a worldview demanded the abolition of this critical ground of Marx's theory:

> The proletariat means what? It means that labour is radicalised on the level of pure and simple commodity, which also reduces the labourer to the same price. As soon as the labourer learns to know himself as such through theory, we can say that this step shows him the way to the status of – call it what you want – a scientist [*savant*]. He is no longer a proletarian *an sich*, if I may say so, he is no longer pure and simple truth, but he is *für sich*, what we call *class-consciousness*. He can even become the Party's class-consciousness where one no longer speaks the truth.[10]

The failure of the Communist Party would then consist in the fact that, in the end, it was the worldview-form which determined the political organisation and sabotaged the invention of a new party-form, and not the other

---

8   V. I. Lenin, 'The Three Sources and Three Component Parts of Marxism' (1913). Quoted in M. Heinrich, *Kritik der politischen Ökonomie. Eine Einführung*, Stuttgart: Schmetterling Verlag, 2005, 24.

9   One can sometimes hear astonishment over the fact that Marx does not use the term 'proletariat' or 'proletarian' in *Capital*. He does not need to because 'labour-power', 'surplus population' and 'industrial reserve army' designate the very same subjective position.

10   Lacan, *D'un Autre à l'autre*, 173.

way around. This political failure is accompanied by an entire set of episte-mological regressions, which have already been mentioned.

The difference between Marx's interpretation of the proletariat as the social embodiment-personification of the truth of labour, and worldview Marxism, which promises to abolish alienation and to constitute a revolutionary subject of cognition, overlaps with the difference between truth and knowledge. The Soviet regime replaced the social embodiment of truth, the proletarian as the true subject of revolutionary politics, with a particular social embodiment of knowledge, the party as the placeholder of the collective subject of knowledge and the Subject of History.[11] Again, the movement of the critique of political economy proceeds exactly in the opposite direction, from the economic forms of knowledge to the progressive deduction of the subject of value, where also the horizon of a possible transformation is outlined, albeit without a prospective insight into the future social order: this is where Marx, too, adopted what Freud called the scientific worldview. Worldview Marxism reverts from this critical perspective by reducing the subject of capitalism back to knowledge, making of the proletarian a *savant*, a scientist, subject of cognition, in which the proletarian knows itself as knowledge. The point of departure is no longer the identity of alienation and structure, which in the end determines the gap between the subject of cognition and the subject of politics. This critical point of departure is now replaced by the hypothesis of a centralised and unalienated Subject of History, which supposedly reaches the highest form of self-consciousness through the Party, another subject supposed to know. The problem is not so much in the introduction of the party but in the fact that the party becomes the privileged embodiment of a presupposed historical knowledge and not an organisation that opens up the space in which the historical and political truth embodied in the working class and in the surplus population can be transmitted. The Party appears as the perfect opposition of what, for instance, Lacan strived to establish through the idea of the School, founded on the imperative of renewing the sharp razor of Freudian truth, the gap between knowledge and truth, and to insist on the inexistence of the Other, which stands for the impossibility of the ultimate abolition of alienation.[12]

---

11   See S. Žižek, 'The Fetish of the Party', in: W. Apollon and R. Feldstein (Eds), *Lacan, Politics, Aesthetics*, Albany: SUNY Press, 1996.

12   Let us recall Lacan's famous intervention during the dissolution of the École freudienne de Paris: 'The Other is missing. It seems funny to me too. I can take the blow though, which gives you a thrill of sorts, but I'm not doing it for that' (Lacan,

By reintroducing the subject of cognition into the critique of political economy through the hypothesis of class-consciousness, worldview Marxism futilely seeks to abolish all forms of alienation and establish authentic intersubjective relations. It thereby regresses into a pre-critical framework. The Party's class-consciousness is the end-result of this movement: one no longer speaks (of) the truth, only (of) knowledge, which is most faithfully embodied in the Party's bureaucratic apparatus. Positive scientific knowledge – and this explains Stalin's tendency to provide an essentially positivistic foundation for dialectical materialism – serves as the point where the subject of capitalism can presumably reach a promised self-realisation beyond alienation.

Freud's theory of the subject saw a similar fate, when the post-Freudians recentralised the subject on the ego and deduced from Freud's *Wo Es war soll Ich werden* an imperative of normalisation and reintegration. Lacan's political struggle against the International Psychoanalytic Association, the psychoanalytic analogue of the Stalinist Party, for which the strong ego is the central instance in mental life, repeatedly turned around the translation of this ambiguous Freudian axiom. Post-Freudians have read it through the lenses of the theory of cognition and in closest compatibility with economic liberalism, while Lacan, in contrast, made it his privileged formula for alienation that constitutes the subject of the unconscious and points towards the real subject of politics.

Aside from all of the humanistic and moralistic appearances, Freud's critique of worldviews brings him suspiciously close to the break that inaugurated Marx's critique of political economy. The lecture on *Weltanschauung* contains a certain repetition of the critical programme from Marx's *Theses on Feuerbach*, which leaves no doubt that for Marx political struggles necessarily address the form of the interpretation of the world, not so much through the all too simple opposition of theory (worldview interpretation) and praxis (political action) but through the actual subversion of the very

---

Television, 134). The inexistence of the Other is both the condition and the ultimate risk of the School – the condition because only the inexistence of the Other can prevent the School or the Party from turning into a Church; the risk because this inexistence is always accompanied by the resistance that pushes the members of the School or of the Party back into the institutional transference, hence into the Church. On the terrain of organisation, the central struggle takes place between the institutional transference that links the organisation back to the hypothesis of the Other, and the political mobilisation of the subject, which is possible precisely because the Other is missing.

praxis of interpretation. Among the many targets of Marx and Freud's critique is philosophy, of which they promote a highly problematic and out dated image. But this detail should not distract us from the fact that the true object of their critique is religion and political economy, their competition with philosophical interpretations, which in the capitalist universe clearly are found in a worse position, discredited in advance as 'self-centred' and 'unprofitable'. Philosophy and science are simply not as successful when it comes to satisfying desire.

For the critique of political economy, the form of interpretation will be no less important as the organisation of the proletariat. And indeed, the transformation of the form of interpretation necessitates the form of organisation. When Marx examines the intertwining of the social form and the commodity form, or Freud the intertwining of the worldview mechanisms and the unconscious mechanisms of satisfaction, this already presupposes an inversion in the form of interpretation, which, in psychoanalysis and in the critique of political economy, supports their critique of appearances and recognises in the commodity form the general envelope of social links and unconscious production.

Another crucial aspect of Marx's critique of appearance, to repeat, concerns the break with the humanism and the essentialism of Feuerbach's conception of alienation. Marx's mature discussion of fetishism no longer departs from the illusion that the commodity form distorts more immediate and authentic social relations. Here it makes sense to repeat the distinction between constitutive alienation – alienation that is equivalent to structure – and constituted alienation – for instance, commodity fetishism, which follows from the misperception of the relation between the appearance of value and the structure that causes this appearance. The doubling of alienation does not prevent their confusion. This is what Marx criticised in Feuerbach. Simultaneously, the twofold character of alienation reveals that constituted alienation functions as a mask or a mystification of the constitutive alienation. The flip side of commodity fetishism is the appearance that there is a more fundamental and unalienated position in the background, a position from which it would be possible to cognise the mistake that determines commodity fetishism – precisely the position of an unsplit and conflict-free ego or consciousness, this common presupposition of political economy, post-Freudian psychoanalysis and scientific Marxism. *Homo oeconomicus*, strong ego and class-consciousness are conceptual and ideological variations of the same attempt to mystify the subjective split produced by the autonomy of discourse.

In distinction to these attempts to abolish alienation, which really do deserve to be called utopian, Marx's critique of political economy contains an effort to think alienation not only as reproduction of the relations of production but also as a structural transformation of the existing mode of production. We cannot overlook that the double meaning of the term 'revolution' is at stake here, the scientific (circular movement of astronomic bodies) and the political (subversion of the given social order). There is also no doubt that constitutive alienation does not address solely the alienation of the subject but above all the alienation of the Other: it makes the Other appear in its split, incompleteness, contradiction and therefore inexistence. The correlate of this inexistence is the existence of the subject, the actual agency of the revolutionary process, which, however, does not assume the position of knowledge but the place of truth, as Lacan persistently repeated. Because the subject is produced, brought into existence in and through the gap in the Other, in other words, because there is a social entity, the proletariat, which articulates a universal demand for change in the name of all (being the social embodiment of a universal subjective position), this very enunciation grounds politics on the link between inexistence, alienation and universality.

Capitalism, by contrast, rooted its politics on the hypothetical existence of the Other (the Market and other economic abstractions), the strong ego of a fictitious economic subject (the narcissism of private interest) and social segregation. Before anyone remarks that we have seen in the communist experiments how the political consequences of inexistence, alienation and universality look in practice, let us recall that the twentieth-century communist regimes failed in all three tasks. They have supported their political projects on the triad of History, class-consciousness (even if they were not all Lukácsian) and the no less intense forms of segregation. The political task of a Party that wants to claim the predicate 'communist' remains in insisting at this interplay of the subject's existence and the inexistence of History, just as for Lacan the politics of his School was rooted in the existence of the subject of the unconscious and the inexistence of the Other. With his critical move, Marx grounded the first theory of the subject that presupposed the total abolition of two central worldview illusions, human essence and social homeostasis, on which the capitalist worldview is grounded. Abstract freedom and abstract equality presuppose an equally abstract human essence, while private property and private interest ground the social consensus, behind which there is nevertheless a fundamental submission of political universalism to the particular interest of capital. The proletariat (the social embodiment of the subject) and class struggle (a concrete manifestation of the inexistence of the Other) represent two critical responses to the construction of a worldview and openly sabotage the undisturbed satisfaction of the insatiable capitalist imperative of creation of value.

Marx addressed the necessity of displacing the struggle from the interpretation of reality – the infamous 'conflict of interpretations' – to the form of interpretation in his often cited and almost as often misunderstood 11th thesis on Feuerbach: 'The philosophers have only *interpreted* the world, in various ways; the point is to *change* it'.[13] The thesis formulates the opposition between interpretation and change, theory and praxis, philosophy and revolutionary politics. Here, worldview Marxism is disqualified from the very outset. It may have brought about a revolutionary change but it adopted an interpretation of history that pushed it back in the centralised and totalising framework of a worldview. Even a reactionary thinker like Heidegger understood that Marx's final thesis in fact questions the dichotomy between thinking and action and conditions the actual change of the world with the change of the *form* of interpretation, thereby articulating a demand for a new *form* of philosophy that would account for the change.[14] Behind the apparent opposition of theory and praxis, the 11th thesis opposes two heterogeneous logical regimes of interpretation. All past philosophies presumably remained within the *dispositif* of worldview interpretations, where the change, the conflictuality of the historic movement is excluded from interpretation, or where History and Reality know no contradiction.[15]

Looking back at the history of philosophy, one can, of course, immediately object that it would be difficult to find philosophers who were merely occupied with the static interpretation of reality, without raising the question of political change: from Plato's ideal state, theorised on the background of

---

13   Marx, *Early Writings*, 423.

14   See M. Heidegger, *Reden und andere Zeugnisse eines Lebensweges*, Frankfurt am Main: Klostermann, 2000, 703–4.

15   For this reason the expression 'worldview' should be understood literally: a view that can be assumed only by stepping out of the world, an impossible metaposition. The critique of worldviews addresses the 'gaze of the world', the impossible point where the world supposedly coincides with itself. This point is nothing other than fantasy, which brings us back to Freud's thesis that the function of worldviews consists in creating conditions for the satisfaction of the unconscious desire.

the crisis of Greek *polis*, via Descartes's foundation of philosophy on the changes introduced by scientific modernity, up to Kant, Fichte and Hegel's enthusiasm for the French Revolution. Philosophers seem to have been more preoccupied with thinking possible changes rather than interpreting the given order and filling the gaps in reality.[16] But, as already stated, the problem of the critical interpretation in Marx concerns first and foremost the closed world of universal commodification, where the commodity form is the ulti-mate horizon of other forms of thinking and where the change already is the actual state of things, the permanent revolution mentioned by the *Communist Manifesto*. Reality already includes change, but what the critique of interpre-tation envisages is an articulation of political theory and practice that departs from the formalisation of the structural contradictions that determine the functioning of social links, as well as the consequent abolition of the hypo-thetical Other and of the centralised model of subjectivity. The *Theses* target young Hegelians and political economists, and not so much philosophy as a whole. Marx's insistence that a materialist theory of the subject conceives the latter as a consequence of social relations and not on a false hypothesis of an abstract human essence indicates that the displacement of the accent from interpretation to change should also be read as a shift in the understanding of change itself. In the capitalist-scientific universe where reality essentially comes down to permanent change, the latter loses its a priori revolutionary character. The structural change that could bring about a new social link, abolish the abstract universality of commodity form and construct a new figure of political subject presupposes a correct interpretation of the given logic of change, the conditions of the permanent capitalist revolution. Again, the point of departure should be that 'the Other is lacking' (Lacan), and from this viewpoint it is not astonishing that a major portion of philosophy seems to fall into the totalising regime of interpretation.

In his critique of worldviews, Freud outlines their three central func-tions and exemplifies them in reference to the conflict between modern science, the motor of revolutionary changes in the register of knowledge, and Christianity, the most persistent and consistent worldview in history, which successfully integrates every change in its form of interpretation:

> If we are to give an account of the grandiose nature of religion, we must bear in mind what it undertakes to do for human beings. It gives them

---

16   M. Dolar, 'Interpreting and Changing the World', Iaspis, Stockholm, 18 April 2013.

information about the origin and coming into existence of the universe, it assures them of its protection and of ultimate happiness in the ups and downs of life and it directs their thoughts and actions by precepts, which it lays down with its whole authority. Thus it fulfils three functions. With the first of them it satisfies the human thirst for knowledge; it does the same thing that science attempts to do with *its* means, and at that point enters into rivalry with it. It is to its second function that it no doubt owes the greatest part of its influence. Science can be no match for it when it soothes the fear that men feel of the dangers and vicissitudes of life, when it assures them of a happy ending and offers them comfort in unhappiness . . . In its third function, in which it issues precepts and lays down prohibitions and restrictions, religion is furthest away from science. For science is content to investigate and to establish facts, though it is true that in its application rules and advice are derived from the conduct of life.[17]

The knowledge of a worldview satisfies the desire for knowledge much better than science, with its epistemological revolutions and instabilities. Worldviews, in addition, produce meaning, which satisfies the desire for persistence; and, finally, they generate order, which satisfies the desire for security, excluding the change from the realms of reality. A worldview first and foremost produces a reality that appears to function, a reality without lack or negativity.[18]

With these three achievements in mind the contrast between Marx's critique of political economy and worldview Marxism becomes even more striking. Marx precisely does not 'solve all the problems of human existence based on an underlying hypothesis'; on the contrary, he formulates the central problem of modern political thought: commodity form as the ultimate horizon of social relations in capitalism. The ruling ideologies insist that Marxism is a worldview, the object of which is not the way things are, the 'question of being', but the way things should be, the question of change, not the present but the future. However, Marx's critique is

---

17 Freud, *Standard Edition*, Vol. 22, 161–2.

18 We can note in passing that the three functions perfectly overlap with the three Lacanian discourses: production of knowledge pertains to the hysteric's discourse, where the subject addresses the master precisely with the desire to know; production of meaning points to the university discourse, where knowledge supports the totalisation of reality; and finally the production of order is intimately related to the master's discourse as the fundamental social link.

neither a worldview nor a utopian theory. It is rather a reclaiming – as an object of thinking and as the condition of politics and revolutionary change – of an irreducible negativity that traverses social and subjective reality, and of which no one can be excepted: there is no metaposition that would ground politics on positive knowledge, but there is the subjective position, which grounds politics on conflictual truth. The notion of class struggle replaces the old, inadequate questions and answers, the social or the economic contract, with a new, radicalised problem: rather than being backed by some mythical contract, convention or relation, society rests on an irreducible struggle and social non-relation. Capitalism exploits this non-relation, but it can do so only under the condition of mystifying the actual source of wealth with a multitude of ideological fictions, fantasies and fetishisations.

In political economy, Marx uncovers the same three tendencies that, according to Freud, support the efficiency of religion. These three tendencies come down to the endeavour to ground the market on stable and predictable laws, which turn it into a positive Other that will support a fully functioning social relation. The association of economy with religious mechanisms is most evidently formulated in the famous lines of *The Poverty of Philosophy*, where Marx describes the metaphysical-theological tendencies of political economy:

> Economists have a singular method of procedure. There are only two kinds of institutions for them, artificial and natural. The institutions of feudalism are artificial institutions, those of the bourgeoisie are natural institutions. In this, they resemble the theologians, who likewise establish two kinds of religion. Every religion which is not theirs is an invention of men, while their own is an emanation from God. When the economists say that present-day relations – the relations of bourgeois production – are natural, they imply that these are the relations in which wealth is created and productive forces developed in conformity with the laws of nature. These relations therefore are themselves natural laws independent of the influence of time. They are eternal laws which must always govern society. Thus, there has been history, but there is no longer any. There has been history, since there were the institutions of feudalism, and in these institutions of feudalism we find quite different relations of production from those of bourgeois society, which the economists try to pass off as natural and as such, eternal.[19]

---

19   K. Marx, *Selected Writings*, Oxford: Oxford University Press, 2000, 226–7.

Smith's figure of the invisible hand remains the best expression of this meta-physical aspiration of political economy. In the market, it presupposes a pregiven rational knowledge, which makes the market appear as an autonomous subject. When Marx later describes the relation of political economy to the capitalist abstractions as fetishist, he implicitly situates this relation, not on the level of perversion, but on the level of *transference*. In order to envisage the persistence of this attitude in political economy, one merely needs to recall the jargon of contemporary advocates of neoliberal reforms. As the crisis persists, we get bombarded by warnings that radical measures are needed in order to 'send a positive signal' to the markets. The function of reforms and of austerity measures is to 'calm the markets'. The formulations are more than mere rhetorical figures; they actually demonstrate the fetishist disavowal that Octave Mannoni condensed in the famous phrase *Je sais bien, mais quand même:*[20] I know very well (that the markets are mere constructions and human inventions) but nevertheless (I believe that they are autonomous and capricious). A double mistake is at work here: yes, the markets are human inventions, but they contain an autonomous dimension, which determines social and subjective reality, and this autonomy is not correctly situated. The reason lies in the fact that political economy, in its apparent rationality and false scientificity, inevitably contains the inversion of the aforementioned fetishisation: I know very well that the markets are autonomous and capricious, but I nevertheless believe that they are mere constructions and human inventions.

In any case, the autonomy of the structural relations that support the functioning of the market is not taken seriously. Political economy in the same move fetishises economic abstractions as autonomous entities and relativises the dimension of causality in this autonomy by regressing back to the false sobriety of conventionalism. The fact is that the economic crisis does not undermine the fetishist relation to the market, it does not unveil the inexistence of the market Other; on the contrary, the more the crisis unveils the instability of the markets, the more the Market receives a surplus of positive existence. What nevertheless becomes observable is that the capitalist Market seems to be much closer to the God of the Old Testament than to the benevolent and abstract God of philosophers and political economists: not the neutral and self-regulating knowledge of the invisible hand but a desiring God that demands constant sacrifice, not a homeostatic order but a negativity, whose consequences are devastating.

---

20   O. Mannoni, *Clefs pour l'imaginaire, ou l'Autre scène*, Paris: Seuil, 1969, 9.

In addition, the imposition of economic reforms and austerity measures as inevitable and quasi-metaphysical necessities recalls the privileged
appearance of class struggle in the first volume of *Capital*, where its paradigm is the struggle for the length of the working day. Is today this struggle
not indicated in the debates regarding the length, not of the working day,
but of the working life? One can repeat Marx here: capitalists have their
own idea of the ultimate limit of the working life. Evidently a working life
cannot be longer than biological life: the ultimate end of the working life is
biological death. However, death can be postponed through the improve-
ment of life conditions and medical interventions, biopolitics and so on.
The argumentation for the extension of work periods comes down to the
argument that the life expectancy in Europe is today longer than it was in
the past, the population grows older, and for this reason the neoliberal
reforms are said to be inevitable. Every extension of the working life abolishes past achievements of the worker's struggles in a more efficient
manner that an extension of the working day ever would. Life and work
become inseparable; the entire lifespan is transformed into the precarious
life in work.

THE LABOUR THEORY OF THE UNCONSCIOUS

Freud's critique of worldviews stands in continuity with the main conclusions of the *Interpretation of Dreams*. It is well known that this work, in
which Freud for the first time systematised his theory of the unconscious,
turns around an apparently banal statement: dreams are wish-fulfilments.
Yet behind this simplicity lies a complex structure that reveals the problematic status of this 'wish'. Before entering the discussion of the Freudian
dream analysis, we should recall the specificity and the epistemological
weight of the Freudian approach in relation to his predecessors. Freud
was certainly not the first one to attribute a theoretical value and meaning
to dreams. The theoretical tradition goes back to Aristotle, and in the first
sections of his work Freud leaves no doubt that he did his homework
when presenting an exhaustive and detailed account of the past
approaches, including psychology, philosophy, literature and so on. The
Interpretation of Dreams proposes to move beyond their meaning to the
formal mechanisms that can be recognised in the dream processes,
thereby isolating their function of satisfaction. In doing so, Freud discovers that behind the production of meaning, narration and visualisation

there is another level of the dream text and another production. Here I want to focus on two main features of the Freudian notion of the unconscious, the already mentioned dimension of production, immanently doubled in the production of meaning and the production of satisfaction, and the central role of unconscious labour in the process that supports the satisfaction of the unconscious tendency. The fact that the longest chapter of the *Interpretation of Dreams* engages with *Traumarbeit*, dream work, should be taken seriously. Psychoanalysis begins with a labour theory of the unconscious.

The first complication is already on the level of terminology. In the book, Freud does not talk about desire (*Begierde*) but wish (*Wunsch*). This terminological choice makes the structural point of Freud's analysis of satisfaction more difficult to grasp, since *Wunsch* in everyday use designates a desire that aims at a specific object, while *Begierde* appears as desire without a strictly determined object. From this nuance, practically all Freud's troubles in 'selling' the idea of an unconscious wish to the scientific community emerge, a wish that is not simply without an object but, at the same time, does not aim at an empirical, immediate or concrete object either. The unconscious desire is neither *Wunsch* nor *Begierde* but somehow a third category that both abolishes and complicates the dichotomy of the presence and absence of the object, or, more precisely, demands a rethinking of what an object is.

Wish-fulfilment results from the manipulation of psychic material, the 'day residues'. This requires a consumption of energy that can, in the end, be quantified and hence understood in terms of labour-power. This explains Freud's strong interest in energetics, which became crucial in his later efforts to construct an energetics of the drives but is already present in his abandoned early attempt to ground a (positivist) scientific psychology (1895). The idea of unconscious production, approached through the notion of labour-power, thus forms the central difference between Freud and his predecessors, who saw in the unconscious either unclear representations or psychic depth, subconsciousness. The unconscious labour also cannot be conceived without the double character of labour in capitalism. In English, this division is inscribed into language, 'work' and 'labour', which cover both aspects of commodities, use-value and exchange-value. This linguistic inscription was already pointed out by Engels in an editorial footnote to Marx's *Capital*: 'Labour which creates use-values and is qualitatively determined is called "work" as opposed to "labour"; labour which creates value and is only measured quantitatively is "labour", as opposed to "work".[21] Engels accentuates the opposition between qualitative and quantitative labour, between sensual qualities and discursive matter. A commodity does not merely abolish or solve the contradiction between both poles, thereby becoming matter with qualities; it consists only as this split. Engels's comment relates to the passage in which Marx links the two aspects of commodity with labour and production:

> On the one hand, *all* labour is an expenditure of human labour-power, in the physiological sense, and it is in this character of being equal, or abstract, human labour that it creates and forms the value of commodities. On the other hand, *all* labour is an expenditure of human labour-power in a particular form and with a definite aim, and it is in this character of being concrete useful labour that it produces use-values.[22]

Here Marx most clearly situates the split in labour: *all* labour is on both sides at the same time; the question is therefore not that the commodity form would in any way encroach labour and introduce its inadequate representation. We are dealing with a parallax structure, according to which labour appears first on one side and then on the other, once as abstract matter, labour-power, once as concrete form, labour-process. In the same move Marx shows that his mature critical materialist orientation implies a more sophisticated and openly anti-empiricist notion of matter, which privileges the apparently 'abstract' discursive materiality, where labour-power and surplus-value can finally be thought as real discursive consequences, over the misleading 'concrete' empirical materiality, whose product is an apparently univocal commodity.

With the division between abstract and concrete labour in mind, unconscious labour falls on the side of abstract labour, notably because it cannot be associated with a concrete psychological agent. Freud will additionally complicate the matter by showing that unconscious production is not univocal either. It brings about two achievements and is itself internally doubled. The satisfaction of desire thus contains two satisfactions, in accordance with the double character of commodities, which now reflects on the couple 'wish' and 'desire'. The minimal difference between meaning and satisfaction conserves the division of use-value and value, as is also the case with meaning and linguistic value in Saussure. This difference is

21   Marx, *Capital*, Vol. 1, 138.
22   Ibid., 137. Translation modified.

noticeable in Freud's emphasis on the quantitative factor in dream work and his insistence that the imaginary aspect of dreams should not seduce us in believing that nothing logically different takes place behind the visualisation:

> The dream-thoughts and the dream-content are presented to us like two versions of the same subject-matter in two different languages. Or, more properly, the dream content seems like a transcript of the dream-thoughts into another mode of expression, whose characters and syntactic laws it is our business to discover by comparing the original and the translation. The dream-thoughts are immediately comprehensible, as soon as we have learnt them. The dream-content, on the other hand, is expressed as it were in a pictographic script [*Bilderschrift*], the characters of which have to be transposed individually into the language of the dream-thoughts. If we attempted to read these characters according to their pictorial value [*Bilderwert*] instead of according to their symbolic relation [*Zeichenbeziehung*], we should clearly be led into error.[23]

Dreams are like commodities: hieroglyphs (the actual meaning of *Bilderschrift*), where meaning and value should be differentiated. Hence Freud's insistence that we should pass from the imaginary to the symbolic, the focus on *Zeichenbeziehung*, the relation between signs independently from their meaningful and adequate relation to images. Just like commodities, dreams, too, appear as an unproblematic universal experience that everyone seems to understand spontaneously. The more their formal analysis progresses, the more their complexity becomes apparent and the deeper the gap between their pictographic script, the imaginary aspect of dreams, and their structure. And again, just as commodities, dreams bring together two languages, not the original and the translation but the language of values and the language of meaning (need, communication), which in the end resume the split within one and the same language. These two levels do not overlap, their interaction is merely accidental, but they both need to be taken into account in order to understand unconscious production, just as we cannot simply omit use-value from the production of value, since we thereby lose the entire paradox of the commodity form. Focusing only on the sequence of dream images, the product appears to us senseless and worthless, without meaning or value, and the 'science of dreams' (as Freud's

---

23 Freud, *Standard Edition*, Vol. 4, 277.

volume was initially titled in French translation) is only possible through the shift from the appearance of meaning to the logic of value. The science of dreams is also a science of value. With this move, Freud outlines the structural background that supports both the production of meaning in a seemingly senseless sequence of images, and the articulation of a demand for satisfaction that aims beyond the meaning of dreams and that can solely open up the 'royal road to a knowledge of the unconscious',[24] the autonomy of the signifier that marked Lacan's first return to Freud. The *Interpretation of Dreams* without any doubt grounds psychoanalysis as a logic and not as a hermeneutic of the unconscious.

Let us move on to unconscious labour. The dream work stands for various formal operations. Freud names them condensation, displacement, consideration of representability and secondary elaboration. Unconscious labour is already implied in the inverted relation between concrete and abstract labour, which prevents the identification of unconscious labour with the psychological subject. Marx pointed out the fundamental achievement of the capitalist decentralisation of labour when he claimed that the capitalist and scientific development of the means of production does not free the labourer from labour but instead frees labour of its content, which means that labour is freed first and foremost of the empirical labourer, while the inverse, the liberation of the labourer from labour, appears as an impossible task. The liberation of labour radicalises the dependency of the labourer on labour, it accomplishes the transformation of the subject into labour-power, a commodified, capitalist subject. There is more at stake in this asymmetry than the fact that abstract labour simply becomes the privileged representation of all concrete forms of labour, or that exchange-value abstracts from use-value, thereby making of labour, too, an abstraction. Because of the asymmetrical relation between abstract and concrete labour, no return to concrete and presumably more authentic forms of labour will abolish the alienation of labour. The alienation of labour is, of course, not a result of capitalism, no more as is discursive alienation. What is its achievement, though, is the objectification of this alienation in a specific commodity.

From a psychoanalytic perspective, this objectification of alienation, its materialisation in a commodity, unveils a major feature of capitalism, namely that it places the subject in the position of the object that satisfies the Other's demand for production, the object that is consumed by the

24   Freud, *Standard Edition*, Vol. 5, 608.

Other for the extraction of surplus-object – this, precisely, is Lacan's definition of perversion. As labour-power, a commodity consumed for the production of value, the subject is deprived of its subjective position. Commodification of labour means as much as imposing a perverse position on the subject, demanding from the subject to assume the position of the object of the Other's *jouissance*.[25] The main achievement of Marx's labour theory of value consisted in the fact that it reclaimed the subject's position, hence reintroducing the position of the subject in the commodity world and abolishing another imposed fantasy, according to which capital is the true subject of the valorisation process.

At this point we can add another remark regarding Marx's labour theory of value, for which we hear that it lost its importance in times of financialisation and proliferation of new technologies. Such declarations risk blurring the difference between the political-economic labour theory (Smith and Ricardo) and its Marxian reformulation. The reason why Marx's theory of value preserves the predicate 'labour' is not so much in the simplistic idea, according to which labour would be the central economic category and the privileged source of value. This is what a certain branch of classical political economy seemed to have claimed – and it was wrong. Rather, the main achievement of Marx's theory of value concerns the fact that it recognises in labour *the* process, the analysis of which demonstrates that the source of value lies in inequality, exploitation and hence in social non-relation. However, in order to think the source of value rigorously we also need to acknowledge the participation of all the fetishist fantasies in this process – and this is another main achievement of Marx's labour theory of value. The logic of value can only be thoroughly thought in parallel with an elaborate logic of fantasy. The labour theory of value thus becomes a component of a critical science, which repeatedly evolves around the interdependency of exploitation and mystification of exploitation, which both reach their peak in the fetishisation of capitalist abstractions. Marx's labour theory has never been more theoretically urgent and more practically relevant than in today's financial capitalism.

Unconscious labour and abstract labour both lack concrete personification and embodiment, since their materiality consists in labour-power, which the discursive apparatus isolates in the living body and which the signifier or value represents independently from the relation to the signified. Because of

---

25   I rely here on D. Hoens, 'A Subject Staging Its Own Disappearance: A Lacanian Approach to Phantasm and Politics', unpublished paper.

this lack of concrete embodiment, Marx and Freud produced two 'fetishisa-tions', that is, they forced two social personifications of abstract and unconscious labour. Marx could only invent the social symptom by fetishis-ing the proletariat and the industrial reserve army as the point where the contradictions of the capitalist structure become empirical. This, of course, entails the misunderstanding that Marx's critique descends from the realm of metaphysical abstractions to the concrete analysis of social conditions and to concrete men and women. The fetishisation in question maybe repeats the very same operation as commodity fetishism, but it articulates something that one might call *Marx's hypothesis*: the individual who is affected by capi-talism is the same as the one who constitutes the subject of value.[26] This clearly inverts the fetishist hypothesis, according to which the subject of capi-talism is capital itself. The sameness of the industrial proletariat and of the subject of value implies that the industrial labourer, in a given historic moment, the industrial revolution, embodies the split in the subject of labour and the alienation introduced by the capitalist organisation of production. Their hypothetical sameness does not contradict the fact that the subject of value designates the radical alienation of the individual that embodies it.

For Freud, the same privilege, equally in the given historical moment, comes to the hysteric, who from *Studies on Hysteria* (1895) onward assumes the same function as Marx's proletariat. The hysteric does not merely embody the symptom; she *is* the epistemological and the social symptom, e.g., for medical knowledge, which sees in her either a pseudo-illness, simu-lation and hypochondria, or an inexplicable enigma, around which an entire spectacle is organised: Charcot's presentations of cases in the Parisian hospital La Salpêtrière had the status of theatre performances and attracted not only other scientists but also the lay public. In the nineteenth century, hysteria was the limit of scientific discourse, the point where the primacy of medical knowledge was suspended because the causes of the hysteric symp-tom cannot be traced back to anatomical origins solely. It was only Freud, who succeeded in theorising the hysteric as a social symptom, which on the epistemological level introduced a shift from the paradigm of the 'medical gaze'[27] to the paradigm of the 'analytic ear', in other words, from the primacy

---

26 I am here paraphrasing what Lacan describes as his hypothesis: 'My hypothesis is that the individual who is affected by the unconscious is the same as the one that constitutes what I call the subject of a signifier' (Lacan, *Encore*, 142, translation modified).

27 M. Foucault, *Naissance de la clinique*, Paris: Presses Universitaires de France,

of vision and observation to the primacy of speech and listening, and finally, from vulgar materialism to critical materialism. The hysteric is, indeed, Freud's proletarian.

The notion of dream work is supposed to explain the logical mechanism of fulfilment and the structure of desire. The question that occupies Freud is why does the unconscious need to work on a detour of displacements and condensations, censorship and deformations, in order to reach satisfaction. Why can there be no unmasked and undistorted satisfaction? In order to answer this question, Freud makes the hypothesis that the relation between unconscious desire and the demands of reality involves a contradiction. Due to this contradiction, the dream work produces double conditions for the satisfaction of desire, whereby the split in commodity form serves as the most comfortable means by which to overcome the contradiction between desire and reality. In the apparent satisfaction, an 'other satisfaction'[28] begins to show. This internally double satisfaction is reached through the manipulation of the day's remains, the material that accumulates on the borders of consciousness, in the preconscious, this grey zone between consciousness and the unconscious. In this intermediate space we come across wishes that can still be consciously formulated. For this reason, one could reproach Freud insofar as his analysis of dream samples exaggerates their meaning. The discussed cases only contain fulfilments of banal, simple and naïve desires. Freud's dream of Irma's injection, this crown example that is supposed to demonstrate the revolutionary character of his discoveries, unveils his attempts to shirk responsibility for the failed treatment of his hysteric patient. Children's dreams, another example that confirms the wish-fulfilment theory, are only concerned with concrete objects (sweets, toys and so on). Almost all examples seem to be badly chosen and speak against the reality of the 'other satisfaction'. They leave the impression that the desire in question is simply preconscious, temporarily dropped out of consciousness and attention but did not change its character in any way. It still aims at the same concrete object and remains intertwined with the content of the day's remains. And most importantly, at least for Freud's critics, there is absolutely no trace of sexuality, not to speak of infantile sexuality, and there is no reason to complicate the matter with repression and censorship.

1963, 107.
   28   Lacan, *Encore*, 49.

Freud anticipates precisely such criticisms when he writes: 'It will then *appear* as though the conscious wish alone has been realised in the dream',[29] a concrete satisfaction that assumed a hallucinatory and performative form. The emphasis is on the appearance that pushes a certain type of satisfaction into the foreground. This appearance is the same as the one that unites both aspects of the commodity and masks the structural gap between use-value and exchange-value. In accordance with this, the dream form implies two satisfactions, of which one depends on its apparent immediate meaning and another on its linguistic value. The move from quality to quantity entails a shift in the object form. Lacan's object *a*, the object of desire, is an object without qualities that presupposes the autonomy of value. Thereby it becomes clear that the discovery of this object is possible only under the condition of the commodity form in the universe of capitalism and modern science. Before the object of desire appears either as an unattainable transcendent Thing (*das Ding* that Lacan discusses in reference to the status of the Lady in the medieval courtly love) or as an immanent *agalma* (like in the transference relation between Socrates and Alcibiades in Plato's *Symposium*). The object *a*, neither transcendent nor immanent, remains unthinkable outside modernity and is so to speak a modern invention, a consequence of the foundation of science on universal mathematisation and of the social relations on quantification and mass production.

The hallucinatory fulfilment in dreams shows that the satisfaction was postponed and that the fulfilment presupposes a renunciation of immediate satisfaction, as in the case of children's dreams. The postponement exposes a shift within satisfaction, which remains invisible in the wish-fulfilment and in relation to which the immediacy of wish relates as a mask. In other words, the manifestation of desire is always mediated through the apparent immediacy of wish. Desire parasites the use-value of objects. We can already notice that the relation between the conscious and the unconscious 'wish' is also inscribed into language: the pair 'wish-desire' perfectly corresponds with 'work-labour', just as the production of use-value and the production of value overlap with satisfaction and the other satisfaction. Wish can still be attributed to consciousness because its object is concrete, whereas desire appears to be without an object, as long as it is not associated with the quantitative and abstract character of the commodity form. Freud's dream analyses simply attempt to demonstrate that the

---

29   Freud, *Standard Edition*, Vol. 4, 553.

'unconscious wish' *does* have an object because it finds satisfaction in the surplus produced through the manipulation of psychic material. The name of this object is also at hand – it is simply *Lust,* pleasure. Although Freud will soon discover that the status of this unconsciously produced pleasure is more problematic than it seems.

After pointing out the appearance that masks the other satisfaction, Freud finally introduces the already mentioned economic comparison, which should illustrate the nature of the unconscious desire and make his concept of the unconscious more understandable. 'I am now in position to give a sharp description' – sharp because the appearance needs to be put back into focus in order to make desire present – 'of the part played in dreams by unconscious wish'.[30] He admits that there are dreams in which the stimulation comes from the day's remains, hence from use-value, although this trigger is not enough for the dream formation. For instance, in Freud's dream of Irma's injection, his concern about the patient's state was not enough. He then has recourse to the comparison of unconscious production with capitalist production that is worth repeating here:

> The *motive force,* which the dream required, had to be provided by a wish; it was the business of the worry to get hold of a wish to act as the motive force of the dream. The position may be explained by an analogy. A daytime thought may very well play the part of *entrepreneur* for a dream; but the *entrepreneur,* who, as people say, has the idea and the initiative to carry it out, can do nothing without the capital; he needs a *capitalist* who can afford the outlay, and the capitalist who provides the psychical outlay for the dream is invariably and indisputably, whatever may be the thoughts of the previous day, *a wish from the unconscious.*[31]

Freud does not say what the Freudo-Marxists will claim later, that the unconscious explains capitalism; he states precisely the opposite: it is capitalism that elucidates the unconscious. The unconscious discovered in the *Interpretation of Dreams* is nothing other than the capitalist unconscious,

---

30 Freud, *Standard Edition*, Vol. 5, 560. Translation modified.

31 Ibid. 560–1 (Freud's emphasis). Freud was clearly aware of the weight and the implications of his comparison, since he referred to it on two other occasions. The passage from the *Interpretation of Dreams* is directly quoted in the analysis of the Dora case (1905) and rephrased in the *Introductory Lectures on Psychoanalysis* (1916–17).

the intertwining of unconscious satisfaction with the structure and the logic of the capitalist mode of production.

Freud seems to make a similar move as Saussure. The reference to the capitalist and the entrepreneur (*homo oeconomicus*) makes the entire comparison sound more like 'Freud with Smith' rather than 'Freud with Marx'. According to classical economic liberalism, the encounter between the capitalist and the labourer takes place in a free space of equal opportunities and is actualised through the act of exchange: money for commodity, one abstraction for another. The same encounter echoes in the unconscious: psychic energy is exchanged for the idea contained in the day's residues. We can mention in passing that in one of his later texts Freud will describe the 'psychic energy', in the meantime renamed libido, as the standard 'currency' of psychic life.[32] Everything can be translated into this mental general equivalent. The situation is nevertheless more complex than Freud's comparisons seem to suggest. Unconscious labour is incompatible with *homo oeconomicus,* so it does not even appear in the comparison. However, the discussion of dreams leaves no doubt that the 'only essential thing in dreams is the dream-work that has influenced the thought-material'.[33] In Freud's example, the association of the capitalist with the 'wish from the unconscious' is more crucial because it exposes an essential feature of the capitalist. Unlike the entrepreneur, who conserves the reference to the economic subject of cognition, the capitalist is identified with decentralised desire, which brings the comparison closer to Marx's description of the capitalist as the personification of the impersonal and systemic imperative of constant growth and of profit-making. Freud also mentions other possible relations between the capitalist and the entrepreneur, from their complete difference, their lesser or greater overlapping, to situations in which several entrepreneurs address the same capitalist or several capitalists support the same entrepreneur. These combinations do not change anything in the underlying relation itself, although they do blur the fact that Freud constantly speaks of unconscious desire in the singular. There is no multiplicity of desires, in contrast to wishes, but one single unconscious desire, which comes down to one insatiable imperative. It also becomes apparent that this

---

32   See Mai Wegener, 'Why Should Dreaming Be a Form of Work?', in: S. Tomšič and A. Zevnik (Eds), *Jacques Lacan: Between Psychoanalysis and Politics*, London: Routledge, 2015, 169–71.

33   Freud, *Standard Edition*, Vol. 15, 223.

singular desire does not imply a subject: desire is precisely a 'process without a subject'.[34]

Rather than explaining unconscious production, the comparison focuses on the appearance. The actual complication emerges when the labour theory shows that the unconscious is split between desire and labour. This double character contains a further aspect that distinguishes the Freudian notion from other possible conceptions. First, the unconscious is placed in a relation of dependency on the social structure. Then this mark is interpreted as a contradiction, the constitutive split of One into Two that Freud already pushed into the foreground in his early work through the notion of the 'psychic conflict'. When Freud applies the social link between the capitalist and the labourer to the unconscious, he literally repeats Marx's move in *Capital,* where they are both progressively detached from the psychological personages, describing processes rather than persons. The unconscious desire shows that the capitalist enters the stage as an anomaly in the field of mastery: a headless master.[35]

As already mentioned, Freud classifies the dream work by four basic operations. His analysis shows that these operations take place on two different levels. The ground level is the condensation work and the displacement work: the two fundamental aspects of unconscious labour that match

---

34   L. Althusser, *Essays in Self-Criticism*, London: New Left Books, 1976, 99. Althusser uses the expression in reference to history. Here a minimal difference with the Lacanian readings of Marx emerges. Lacan, too, rejects the existence of a transcendental and unchangeable subject of history, but for him there nevertheless is a subject of history. Consequently, History does not exist, at least not as an abstract history of the One but as a decentralised history of negativity (recall that, for Althusser, Marx's epistemological contribution consists in the decentralisation of history, the abolition of its teleological movement). Lacan's neologism *hystoire*, a wordplay on history and hysteria, encapsulates this orientation.

35   Because the efficiency of the capitalist discourse is based on this specific transformation of the feudal master into the capitalist and the serf into the proletarian, Lacan will later claim that capitalism progressively reveals the very essence of the master, namely that he does not know what he wants. In the figure of the capitalist, the master is reduced to the bare imperative that requires productive labour: 'In the master's discourse, for instance, it is effectively impossible that there be a master who makes the entire world function. Getting people to work is even more tiring, if one really has to do it, than working oneself. The master never does it. He gives a sign, the master signifier, and everybody jumps. That's where you have to start, which is, in effect, completely impossible. It's tangible every day' (Lacan, *The Other Side of Psychoanalysis*, 174).

the two main linguistic operations, metaphor and metonymy. Freud privileged these processes in another comparison with social labour: '*Dream displacement* and *dream condensation* are the two skilled workers [*Werkmeister*] to whose activity we may in essence ascribe the form assumed by dreams.'[36] The processes appear as a form of knowledge: savoir faire, knowledge without reflection, unknown knowledge. This is what differentiates the unconscious labourer from the entrepreneur, who still remains in the paradigm of the subject of cognition, for which political economy assumes that it possesses knowledge both of his or her inner interests and of the external market relations.

The other two operations, consideration of representability and secondary elaboration, appear as a repetition of condensation and displacement within the imaginary. Freud points out that this imaginary dimension is not reducible visualisation, when during his discussion of secondary elaboration he evokes the very same lines in Heine that will three decades later serve him in his critique of *Weltanschauung*:

> The thing that distinguishes and at the same time reveals this part of the dream-work is its *purpose*. This function behaves in the manner, which the poet maliciously ascribes to philosophers: it fills up the gaps in the dream-structure with shreds and patches. As a result of its efforts, the dream loses its appearance of absurdity and disconnectedness and approximates to the model of an intelligible experience. But its efforts are not always crowned with success.[37]

The second stage of dream formation is related to this totalisation. Here the dream receives consistency and narration, which makes it comparable to the 'intellectual construction' of worldviews and even more so with the use-value of commodities. But the tendency of labour is not necessarily the same as in metaphor and metonymy, since it tries to fill the gap between use-value and exchange-value, between meaning and value of the unconscious formation. Freud underlines this minimal discrepancy by indicating that the task of secondary elaboration is to abolish the appearance of absurdity, which becomes striking once the 'value of *jouissance*' (as Lacan translates exchange-value in *Seminar XIV*) is entirely separated from meaning. On the level of secondary elaboration and the consideration of

36   Freud, *Standard Edition*, Vol. 4, 308. Translation modified.
37   Freud, *Standard Edition*, Vol. 5, 490.

representability, the value of dreams appears in their meaning: *jouissance* assumes the form of *joui-sens* (enjoyed meaning, to refer to another Lacanian wordplay).

When Lacan replaced Saussure with Marx, he directed psychoanalysis back to the figure of the unconscious labourer and thereby radicalised the implications of his own introduction of the subject. This orientation is most lucidly formulated in *Television*, where Lacan leaves no doubt that psychoanalysis and the critique of political economy come across the same subject:

> Does the unconscious imply that it be listened to? To my mind, yes. But this surely does not imply that, without the discourse through which it ex-sists, one judges it as knowledge that does not think, or calculate, or judge – which doesn't prevent it from being at work (as in dreams, for instance). Let's say that it is the ideal worker, the one Marx made the flower of capitalist economy in the hope of seeing him take over the discourse of the master; which, in effect, is what happened, although in an unexpected form. There are surprises in these matters of discourse, and that is, indeed, the point of the unconscious [*le fait de l'inconscient*].[38]

That the unconscious implies listening does not make psychoanalysis a dialogue in which it would regress back to some abstract and ideal communicative model, as various forms of psychologies and psychotherapies have done. What is at stake is that the truth regains the power of speech.[39] The subjective manifestations of its speech are inhibitions, symptoms and anxieties that the discourse causes in the body. The speaking truth, the power of truth to be more than mere facticity or truth-value, is the main terrain where psychoanalysis encounters Marxism and the figure of the labourer is the privileged conceptual embodiment of this encounter. Practically all of Lacan's texts from 1969 onwards address this intertwining of the unconscious subject and the capitalist labourer, thereby indicating that the transformation of the subject that psychoanalysis strives to produce in its praxis stands in immediate continuity with the political question of social change. It is not surprising that *Television* defines one of the psychoanalytic goals as the 'way out of capitalist discourse', to which Lacan adds that it 'will

---

38   Lacan, *Television*, 16.

39   'I, truth, speak' was the famous prosopopoeia of truth that Lacan proposed in 'The Freudian Thing' (Lacan, *Écrits*, 408–11).

not constitute progress, if it happens only for some'.[40] In political matters, psychoanalysis envisages the same universalism as Marxist politics.

Lacan condenses Freud's analysis of the relation between unconscious desire, dream work and capitalism by speaking of the ideal labourer, an expression that explores the flip side of the homology between unconscious production and capitalist production. The ideal labourer is not the same as the subject of alienation. It stands for the multiplicity of operations that take place among the signifiers, to which a decentralised form of knowledge can be attributed. The ideal labourer does not know itself as a form of knowledge, but this does not prevent it from accomplishing its task. The subject of labour only enters the stage as far as the unconscious does not merely imply labour but also listening, the enunciation of truth that sabotages the automatism of unconscious knowledge, of knowledge as 'means of *jouissance*',[41] that is, as means of production. The subject of the unconscious, by contrast, is a disturbance in the regime of knowledge, an anomaly that articulates its enunciation through the symptom: 'There is only one social symptom – each individual is really a proletarian, that is it has no discourse of which to make a social link, in other words, a semblant'.[42] The real status of each individual as subject in the capitalist mode of production coincides with what Marx strives to address through the proletariat. The proletarian is 'the subject as a *response* of the real'.[43] Here we again encounter the echo of Marx's subject-hypothesis that orthodox Marxism later abolished through the identification of the proletariat with the subject of knowledge. To paraphrase Hegel, the worldview Marxism theorised the proletarian merely as substance (class-consciousness) and no longer as subject (labour-power). Instead of transforming the capitalist subject, class-consciousness transformed the ideal labourer, making of its unknown knowledge a reflected 'scientific' knowledge. This, too, is the surprise that Lacan alludes to in *Television*: the historical and the structural development goes from the master's discourse, whose modern version is capitalism before the second industrial revolution, to the university discourse in post-industrial capitalism, where it is precisely knowledge, hence the ideal labourer, that assumes the position of the master. The same structural shift was accomplished in the Soviet Union, where the knowledge of the Party,

---

40   Lacan, *Television*, 16.
41   Lacan, *The Other Side of Psychoanalysis*, 39.
42   Lacan, 'La troisième', 18.
43   Lacan, *Autres écrits*, 459 (my emphasis).

the historic embodiment of the proletarian class-consciousness, became the privileged discursive agent.

Lacan's conclusion is thus: the proletarian is the subject of the unconscious. Marx and Freud undoubtedly placed their wager on the revolutionary potential of this figure. For Marx, the political task of the industrial proletariat consists in its realisation, that is, its self-abolition through the abolition of labour-power, which would produce a new social link and a new figure of subjectivity. Freud, too, thought that the discovery of the unconscious would initiate a transformation that is both epistemological and social. His critiques of religion in *The Future of an Illusion*, of politics in *Group Psychology and the Analysis of the Ego*, and of capitalism in *Civilisation and Its Discontents* were directed against the social structures that are rooted in the relations of domination. The revolutionary potential of the subject of psychoanalysis was supposed to demonstrate that the ego is not a master in his own household, and thereby to overthrow the 'I-cracy' (Lacan) that marked the modern philosophies of consciousness and on which economic liberalism grounded its *homo oeconomicus*.

Lacan clearly assumes a more realistic position and detects the political failure of Marxism and Freudianism. The proletarian, this privileged figure of social and unconscious labour, did indeed accomplish a social and an epistemological revolution, but this revolution essentially took place in the relation between power and knowledge. The liberation of labour introduced a social system in which abstract knowledge assumed the position of the master. The ideal labourer meanwhile changed its appearance and turned into a figure of domination both in capitalism (the expert, the Eurocrat) and in Stalinism (the party bureaucrat). Marx in fact predicted the possibility of such a course of events. In the first volume of *Capital*, the capitalist transformation of labour is accomplished in the technological organisation of production, the inversion of the relation between the labourer and the machine. When Marx writes about the use of machines in capitalism, he thematises constantly the essential role of scientific knowledge in the progressive social implementation of capitalist abstractions. The importance of machines is not in their material presence but in the fact that they exemplify the productive nature of knowledge in capitalism, knowledge as a means of production and as a tool of modern power relations. For this reason, Marx assumes a reserved position towards the Luddite movement. His main concern was that they mistakenly saw the problem in machines themselves and not in the new social role of knowledge that these machines actualise in the production process. Their immediate attack on the machines could indeed be considered the flip side of the capitalist fetishisation of machines as the producers of surplus-value.[44]

Lacan's ideal labourer translates Freud's skilled worker, condensation and displacement, the logical operations that do their labour, without knowing themselves as a form of knowledge. The designation of the ideal labourer as 'knowledge that does not think, judge, or calculate' immediately evokes a crucial passage from the *Interpretation of Dreams*, where Freud provides a condensed account of the dream work from the viewpoint of secondary elaboration and draws the following conclusion:

> Two separate functions may be distinguished in mental activity during the construction of a dream: the production of the dream-thoughts, and their transformation into the content of the dream . . . However many interesting and puzzling questions the dream-thoughts may involve, such questions have, after all, no special relation to dreams and do not call for treatment among the problems of dreams. On the other hand, the second function of mental activity during dream construction, the transformation of the unconscious thoughts into the content of the dream, is peculiar to dream-life and characteristic of it. This dream-work proper diverges further from our picture of waking thought than has been supposed even by the most determined depreciator of psychical functioning during the formation of dreams. The dream-work is not simply more careless, more irrational, more forgetful and more incomplete than waking thought; it is completely different from it qualitatively and for that reason not immediately comparable with it. It does not think, calculate or judge in any way at all; it restricts itself to giving things a new form.[45]

The double character of unconscious labour is striking, but the actual object of dream work is the form and not the content, the very same form that supports the satisfaction of unconscious desire. The transformation of

---

44 Of course, this is a one-sided 'pessimistic' view of the Luddites. For a more exhaustive discussion see E. Hobsbawm and G. Rudé, *Captain Swing*, London: Verso, 2014. For Marx's critique of the Luddites, the following passage from *Capital* (Vol. 1, 554–5) is representative: 'It took both time and experience before the workers learnt to distinguish between machinery and its employment by capital, and therefore to transfer their attacks from the material instruments of production to the form of society which utilizes those instruments.'

45 Freud, *Standard Edition*, Vol. 5, 506–7.

preconscious material involves a production of appearance that will not only lead to the satisfaction of desire but will literally mask desire in a wish. Dream work essentially consists in creating the conditions for this masking, which also codifies other satisfaction into satisfaction, exchange-value into use-value, and finally *jouissance* into pleasure. 'Dreams are wish-fulfilments' is therefore anything but an innocent statement.[46]

The supposedly enigmatic character of dreams is of no particular interest to Freud. He explains it as an effect of the form of the dream itself. This is why psychoanalysis does not interpret dreams by giving them meaning. The hermeneutic strategy would focus on the content and in doing so overlook the mechanism of the dream production, the labour and the subject of labour. Thereby it would fetishise dreams by attributing them a deeper meaning. It is interesting to observe how Freud rejects the appearance of enigma and the postulate of irrationality in the procedures of the dream. He implicitly refers to the difference between concrete and abstract labour: dreams display the pure form of rationality because the labour that produces them is stripped of positive qualities like thinking, calculating and judging, qualities that still define the subject of cognition. Because the dream work merely accomplishes its task, it is careful, correct, unforceful, and thus ideal: labour without qualities.

Something nevertheless goes wrong in this dream factory, and this is yet another aspect of surprise that the unconscious introduces into discourse. Freud soon discovered that not all dreams confirm the general scenario of wish-fulfilment. He came across dreams that reproduced traumatic experiences, for instance those reported by war neurotics or the sexually abused; and finally there is the famous dream of the burning child that Freud initially took as an example of wish-fulfilment. By constantly returning to a traumatic experience – war, abuse, death and so on – these dreams unveil the compulsion to repeat. With this discovery, traumatic neurosis turns out to be the collateral damage of capitalism. Cultural discontent will immediately become the main theme of Freud's critique of

---

46   Lacan will translate this Freudian lesson in the general axiom: *le désir de – est le désir de l'Autre* (Lacan, *Autres écrits*, 207). The meaning of this claim is double: 'desire is desire of the Other' accentuates the dimension of alienation and places the doubling on the level of desire at the forefront, the relation between the subject and the Other, the fact that there is no subject of desire and that desire is inscribed in the Other and belongs to the Other; but the axiom also means that 'desire of', desire that seems to aim at a concrete object, is 'desire of the Other', desire that actually aims at the surplus-object.

modern culture. The dreams that do not confirm the general *dispositif* bear the character of awakening, sabotaging the production of *jouissance*. In this respect the unconscious is not reducible to one single discursive structure. It already raises the question of its exit.

When Lacan reaffirmed the linguistic structure of the unconscious, he introduced the term that brings together Marx and Freud's analysis of labour. This is the function of *ça parle*, it speaks. The psychoanalytic intervention operates on three levels: thinking, working and speaking. Discussions of psychoanalysis often mention that Freud's invention consisted in the fact that he listened to the speech of his hysteric patients, who revealed to him the secret of the unconscious: the hysteric symptom speaks and by speaking enunciates the truth of the discourse that determines it. This enunciation already inhibits the mechanism of satisfaction. In this psychoanalysis most directly coincides with Marx's discovery that in labour, too, an enunciation takes place, which articulates the truth of the capitalist relations of production. This is where Marx's invention of the social symptom gains its full weight for psychoanalysis. The symptom is the encounter of the proletarian and the subject of the unconscious, of the labourer and the speaking being.

LUSTGEWINN

Only four years after the publication of the *Interpretation of Dreams*, its lessons found a further development in the elaboration of the libidinal unconscious. In 1905, Freud published two apparently unrelated books, *Jokes and Their Relation to the Unconscious* and *Three Essays on the Theory of Sexuality*. While the book on jokes continues the direction of the *Interpretation of Dreams*, both method- and style-wise, the *Three Essays* replace the reference to language with the body, and the structural analysis of satisfaction with the theory of sexual development. The press welcomed the first book, while the discussion of sexuality encountered resistance and discontent. Despite apparent differences, the two works nevertheless meet in the introduction of the Freudian notion of *jouissance*, condensed in the expression *Lustgewinn*, pleasure gain or pleasure profit, in which it is not difficult to recognise the conceptual mediator between Lacan's surplus-*jouissance* and Marx's surplus-value. With this notion, Freud finally names the object of the unconscious production and the object that satisfies the unconscious tendency. Both works also intersect in that they introduce the tendency that will henceforth occupy Freud's theoretical work and call for the elaboration of a metapsychology: the drive and its topological paradoxes. *Lustgewinn* and the move towards *Trieblehre*, the theory of the drive, overcame the opposition between structure and anatomy, situating psychoanalysis in the grey zone their intersection. Freud thereby inaugurated the direction that Lacan came back to when defining the signifier as an apparatus of *jouissance*.

Freud from the very outset approached the *modus operandi* of the mental apparatus through economic metaphors. As his theories became more complex, this economic reality, too, displayed its antagonistic features more and more, one of them being the tendency of the unconscious production towards the absolutisation of the production of *jouissance*. 'Our mental activities', writes Freud in one of his later texts, 'pursue either a useful aim or an immediate pleasure gain',[47] again in accordance with the distinction between use-value and exchange-value. The analysis of dreams has already shown that the satisfaction of desire does not address the use-value of the day residues but aims at the value of *jouissance* they obtain through the dream work, placing unconscious labour in equivocity with unconscious desire. The term *Lustgewinn* defines pleasure as surplus, hence as something that the mental activities reach beside their tendency to usefulness. Seen from the perspective of use-value and of the need it presupposes, pleasure appears as an affection that accompanies the abolition of a bodily stimulus and the decrease of a tension. From the viewpoint of value, however, pleasure is no longer a more or less accidental side effect but *the* object of satisfaction. As such, *Lustgewinn* does not relate to any quality, which also implies that it has no corresponding need. The shift from usefulness to uselessness that directs the Freudian concept of *Lust* explains why Lacan translated the German term with '*jouissance*' and not 'pleasure'. From the very outset it is clear that a fundamental subversion is at stake in *Lustgewinn*, which is not an insignificant side effect of satisfaction. The satisfaction of needs is always-already parasitised, colonised and subverted by the satisfaction of unconscious tendencies (desire and drive), whose existence depends on the autonomy of the signifier and of value.

The connection of pleasure with use-value, the definition of commodity as what satisfies a need and serves as a source of pleasure is also Marx's

---

47   Freud, *Standard Edition*, Vol. 19, 127. Translation modified.

point of departure, where different types or qualities of needs are equated in the following way:

> The commodity is, first of all, an external object, a thing which through its qualities satisfies human needs of whatever kind. The nature of such needs, whether they arise, for example, from the stomach or from fantasy, makes no difference. Nor does it matter here how the object satisfies these needs, whether directly as a means of subsistence, i.e., an object of consumption, or indirectly as a means of production.[48]

Hasty psychoanalytic readings will conclude that Marx begins his analysis of commodity form by foreclosing the dimension of desire and hence of the subject[49] because he simply equates the immediate bodily needs and the needs that are symbolically mediated and in the last instance rooted in fantasy – hence needs and desires in the strict sense. However, this is precisely what Marx does not do. By exposing the double character of commodities, he introduces the equivocity between both regimes of value and the tendencies of satisfaction, which will in the end relativise the non-fantasmatic status of need and use-value. Marx introduces his developments with the claim that, in order to analyse the qualitative aspect of commodity, we first need to abolish the division of immediate and mediated satisfaction, on the one hand, and physiological and psychological satisfaction, on the other. The commodity form becomes the universal source of pleasure: in the modern universe 'there are only commodity pleasures';[50] there is thus one single satisfaction, which is nevertheless internally complicated due to the split of commodity between 'qualities without matter' and 'matter without qualities', to repeat Milner. If even fantasies are marked by use-value, the inverse is no less true, exchange-value colonises physiological or psychological needs. The complication envisaged by Marx is thus apparent. In order to understand any satisfaction whatsoever, one first needs to analyse the structure of commodity. A useless object such as a diamond is evidently fetishised, but this fetishist relation is accompanied by

---

48   Marx, *Capital*, Vol. 1, 125. Translation modified.

49   See, for instance, P. Martin, *Argent et psychanalyse*, Paris: Navarin, 1984, 15–16. Martin proposes another highly problematic thesis, the identification of money with the master-signifier, thereby neglecting its actual status as the fetish-object.

50   Milner, *Le triple du plaisir*, 76.

a fantasmatic need. Desire traverses the need and is supported by the fantasmatic screen of usefulness. The simultaneity of the satisfaction of needs and the other satisfaction (of desire and drive) unveils the coupling of two heterogeneities in a unified object, one of the functions of fantasy being precisely to link the non-linkable. Through this fantasmatic link, the use-value and the exchange-value contaminate each other and make the object in question *sehr vertrackt*, as Marx writes, complicated, fuzzy and even insane.[51]

When Marx equates the physiological need (stomach) with the intel-lectual need (fantasy), he indicates that the need should not be understood as quasi-natural. With need we already entered the discursive field, and need cannot be exactly isolated from its dialectical relation with demand and desire. There are no innocent needs, the satisfaction of which would not be structurally determined. Going back to Freud, his distinction between usefulness and pleasure shows that the satisfaction of needs could only cause pleasure as a side effect and that this side contains no pleasure-gain. Usefulness and need remain in the perspective of what Freud describes as the reduction of tension, or the abolition of bodily affection, which still suggests that the mental apparatus contains an essen-tially self-regulatory tendency towards homeostasis, the Aristotelian right measure. In order to speak of pleasure-gain, a third term must stand between need and satisfaction: discourse (social link, difference). There is no *jouissance* without discourse, and there is no other *jouissance* than a discursive one. Lacan emphasises this in the aforementioned translation of exchange-value with the value of *jouissance*. From the viewpoint of discourse, needs and their satisfactions are always-already stained with the other satisfaction that is tied to the libidinal body and to the materi-ality of the signifier. The concreteness of the object, whose qualities are supposed to cause pleasure, fades, and what counts is only the 'abstract' object, which finally inverses the relation between pleasure and tension. This is where the structure of the mental apparatus approaches the

---

51 The best example of the fantasmatic intertwining of both tendencies and the insanities it encourages is collecting and its possible deviation into hoarding. Gérard Wajcman analysed both activities in relation to desire, which still does not entirely eliminate the qualitative aspect of collected objects, such as artworks, antiquities, books and so on. See G. Wajcman, *Collection*, Paris: Nous, 1999, 32. For Wajcman, the minimal formula of collecting is: objects + desire, whereby, of course, desire aims at a singular Object beyond the multiplicity of objects.

capitalist economic model. In the other satisfaction, tension is no longer reduced but increased. The satisfaction of needs is of minor importance and is entirely integrated in the other satisfaction, as its internal, quasi-fictional moment. The unconscious tendency and the capitalist drive for self-valorisation first and foremost demand a constant production of surplus and a constant growth in tension. This is one of the main features of the Freudian notion of the drive, which demands a thorough re-elaboration of the functioning of the mental apparatus and the abolition of the initial homeostatic model.

The dialectic of value shows that use-value relates to exchange-value in a similar way as appearance to logic. Freud will come to an astonishingly similar conclusion: 'What is useful is itself (as is well known) only a circuitous path to pleasurable satisfaction.' Dreams fall into this category, whereby Freud reminds his reader that it would be wrong to consider dreaming an activity that merely concludes and resolves the day's preoccupations in a hallucinatory (performative) way: 'That is the business of preconscious thought. Useful work of this kind is as remote from dreams as is any intention of conveying information to another person.'[52] Dreams minimise the usefulness and the referentiality of the signifier. Instead, they intensify its autonomy and causality. In this respect, capitalism, too, is an eternal dream, or rather a perpetuated nightmare, from which it appears impossible to wake up.

Once desire and the drive enter the picture, every satisfaction of needs seems problematic: 'All the needs of speaking beings are contaminated by the fact of being involved in an other satisfaction that they may not live up to.'[53] The commodity form is the privileged materialisation of this distortion, and even when Marx discussed the developed form of this contamination, fictitious capital, where the creation of value out of value (M – M') becomes the rule of production, he nevertheless repeated the critical gesture from the first volume, according to which the self-engendering appearance of capital is grounded in the fetishist fantasy of direct overlapping of quality and value. Freud took the same direction in his move beyond the pleasure principle, from the homeostatic to the conflictual conception of the psychic apparatus, where *jouissance* appears to be deprived of all referentiality and becomes its own subject. But it would be wrong to conclude that in the libidinal unconscious the negative subject of the

---

52 Freud, *Standard Edition*, Vol. 19, 127.
53 Lacan, *Encore*, 49.

signifier is abolished, that the unconscious labourer vanishes, or that the repressed unconscious tendency becomes its own productive labourer. This would be fetishisation of *jouissance*, homologous to the fetishisation of financial abstractions.

Freud discovered in the production of pleasure-gain a transformation of pleasure. No satisfaction of needs can produce pleasure as profit because the pleasure that accompanies the satisfaction of needs merely signals the re-establishment of the supposedly homeostatic order that turns out to be fictional from the viewpoint of the other satisfaction. The keyword here is homeostasis, which Freud in 1905 still believed determined the overall functioning of the mental apparatus. *Lustgewinn* is the first sign that the homeostasis of the pleasure principle is mere fiction. Nevertheless it demonstrates that no satisfaction of needs can produce more pleasure, just as no surplus-value can logically follow from the circulation (C – M – C). Surplus-*jouissance*, the connection of pleasure with profitmaking, does not simply undermine the supposedly homeostatic character of the pleasure principle; it shows that the homeostasis is a *necessary* fiction, which structures and supports unconscious production, just as the imaginary achievement of worldview mechanisms consisted in providing an enclosed whole, without cracks in its overall construction. *Lustgewinn* is Freud's first conceptual confrontation with what will later be situated beyond the pleasure principle, the compulsion to repeat, and what will introduce the psychoanalytic equivalent to the circulation (M – C – M').

The introduction of *Lustgewinn* retroactively explained the status of pleasure and satisfaction in the *Interpretation of Dreams*, but it also complicates the matter because unconscious desire was replaced by the drive. In both cases, the surplus-object functions differently. On the level of desire, it appears as lack, absence and negativity. This appearance is linked to the metonymic structure, which makes the object shift from one concrete embodiment to another. Wajcman extensively elaborated this logical articulation in the case of the collector and the miser.[54] The structure of collection remains open because the object of collecting is not identical to the collected

---

54 Wajcman, *Collection*, 32. The figure of the miser is slightly more ambiguous, as it can be placed at the very intersection of desire and drive, as Marx also notes. This link was extensively analysed by M. Dolar (*O skoposti*, Ljubljana: Analecta, 2002), who defined the miser as someone who believes to have discovered the truth of desire, although this truth is *de facto* realised in the drive.

objects. No object is *the* object that would totalise the collection, thereby bringing about *the* satisfaction of desire. Another case is provided by Freud's dream analysis, where the reality of unconscious desire depends on the association of apparently disparate elements. Desire coincides with its own interpretation, the combination of the material from the day's remains and with the codification of its insistence. One way to meet the surplus is thus through the metonymic movement, where the encounter with the object always fails: no object is *the* object of desire, and, consequently, the surplus is always confronted in the form of a lack. For the unconscious desire, the surplus is never enough surplus; it cannot be associated with one object alone. It is only in relation to the drive that the surplus appears positive. Instead of the metonymic shifting and withdrawing of the object, the drive is structured through circulation and repetition.

The paradoxes of the drive were not an unknown for Marx, whose manuscripts already contained the connection between the structure of the drive, the abstract nature of the general equivalent and the production of surplus-value:

> Money is therefore not only *an* object, but is *the* object of greed . . . Greed as such, as a particular form of the drive, i.e., as distinct from the craving for a particular kind of wealth, e.g., for clothes, weapons, jewels, women, wine, etc., is possible only when general wealth, wealth as such, has become individualised in a particular thing, i.e., as soon as money is posited in its third quality. Money is therefore not only the object but also the fountainhead of greed. The mania for possessions is possible without money; but greed itself is the product of a definite social development, not *natural*, as opposed to *historical*.[55]

The drive is intimately linked to the double status of the general equivalent – as a means of exchange and as a particular use-value that totalises the universe of objects. Unlike desire, whose object is not yet identified with a particular embodiment and therefore supports the structure of metonymy, the drive presupposes the paradox of concrete universality, what the general equivalent is supposed to be. The desire for the object (wealth) thus accumulates a collection of objects that embody value – it focuses on the *objects of value* and not on *value as object*. The drive, on the other hand, is fixated on *the* object, the general equivalent,

---

55   Marx, *Grundrisse*, 222.

which due to its paradoxical status – being both singular and universal, a commodity and a Commodity in which all commodities are reflected – supports the infinitisation of satisfaction, which is to say, its impossibility and endless perpetuation. The capitalist drive for self-valorisation is an unsatisfiable demand, to which no labour can live up to. Marx also made an important point when he detached the notion of the drive from its biological or physiological connotation. He entirely conditioned it with the social existence of the general equivalent and with historical development. The capitalist drive is therefore not the only possible drive. There is something like a history of the drive, a historical transformation of fixations, which alters the social articulation of the drive together with the function of the general equivalent in the predominant mode of production. In Plato and Aristotle, the problem of the drive is indicated, although in the universe of antiquity this problem was not the same as in the capitalist universe, where the mode of production is based on the mathematisation of surplus-value and on the unleashing of the demand for self-valorisation in the form of fictitious capital. The old spirit of usury is by far no embryonic form of the modern spirit of capitalism, even if both can be explained through the existence of the general equivalent. Let us recall another crucial passage from the *Grundrisse*:

> Hunger is hunger, but the hunger gratified by cooked meat eaten with a knife and fork is a different hunger from that which bolts down raw meat with the aid of hand, nail and tooth. Production thus produces not only the object but also the manner of consumption, not only objectively but also subjectively. Production thus creates the consumer. Production not only supplies a material for the need, but it also supplies a need for the material.[56]

Marx again aims at the historical and the social transformation of the drive, leaving no doubt that the placement of the drive at the intersection of presumably natural need and its cultural articulation can be considered a predecessor of the psychoanalytic notion, for the Freudian notion of the drive is *not* the hunger that swallows raw meat but the hunger that reaches satisfaction through the *montage* of cooked meat, cutlery and table manners. Indeed, Lacan brought this to a crucial point when he compared the drive to a surrealist collage, underlining that the montage of the heterogeneous

---

56   Ibid., 92.

elements contains a differentiation between the *aim* and the *goal*, so again between use-value and exchange-value.[57]

Let us now pass over to Freud's discovery of surplus-*jouissance* in his analyses of jokes and humour. In *Jokes and Their Relation to the Unconscious*, the production of surplus is discussed in the social context. Freud emphasises this at the very beginning when he justifies the fact that, after already writing on dreams and failed actions, he dedicated another scientific study to an apparently marginal and insignificant object. The scientific discussion of jokes can be justified by the fact that a 'new joke acts almost like an event of universal interest'; a joke is never merely a joke – it is a 'social process'.[58] It codifies nothing less than the relation between the unconscious and the social link. Unlike dreams, which appear to be a private activity of the dreamer and where the presence of social mechanisms is harder to demonstrate (after all the function of dreams is to preserve sleep, the withdrawal from the social), jokes immediately point towards a social framework; they reveal the structure of social relations and the social economy of surplus-*jouissance*.

The matter is, of course, more complicated. It is not that the unconscious is more social in jokes than in dreams, and that one changes the register of the individual unconscious for the social unconscious. On the contrary, for Freud, dreams and jokes present two cases of the same discursive condition. The discussion of jokes in no respect shifts from the individual to the social; instead, it demonstrates that the unconscious stands beyond the division between interiority and exteriority, individuality and society, private and public. If dreams revealed the inscription of the social link into the unconscious, jokes demonstrate the manifestation of the unconscious in the social link, two sides of the causality of the signifier.

The analysis of jokes is introduced with the note that their character is not linked to a specific thought but to their form of expression, wording (*Wortlaut*). The entire focus is on the role of equivocity, which actualises the split between meaning and value. The efficiency of jokes depends on how *Witzarbeit*, the unconscious labour in jokes, forms the word. Unconscious production is again directed by condensation and displacement, but in this case their combination reveals an economic paradox.

---

57   See Lacan, *The Four Fundamental Concepts of Psychoanalysis*, 169, 179.
58   Freud, *Standard Edition*, Vol. 8, 15, 140.

Different joke techniques meet in a common strategy, which consists of the multiple use of the same material, the recycling of the given. Equivocity, double meaning or wordplay, combines different contexts in the same product. The multiple use of the same material characterises the non-metaphorical use of condensation: 'play upon words is nothing other than a condensation *without* substitute-formation'. In this transformation of condensation, Freud encounters the economic tendency towards saving: 'All these techniques are dominated by a tendency to compression, or rather to saving. It all seems to be a question of economy. In Hamlet's words: '"Thrift, thrift, Horatio!"'[59] From this perspective, the unconscious labourer appears as the ideal saver, whose tendency to condensation is supposed to produce a surplus: save in order to create profit and to stabilise economic relations. Sounds rather familiar.

The tendency towards saving is declared to be the general characteristic of joke techniques, although there is something economically inefficient in this form of saving, since the entire process is accompanied by displacement. In order to explain the apparent absurdity of unconscious saving, Freud recurs to the following economic comparison:

> The economies made by the joke-technique do not greatly impress us. They may remind us, perhaps, of the way in which some housewives economise when they spend time and money on a journey to a distant market because vegetables are to be had there a few farthings cheaper. What does a joke save by its technique? The putting together of a few new words, which would mostly have emerged without any trouble. Instead of that, it has to take the trouble to search out the one word which covers the two thoughts. Indeed, it must often first transform one of the thoughts into an unusual form which will provide a basis for its combination with the second thought. Would it not have been simpler, easier, and, in fact, more economical to have expressed the two thoughts as they happened to come, even if this involved no common form of expression? Is not the economy in words uttered more than balanced by the expenditure on intellectual effort? And who saves by that? Who gains by it?[60]

Saving turns into spending and the unconscious appears as an ideal consumer. The problem is that metonymic movement creates long detours and actualises a tendency to spend. The combination of both operations,

---

59 Ibid., 42.
60 Ibid., 44.

condensation and displacement, saving and spending, thus produces an apparent contradiction, an economic absurdity. Freud's analysis shows that jokes generate a loss in order to reach pleasure-profit. The surplus is produced at the background of the interdependency between spending and saving, and the housewife metaphor is pertinent only in so far as it shows that saving should not be regarded as the ultimate goal of the process but as something that can as well be considered a form of spending, a production of surplus that differs from what would be the accumulation of savings. The appearance of saving masks that there is a different kind of production in the background. Similarly, the imperative of economic cuts and restrictions is the inevitable flip side of the imperative to produce surplus. The house-wife example shows that the profit should not be attributed to the housewife but to the entire procedure. Economy can make profit because she is losing money in a seemingly rational economisation.

This structural operation is deployed in the social dimension of jokes. Jokes 'should not, after all, be described as pointless or aimless, since [they have] the unmistakable aim of evoking pleasure in [their] hearers'. They cause pleasure, and this feature entails a shift from usefulness to useless-ness. At this point, things complicate for the same reason as in dreams. The pleasure in jokes is reached through detour and at the background of the preceding renunciation of pleasure: 'If we do not require our mental appa-ratus at the moment for supplying one of our indispensable satisfactions, we allow it itself to work in the direction of pleasure and we seek to derive pleasure from its own activity.'[61] When the mental apparatus does not satisfy needs, it produces pleasure, but it is impossible to determine when one activity ceases and the other begins. Production needs to be associated with a problematic tendency, which opens up three possibilities: either the tendency is innocent (which is questionable in itself; why would it then be masked?), or jokes serve either a hostile or an obscene tendency (aggres-sion or exposure). The procedure is marked by a libidinal investment that points back to the drive, this new object of study in connection to uncon-scious formations and, one could say, a new metaphor of the capitalist, the unconscious investor that has now replaced desire. Desire did not know what it wanted and has metonymically shifted from one object to another; the drive, however, 'knows' what it wants. It is fixated on the object.

As an example in which the hostile and the obscene tendency are combined, Freud mentions smut, where the psychoanalytic gaze meets

---

61   Ibid., 95–6.

unconscious production and its object at its purest. This is also where the third person that supports the mechanism of jokes and reveals the importance of the social link in the production of *jouissance* finally enters the picture. Three persons condition the manifestation of an unconscious tendency: the narrator, the target of the joke, and the listener. Freud makes an important remark that the person who tells the joke is not the same as the person who enjoys its effects. The production of *jouissance* is outsourced to the side of the passive listener. It is tied to what is heard and to the combination of the aggressive and the obscene content that does not match any need. In order to illustrate this structure, Freud proposes a detailed analysis of smut:

> We know what is meant by 'smut': the intentional bringing into prominence of sexual facts and relations by speech . . . It is a further relevant fact that smut is directed to a particular person, by whom one is sexually excited and who, on hearing it, is expected to become aware of the speaker's excitement and as a result to become sexually excited in turn. Instead of this excitement the other person may be led to feel shame or embarrassment, which is only a reaction against the excitement and, in a roundabout way, is an admission of it. Smut is thus originally directed towards women and may be equated with attempts at seduction. If a man in a company of men enjoys telling or listening to smut, the original situation, which owing to social inhibitions cannot be realised, is at the same time imagined. A person who laughs at smut that he hears is laughing as though he were the spectator of an act of sexual aggression.

We can remark here that, once the signifier is envisaged as an apparatus of *jouissance*, language appears as an endless smut. Now Freud's conclusion:

> When the first person finds his libidinal impulse inhibited by the woman, he develops a hostile trend against that second person and calls on the originally interfering third person as his ally. Through the first person's smutty speech the woman is exposed before the third, who, as listener, has now been bribed by the effortless satisfaction of his own libido.[62]

Smut lacks the formal conditions of a joke. While a joke would make a long detour in order to mask the sexual insinuation with a sophisticated

---

62   Ibid., 97, 100.

metaphor, smut openly talks about sexuality, 'the uttering of an undisguised nudity gives the first person enjoyment and makes the third person laugh'. Here Freud very quickly discovers that smut leads to the very core of social segregation. For Freud, who speaks here as a sincere bourgeois, the satisfaction through smut characterises the common man, while in the upper classes smut is tolerated only on the condition that it appear as a joke, with a complex codification of obscene content through condensation and displacement. In smut we encounter the zero level of metaphor and metonymy, while in refined social circles smut is transformed into an allusion. The common point between smut and joke nevertheless remains the satisfaction of the drive in face of an obstacle: 'They circumvent this obstacle and in that way draw pleasure from a source which the obstacle had made inaccessible.'[63] The social context shows that the first case, the use of smut among the common men, only apparently differs from its sophistication in the upper classes. The inhibition of the drive is not weaker among the workers and the peasants. When Freud inclines to the conclusion that the common man is one step closer to the satisfaction and that he enjoys more than the upper classes, he repeats a typical bourgeois prejudice, yet he also shows that the inhibition is structural and that both smut and jokes are conditioned by the discrepancy between the need and the demand, pleasure and *jouissance,* usefulness and uselessness. If we imagine a situation in which the narrator is confronted with the object of smut, the conditions of the production of *jouissance* are abolished. What the narrator confronts in this case is castration. He can enjoy only through the third person, which introduces the dimension of the Other, where the linguistic equivocity produces the narrator's own pleasure-gain in the listener. There is no difference between the upper and the lower classes, as far as their relation to *jouissance* is concerned. In both cases, sexuality and violence need to be masked in order to support the production of *jouissance,* even if this masquerade means that sexuality is masked into sexuality and violence into violence, as in the case of smut.

Smut is in no respect more authentic from a sophisticated joke. It merely shows that the immediate addressing of sexuality, the obscenity of the smut, masks the impossibility of immediate satisfaction because sexuality does not correspond to any need. Lacan's axiom 'There is no sexual relation' implies precisely that there is no sexual need. Sexuality is *the* field where the production of *jouissance* takes place. The procreative

---

63   Ibid., 101.

'use-value' of sexuality is mere fiction. For this reason, the superego, too, does not prohibit enjoyment, it demands it, and when Lacan proposes his minimal prosopopoeia of the superego (*Enjoy!*) he actually spells out the echo of capitalist imperatives in the mental apparatus, the obscenity of the capitalist superego. The unsatisfiable demand for more, for the constant and uninterrupted production of surplus emerges from the gap in the Other, which points to the cut between use-value and exchange-value that the commodity form imposes on every object in the capitalist universe. Or to formulate it with the main economic lesson of Freud's analysis of humour, the pleasure in jokes does not mean that some lost *jouissance* is regained and the gap between the subject and the object is abolished but that *jouissance* is produced on the background of a structural impossibility of satisfaction.

Freud's crucial political insight was that every social order builds on libidinal economy. Consequently, an important part of efficiency of capitalism derives from the fact that it successfully mobilises the structural deadlocks of libidinal economy – the infamous 'inexistence of sexual relation' – and transforms them in the source of profit. Because its logic of production is coupled to the desire and the drive, it makes little sense, from the psychoanalytic point of view, to insist that capitalism represses sexuality, desire or drive. Quite the contrary, the capitalist mode of production seems to be the first social and economic system in history that created ideal conditions for their social realisation. No wonder, then, that Freud found in the relation between capital and labour the best illustration possible for the unconscious mode of production. Capitalism stretches its consequences in the unconscious, but this does not imply that capitalism *is* the unconscious.

REPRESSION AND PRODUCTION

The reason for the impossibility of immediate satisfaction of the drive lies in *Verdrängung*, repression, in which Freud detects another, probably the most unusual, type of unconscious labour:

> The power which makes it difficult or impossible . . . to enjoy undisguised obscenity is termed by us 'repression' . . . It is our belief that culture and higher education have a large influence on the development of repression, and we suppose that, under such conditions, the psychical organisation

undergoes an alteration . . . as a result of which what was formerly felt as agreeable now seems unacceptable and is rejected with all possible psychical force. The repression labour [*Verdrängungsarbeit*] of civilisation brings it about that primary possibilities of enjoyment, which have now, however, been repudiated by the censorship in us, are lost to us. But to the human psyche all renunciation is exceedingly difficult, and so we find that tendentious jokes provide a means of undoing the renunciation and retrieving what was lost. When we laugh at a refined obscene joke, we are laughing at the same thing that makes a peasant laugh at a coarse piece of smut. In both cases the pleasure springs from the same source.[64]

Freud's description immediately recalls the 'repressive hypothesis' that Foucault criticised in his work. On the one hand stands the labour of repression, which serves higher tendencies striving to preserve the cultural ideals and institutions, and, on the other, the originary yet excluded *jouissance*, the immediate possibilities of enjoyment, which had to be abandoned in favour of cultural progress. Cultural phenomena such as jokes create the impression of bypassing the prohibition and regaining a part of the lost and forbidden *jouissance*. Is this the ultimate point Freud's theory of repression wants to make? The quoted passage certainly supports this, for Freud places the existence of the drive before culture, thereby formulating the hypothesis of a *jouissance* before *jouissance*, an originary *jouissance*, which was subsequently prohibited and mortified by the intervention of the law. Freud's later theoretical endeavours tried to embody this hypothetic *jouissance* in the mythological figure of the primordial father, but his phylogenetic speculations are marked by a complex structure, which questions simplified critical readings. In *Totem and Taboo*, where Freud's main topic of discussion is the birth of law from the originary patricide, the primal father is evidently a personification of originary *jouissance*, but he is equally an instance that imposes originary prohibition – the right to *jouissance* belongs to him only, not to his sons, the subjects of the obscene paternal violence, in which *jouissance* and law are indistinguishable. The primal father can stand for a *jouissance* before *jouissance* only insofar as he is also a law before the law. This fusion of *jouissance* with the law makes him an insatiable instance, demanding renunciation from all other members of the human horde.

Freud's descriptions of this prehistoric father-figure therefore show that his two main features merely exaggerate both tendencies that were discussed

---

64   Ibid., 101. Translation modified.

in relation to jokes, violence and obscenity: violence over his sons and obscene right over all women. The primal father is literally a joke – but a joke that Freud took seriously. Far from resolving the dilemmas that pushed Freud's theories towards an epistemological deadlock, its speculative discussion merely condenses the paradoxes of the actually existing libidinal economy in one hypothetical character. Lévi-Strauss and Lacan already recognised in the tale of originary patricide that Freud adopted from the ethnological and evolutionary context a scientific myth. But in Freud's case, this myth becomes a curious structural equivalent of what Marx strived to address under primitive accumulation, a historical fiction, which strives to outline the genesis of modern antagonisms that determine both subjective and social reality.

The repressive hypothesis, tempting as it may be, and the myth of the primordial father do not succeed in resolving all the immanent contradictions that Freud encounters in unconscious labour, namely that it produces pleasure-gain and creates long detours that apparently sabotage immediate satisfaction. The labour of repression is split between the achievements of condensation and displacement, on the one hand, and those of suppression and censorship, on the other. Unconscious production is conditioned by this discordance, showing that at least one segment of the repression questions its simplified understanding as a force that works from the higher mental or cultural instances (the ego and the superego) on the repressed desires and drives (the id). Being a productive unconscious labour, and even the most general description for the variety of its achievements, repression must be dissociated from the meaning attributed to it by the repressive hypothesis, namely that of suppression and oppression. The misunderstanding is surely encouraged by Freud's initial explanations of repression, but it was strengthened through the translations of *Verdrängung*, in which notably the English and French translators heard oppression and suppression.

One of the main achievements of Lacan's return to Freud consisted in reaffirming the primacy of repression, in terms of productive labour, over the repressed, thereby providing the necessary ground for distinguishing repression from suppression or oppression. Repression may create the conditions for oppression, but it is not its synonym. Far from being instances and institutions of repression, family and society are its products, thereby assuming the same status as the repressed drives and desires. Once repression is distinguished from oppression, its productive character appears double. Freud's book on jokes already showed that repression plays the crucial role in the production of *jouissance*, while the later metapsycholog-ical writings argued that it also constitutes the repressed. Like alienation, repression, as well, is immanently doubled on constitutive and constituted repression, whereby Freud addresses the constitutive repression in the notion of *Urverdrängung*, originary repression.[65] The notion certainly accentuates the transcendental character of repression, which immediately recalls the structuralist transcendentalism of the symbolic. But originary repression goes a step further because it also exposes the inherently twofold structure of repression that, from the autonomy of symbolic structure, deduced two productive achievements.

Before considering the significance of repression for the encounter of psychoanalysis with Marxism, it is necessary to recall the basic accounts of Freud's theory of repression. Repression is revealed as a compromise proce-dure – *Mittelding*, intermediate thing – between escape and condemnation, which already deprives it of the exclusively negative connotation that later readings of Freud ended up privileging. It neither avoids the repressed tendency nor refuses its satisfaction. The central question is why the tendency is repressed in the first place, and the spontaneous answer would most likely be that its satisfaction would cause unpleasure. This is precisely *not* the case:

> A necessary condition of its happening must clearly be that the drive's attainment of its aim should produce unpleasure instead of pleasure. But we cannot well imagine such a contingency. There are no such drives: satisfac-tion of a drive is always pleasurable [*lustvoll*]. We should have to assume certain peculiar circumstances, some sort of process by which the pleasure of satisfaction is changed into unpleasure.[66]

Every satisfaction is *lustvoll*, full of pleasure; there is no satisfaction without the production of pleasure. In order to respond to this dilemma, the notions of the drive and of pleasure need to be questioned thoroughly.

---

65 I propose to translate Freud's *Urverdrängung* as 'originary repression' (rather than 'primary repression') in order to accentuate the reference of *Ursprung*, origin, which Freud here clearly addresses as a crucial epistemological problem. The same point could be made for Marx's notion of *ursprüngliche Akkumulation*, which means 'originary accumulation'. Marx encounters the same temporal and topological paradox in his reconstruction of the historical genesis of capitalism.

66 Freud, *Standard Edition*, Vol. 14, 146. Translation modified.

The Freudian concept of the drive remains controversial even today. The term is adopted from the physiological and biological context, and even from mechanics, just as labour-power, but it describes a phenomenon that, even if traversing the biological body, reaches beyond its limits. In the naturalistic context, the drive stands for a bodily need, which can be traced back to physiological mechanisms. Freud, accordingly, distinguishes between drives that point to a quasi-natural need (e.g., hunger and thirst) – this was probably the reason why *Trieb* was initially translated as 'instinct' – where repression is out of the question, and drives that deviate from this apparently natural satisfaction and are subjected to repression (in this category, Freud situated sexuality):

> Let us take the case in which a drive stimulus such as hunger remains unsat-isfied. It then becomes imperative and can be allayed by nothing but the action that satisfies it; it keeps up a constant tension of need. Nothing in the nature of a repression seems in this case to come remotely into question.[67]

In this physiological sense, hence in relation to the preservation of organism, the drive is entirely reducible to need and cannot become the target of repression. It can be satisfied only by a corresponding action (eating, drinking and so on). The drive that demands the labour of repression is too symbolic to be biological or physiological. This, and nothing else, is the meaning of Freud's claim that the drive 'appears to us as a concept on the frontier between the mental and the somatic' or as 'the psychical representative of the stimuli originating from within the organism and reaching the mind'.[68] This careful placement of the drive – neither physiological nor psychological – sufficiently indicates that Freud aims beyond the classical mind-body dualism, without therefore slipping into a vitalist monism. The drive is the border that from within traverses and splits the body on the physiological and the libidinal, so that we are dealing with some sort of conflictual monism including nega-tivity, precisely the negativity of representation, which brings the materiality of the signifier and the causality that depends on its auton-omy into the picture. As an internal border, which makes the biological equivocal with the linguistic, the drive remains a bodily phenomenon and even appears indistinguishable from the need it translates or

---

67   Ibid., 147. Translation modified.
68   Ibid., 122.

represents. Fusing a physiological stimulus with its representation, the drive becomes a material echo of linguistic autonomy, but it is also what the intervention of the signifier isolates in the tendencies of the organism towards self-preservation. Freud's inquiries circulate around this epistemological deadlock: because the echo is too material, it cannot be declared an idealist entity or a scientific fiction, but because its satisfaction seems to cause unpleasure, which is not the case with physiological needs, something violates the mechanisms of satisfaction. This scandal in the end exposes the minimal gap between the drive and organic needs: the drive is the symbolic isolation of their demand, the imperative for satisfaction that they contain. Detached from its repetitive organic context, the demand for satisfaction assumes a life of its own, and this is where the unpleasurable aspect of satisfaction enters the picture.

Freud was most certainly hesitant regarding the ontological status of the drive. In his *New Introductory Lectures*, he famously wrote that the drive is comparable to a mythological being, and his drive-theory to ancient mythology. Certainly the drive is a hypothesis, which strives to account for the fact that the apparatus of the signifier, which conditions the split between consciousness and the unconscious, does not follow useful goals, the satisfaction of needs, but tends towards immediate pleasure-gain. The drive names the tendency that accounts for a series of material consequences of the signifier, without therefore appearing before the analyst's eyes as a positive substance: 'In our work we cannot for a moment disregard them, yet we are never sure that we are seeing them clearly.'[69] The drive assumes the same ontological and epistemological status as the energy does in physics. Its hypostasis is indispensible, but one can never confront it directly, only observe its consequences, first and foremost the production of pleasure-gain and the conversion of pleasure into unpleasure. The visibility of the drive's satisfaction is comparable to the visibility of entropy, which can be observed only after science has placed the formal language of mathematics over the physical world. The manifestation of physiological needs additionally blurs the visibility of the drive, or better put, because all the bodily needs are channelled through the drive as their privileged representation, they no longer remain unproblematic. The drive is the paradigmatic case of the pun *traduttore*-traditore. It represents (translates) the apparently natural need in an unfaithfully productive way, thereby betraying its satisfaction.

---

69   Freud, *Standard Edition*, Vol. 22, 95.

The translation first and foremost produces a change in the status of pleasure. There is no drive the satisfaction of which would not cause pleasure, although this pleasure is no longer an affect that accompanies the decrease of tension. We can return to Marx's example of the two hungers from the *Grundrisse*. The pleasure that can be associated with the satisfaction of hunger is different from the pleasure that clings to the act of eating. The intertwining of the two imperatives, the need and the demand, in the satisfaction of a physiological need conceals the fact that the demand of the drive is constant, that it repeats the imperative of satisfaction beyond the need. It would be too simple to see in an insatiable hunger that swallows raw food a pre-symbolic natural instinct, which stands opposite to the cultural consumption of food. Bare instinctual life is an imaginary presentation of what takes place behind the apparent satisfaction of physiological needs, the persistence of the imperative beyond every attempt of satisfaction. This feature of the drive did not go unnoticed in Freud: 'A drive . . . never operates as a force giving a *momentary* impact but always as a *constant* one.'[70] The detachment of the imperative from a concrete reference, and consequently the autonomy of the demand, which depends on the autonomy of the signifier, places the drive in discrepancy with every supposedly natural or instinctual need.[71] The demand of the oral drive, isolated in the need for nourishment, persists behind different and apparently unrelated activities such as eating, smoking, speaking, sucking and so on. Due to this persistence, the drive's constant force can only be

---

70   Freud, *Standard Edition*, Vol. 14, 118.

71   The talk about 'instincts' is not without risks, since the very idea of an instinct is built on shaky ground. Lacan briefly addresses this issue in *Television* when he talks of the instinct as a potentially inadequate concept: 'There is no unconscious except for the speaking being. The others, who possess being only through being named – even though they impose themselves from within the real – have instinct, namely the knowledge needed for their survival. Yet this is so only for our thought, which might be inadequate here' (Lacan, *Television*, 5). Animals do not have drives; they only have instincts, which could be considered a 'knowledge in the real', the function of which is to guarantee animals their survival. Lacan's reservation towards this hypothesis is justified: knowledge in the real is, in the end, an ungrounded and unscientific hypothesis. But this does not annul the initial claim: because the drive is conditioned by the autonomy of the signifier, it can be attributed to humans but not to animals. Animals have a language of signs but one cannot claim (yet) that they have the signifier, the autonomy of which, to repeat again, consists in the fact that it relates to another signifier. The conclusion is thus that one does not need to refer to the instinct in order to theorise the drive, and Freud's *Trieblehre* did precisely this: it detached the drive from its biological and physiological context.

experienced as unpleasure, more precisely, as *Lust, die nicht als solche empfunden werden kann,*[72] pleasure that cannot be felt as such. Pleasure that can only be experienced as unpleasure – with this formulation, Freud provides the best definition of what Lacan envisages with his notion of *jouissance*. In the need, displeasure precedes its satisfaction; in the drive, displeasure accompanies satisfaction and *is* the privileged form of pleasure. Satisfaction now takes place in the increase of tension, and this tension is due to the insatiable *Drang*, pressure, which is 'common to all drives; it is in fact their very essence'.[73] The drive as representation of physiological needs comes down to the imperative signifier, S_1, the repressed signifier of *jouissance*.

Here the second essential feature of the drive enters the picture, which clarifies that Marx's opposition between bare hunger and cultivated hunger indeed highlights two immanent aspects of the drive and not the opposition between nature and culture. Under constant pressure, Freud understands the 'amount of force or the measure of the demand for labour [*Arbeitsanforderung*] that it represents'.[74] At the very core of the drive stands a permanent demand for labour, representation of labour-power, hence the Freudian attempt to elaborate an energetics of the drive. This demand for labour explains the simultaneous sameness and difference between pleasure and unpleasure in unconscious satisfaction. At this point, Freud's early analogy with capitalism finds another repetition. Because the unconscious is split between the capitalist and the labourer, the process of satisfaction is necessarily experienced on both ends, pleasure and unpleasure. Yet the one enjoying is not the subject, for as Freud's analyses demonstrate again and again, there is no subject of *jouissance*. There is only the subject of labour, the addressee of the demand for labour. There is no imperative of *jouissance* without the imperative of labour. Consequently, *Labour!* is true meaning of the superego's injunction *Enjoy!* The critical kernel of Freud's labour theory of the unconscious again becomes striking, since Marx's reformulation of the political-economic labour theory of value into a materialist theory of the subject was the first one to establish this interdependency of the two demands that can be associated with capital: the constant demand for surplus-value and the constant demand for labour.[75]

---

72   S. Freud, *Studienausgabe*, Vol. 3, Frankfurt am Main: Fischer Verlag, 2000, 220.

73   Freud, *Standard Edition*, Vol. 14, 122. Translation modified.

74   Freud, *Studienausgabe*, Vol. 3, 220.

75   The identification of capital with the drive does not mean that capital is the

The difference between need and demand is finally reflected at the level of the object. Unlike need, the drive appears to be without an object:

> The object of a drive is the thing in regard to which or through which the drive is able to achieve its aim. It is what is most variable about a drive and is not originally connected with it, but becomes assigned to it only in consequence of being peculiarly fitted to make satisfaction possible.[76]

Lacan later draws attention to this passage in order to explain how the object *a* relates to the montage of the drive. However, we cannot overlook the fact that Freud – prior to Lacan's developments – again hints at the difference between the content and the form, which already backed the mechanism of desire. The drive reaches its satisfaction in the object-form, which corresponds to the autonomy of differences, and based on this displacement the demand for satisfaction can become imperative. The drive becomes a symbolic machine without end, consuming objects for the sake of consumption (i.e., extraction of surplus), and designating the permanent *Entstellung*, deformation and displacement of the need.

Let us now turn to the paradoxes of repression. Freud writes that repression is not an originary defence mechanism but can only become operative once 'a sharp cleavage has occurred between conscious and unconscious mental activity'.[77] Repression already presupposes the unconscious, and its function does not consist so much in supressing, inhibiting or hindering satisfaction but in keeping the drive away from consciousness. The paradox of repression lies in the fact that repression is secondary, despite being constitutive of the repressed. It can only emerge after the scission of the mental apparatus between consciousness and the unconscious has been established, but it is also the necessary condition for this cleavage. The hypothesis of an originary repression is supposed to solve the paradox in the relation between the repression and the repressed:

---

only possible drive and that we are dealing with a closed system from which there is no escape. The structure of the drive can also be associated, for instance, with the miser, which is what Marx does when he traces the transformation of the drive from simple and essentially antisocial hoarding to the accumulation of capital.

76   Freud, *Standard Edition*, Vol. 14, 122. Translation modified.
77   Ibid., 147.

> We have reason to assume that there is an *originary repression*, a first phase
> of repression, which consists in the psychical (ideational) representative of
> the drive being denied entrance into the conscious. With this *fixation* is
> established; the representative in question persists unaltered from then
> onwards and the drive remains attached to it.[78]

What is repressed is not some originary instinctual substance that the
intervention of language would suppress but the signifier of the drive, a
signifier that aims at *jouissance* and on which the translation of the
supposedly physiological need into the symbolic demand depends. Freud
again recurs to the more accessible language of the repressive hypothesis
but in fact targets the autonomy of the signifier. The actual achievement
of originary repression is the *production* of the master-signifier, which is
synonymous to the autonomy of the system of differences, a signifier of
the demand and *jouissance*. The originary repression thus confronts an
impossible task to examine the repressed *in statu nascendi*, the genesis of
the repressed, which is, in the last instance, the same as the genesis of
language. The description of the structure of repression continues in the
following way:

> The second stage of repression, *repression proper*, affects mental derivatives
> of the repressed representative, or such trains of thought as, originating else-
> where, have come into associative connection with it. On account of this
> association, these ideas experience the same fate as what was originally
> repressed. Repression proper, therefore, is actually an after-pressure [*Nach-
> drängen*]. Moreover, it is a mistake to emphasise only the repulsion, which
> operates from the direction of the conscious upon what is to be repressed;
> quite as important is the attraction exercised by what was originally
> repressed upon everything with which it can establish a connection. Proba-
> bly the trend towards repression would fail in its purpose if these two forces
> did not co-operate, if there were not something previously repressed ready
> to receive what is repelled by the conscious.[79]

Constituted repression, the second stage of repression, is productive unconscious labour. All other forms of unconscious labour can be reduced to
repression, which now appears as the satisfaction of the drive rather than its

---

78 Ibid., 148. Translation modified.
79 Ibid.

suppression or obstruction. Here another complication emerges. We are not simply dealing with two different repressions, of which one would be in the past and the other in the present. The historical reading overlooks the topological aspect of repression that is linked to its inherent doubling: in order to have repression, there have to be at least two. A singular repression could not constitute the relation that Freud very precisely describes in reference to attraction and repulsion. The inner moments of every concrete act of repression are originary repression (the constitution of the repressed) and the labour of repression (the satisfaction of the repressed tendency). This double structure can be compared with the chain of signifiers. The cut that produces the split between consciousness and the unconscious is redoubled, as the signifier of the repressed demand for surplus-*jouissance* ($S_1 - a$) and as a difference that relates to another signifier ($S_1 - S_2$), initiating unconscious production and representing the 'amount of demand for labour', labour-power. Repression activity contains both axes of the signifier, representation and production. This internal doubling unveils the parallax that Freud explicitly underlines in the reminder that besides the repulsion from consciousness one should equally acknowledge the attraction that derives from the point of the originary repression, the master-signifier. From the point of view of consciousness, repression *appears* as a defence mechanism that represses in the sense of oppression. The repressive hypothesis absolutises this perspective, and we can find its most contemporary political exemplification in neoliberalism. Did the neoliberal ideology not turn around the idea that the market contains 'creative potentials', which need to be liberated through deregulation? The concept of the free market mobilises the repressive hypothesis, through which capitalism perverts and neutralises the political radicality of modern liberation movements.[80] Only from the position of the subject, which is the position of Freud's labour theory of the unconscious and Marx's critique of fetishism, can repression appear as an operation that conditions the satisfaction of the drive through the double production of the surplus-object and of the alienated subject in a concrete

---

80   It would be false to conclude that all liberation movements come down to the repressive hypothesis. It is necessary to distinguish between repression, which signifies the production of subjectivity, in the case of capitalism labour-power, and the various forms of oppression, which result from this underlying repression. By imposing the universalism of commodity form, capitalism annihilates other forms of subjectivity and universality. Every liberation movement that raises the question of the subject of politics targets repression as a process that involves the production of a concrete form of subjectivity.

form. The drive now no longer appears deprived of its immediate satisfaction, repulsion (rejection) turns into attraction (satisfaction), and unpleasure turns into a specific form of pleasure.

This problematic is not unrelated to Marx, for in the double structure of repression, Freud encounters the same problem that concerns the accumulation of capital. When Marx turns towards the historical conditions of capitalism, he reformulates the question of primitive accumulation, which served classical political economy in its apology for capitalism. Marx unveils its fictional character but then also provides its rational reinterpretation in the context of the historical genesis of the capitalist logic, the transformation of the old spirit of the miser into the modern spirit of capitalism, which deepened the social relations of domination by rooting them in the very relations between things. The modern reification of the master, i.e., its detachment from the old figure of divine sovereign, inevitably brought about the reification of the subject.

The psychoanalytic value of Marx's speculation on the origins of capitalism consists in him exposing the link between *jouissance* and ideology, and more concretely, the rootedness of economic liberalism in the fiction of the subject of enjoyment – a fiction, which remains entirely intact in today's neoliberal condition. Of course, the significance of primitive accumulation is commonly known and has been discussed by several authors.[81] Marx starts from the structural paradox in the relation between accumulation and production. Just as in the case of repression and the repressed, where repression constitutes the repressed that it simultaneously presupposes, the analysis of accumulation contains a vicious circle, in which production and accumulation support each other: there is no accumulation of capital without a preceding production of surplus, but there is no production of surplus without the preceding accumulation of capital either.

Marx first draws attention to the fact that primitive accumulation, as used in political economy, contains a moral lesson, thereby assuming the role of original sin in theology. It thereby also assumes the function of myth, since it strives to address the unattainable historical origin of accumulation of capital – a point that can be grasped only by means of fictitious constructions and fantasies. The tale is grounded on the presupposition of

---

81   See notably J. Read, *The Micro-Politics of Capital*, New York: SUNY Press 2003; Silvia Federici, *Caliban and the Witch: Women, the Body and Primitive Accumulation*, Brooklyn, NY: Autonomedia, 2004; and, more recently, D. Harvey, *A Companion to Marx's Capital*, London: Verso 2010.

jouissance on the side of the proto-proletarian and the equally presupposed renunciation on the side of the proto-capitalist:

> Long ago there were two sorts of people; one, the diligent, intelligent and above all frugal elite; the other, lazy rascals [*Lumpen*],[82] spending their substance, and more, in riotous living . . . Thus it came to pass that the former sort accumulated wealth, and the latter sort finally had nothing to sell except their own skins. And from this original sin dates the poverty of the great majority who, despite all their labour, have up to now nothing to sell but themselves, and the wealth of the few that increases constantly, although they have long ceased to work.[83]

At the beginning there were the ascetic and the consumer: the subject of renunciation and the subject of enjoyment. The political-economic myth thus tries to explain the genesis of positive and negative surplus: surplus-value, originating from abstinence and embodied in the first accumulated wealth, and labour-power, originating from excess, for which the myth claims that it inevitably generates debt. Abstinence helps accumulating the surplus that will finally enable the minority to appropriate the means of production, while *jouissance* creates a negative that will eventually force the majority to sell their own bodies. For political economy this scenario sounds entirely rational: the capitalist forefathers accumulated the minimal wealth through personal sacrifice, so it seems just that their contemporary offspring continue to profit from it without restriction. At the same time, the proletarians are responsible for their own misery because their predecessors wasted more than they possessed, *ihr alles und mehr*. This apparently insignificant formulation is crucial because it envisages the interdependency of *jouissance* and debt, seemingly adopted from religion, hence Marx's comparison of primitive accumulation with the fable of original sin.

The political-economic myth significantly marked recent attempts to legitimise austerity measures, as others have already noticed.[84] The global South was presented as the space of enjoying subjects that the absurd

---

82   The term suggests that the proto-proletarian is in fact an archaic figure of lumpenproletariat.

83   Marx, *Capital*, Vol. 1, 873.

84   See M. Lazzarato, *La fabrique de l'homme endetté*, Paris: Éditions Amsterdam, 2011.

national debts meanwhile turned into an oasis of surplus population; while its counterpart, the global North, and notably Germany, appeared as the land of saving, a success story possible only under the condition that the economic growth is anchored in the constant renunciation of *jouissance*. Of course, everyone could witness that the actual situation was quite the opposite: imposed saving initiates a negative spiral that produces more debt than is possible to repay. This debt is not a moral obligation calling for repayment but actually has a productive function: the austerity measures are supposed to create economic devastation that will strengthen the link between citizens and the structural function of indebted subject. This recent development once again confirms the thesis that the primitive accumulation is not a process in the past but an inner moment of the present that reproduces the conditions of possibility for capitalist accumulation and expropriation. It designates the root of the discursive process that constitutes the individual as a subject of value, just as originary repression addresses the root of the autonomy of the signifier, through which the double production of the subject of the unconscious and of surplus-*jouissance* can be initiated. The scission between consciousness and the unconscious is the Freudian way of addressing this autonomy.

According to the implicit prejudice of the political-economic tale, the labourer continues to enjoy (to laze around and become even more indebted), while the capitalist continues to save (to increase his wealth). Marx introduces a minimal correction to this scenario. The capitalist subject most certainly is in the first instance a subject of debt but never enjoyed as a subject. In other words, the capitalist figure of subjectivity did not emerge from the transformation of some hypothetical subject of *jouissance* into labour-power, as political economists suggest, but from a specific transformation of *jouissance* itself. The abstinence theory of the capitalist highlights this development:

> Accumulate, accumulate! That is Moses and the prophets! 'Industry furnishes the material which saving accumulates'. Therefore save, save, i.e., reconvert the greatest possible portion of surplus-value or surplus product into capital! Accumulation for the sake of accumulation, production for the sake of production: this was the formula in which classical economics expressed the historical mission of the bourgeoisie in the period of its domination . . . If, in the eyes of classical economics, the proletarian is merely a machine for the production of surplus-value, the capitalist too

is merely a machine for the transformation of this surplus-value into surplus capital.[85]

Marx's correction concerns the externalisation of the link between accumulation and saving that already existed in the premodern spirit of the miser. In the foundation of the system lies the imperative of abstinence, which is directly translatable in the imperative of indebting: the subject's duty is to assume and to interiorise the debt created by the *jouissance* of the system – and precisely for this reason Marx remarks that the national debt is the only wealth that enters into possession of all modern nations, i.e., something that belongs to everyone and from which no one has the right to exempt him or herself. While merely a minority personifies systemic *jouissance*, labour-power becomes the sole universal subjective position in the capitalist universe. The political-economic tale of primitive accumulation contains a grain of distorted truth, showing that no *jouissance* precedes renunciation but that there is a strong correlation between the renunciation and the production of *jouissance*, both through generalised indebting.

After criticising the political-economic myth of origin, Marx suggests his own rationalised variant of primitive accumulation. In the reconstruction, which assumes no less than the status of a historiographical fiction, the separation of producers from the means of production is accomplished through 'blood and fire', the constitutive violence that progressively transforms the feudal relations of domination and subjection into the capitalist ones. I am not going to go deeper into Marx's reconstruction of the genesis of capitalism, the accuracy and the general validity of which remains a topic of discussion.[86] What is more important is the logical background of Marx's outline of the historical genesis of capitalism, which in many respects anticipates Freud's topological account of repression. In Marx's reading, the crucial part in the genesis is attributed to the invention of national debt. He places the emphasis on the transformation of premodern religious debt, still embedded in its mystifying metaphysical meaning, into modern debt, founded on public credit and turned into a quantified and meaningless abstraction. This shift is accomplished through the transformation of the logic that grounded the feudal social link, what Lacan called the master's discourse:

85   Marx, *Capital*, Vol. 1, 742.
86   See, for instance, Harvey, *A Companion to Marx's Capital*, 304.

> The starting-point of the development that gave rise both to the wage-labourer and to the capitalist was the enslavement of the worker. The advance made consisted in a change in the form of this servitude, in the transformation of feudal exploitation into capitalist exploitation.[87]

The formal change invents a new form of indebtedness that no longer has economic-metaphysical roots in submission to the feudal lord, the monarch or any other representative of divine power on earth, but instead in the economic inequality that is codified in the apparently unproblematic and concrete act of exchange. The truth of the capitalist worldview is universal indebtedness produced by emptied political categories such as freedom and equality. The invention and social implementation of national debt and public credit amounted to a new discursive production without abolishing the old structure of domination and inequality. It merely transformed the premodern serf into abstract labour-power, a machine to produce surplus-value, and in the same move introduced a new figure of the master, the capitalist, who personifies the machine to transform the surplus-product into capital. This transformation integrates the surplus-product into the social link, introducing a new form fetishisation of social relations, through the fetishisation of objects. In the same move, the feudal master is stripped of his fetish quality, which also means that the new capitalist master no longer depends on concrete personifications. Mastery becomes an abstraction embodied and operative in every object that enters the economic sphere: commodity, money and financial abstractions. If the king had two bodies, the mortal and the sublime, the capitalist has merely one but is therefore endowed, as Marx claims, with the soul of capital.

In capitalism, the subject is indebted to neither the secular nor the divine master, but to the economic system itself. Consequently, capitalism is no realisation of the spirit of Protestantism, as Max Weber argued, but a *cult* of indebting, as Walter Benjamin specified in his famous critical note.[88] If we want to maintain the link between capitalism and religious logic – this still makes sense because of the structural function of debt, which in both cases builds on the equivocity of morality and economy – we nevertheless have to take into account a certain regression in religion: from institutionalised religion of revelation to the no less

---

87   Marx, *Capital,* Vol. 1, 875.

88   W. Benjamin, 'Kapitalismus als Religion', in: D. Baecker (Ed.), *Kapitalismus als Religion,* Berlin: Kadmos, 2009, 15–18.

institutionalised (through central banks, corporations, multinationals, political Troikas and so on) cult. Marx aims at this regression when he reduces the capitalist social link to commodity fetishism: from religion that understands itself as a religion of truth and that essentially is a 'true religion' (Lacan) into 'neo-paganism', an irrational secularised belief in the self-valorising power of capital.

With the transformation of the master into an abstraction, the abstract debt no longer grounds the social link between the master and the serf but instead supports that between the citizen and the state:

> The system of public credit, i.e., of national debts, the origins of which are to be found in Genoa and Venice as early as the middle ages, took possession of Europe as a whole . . . The national debt, i.e., the externalisation [*Veräusserung*] of the state – whether that state is despotic, constitutional or republican – marked the capitalistic era with its stamp. The only part of the so-called national wealth that actually enters into the collective possession of a modern people is the national debt. Hence, as a necessary consequence, the modern doctrine that a nation becomes the richer the more deeply it is in debt. Public credit becomes the *credo* of capital. And with the rise of national debt-making, lack of faith in the national debt takes the place of the sin against the Holy Ghost, for which there is no forgiveness.[89]

With the genesis of the national debt, Marx's analysis of primitive accumulation most definitely changes its character. While the description of the constitutive violence over the English rural population remained in imaginary historical coordinates and in the horizon of repressive hypothesis, just as Freud's early accounts of repression, the focus on national debt turns towards the logical displacement in the social mode of production, which inevitably comprises the production of labour-power as a specifically capitalist form of subjectivity: the sole subject that corresponds to the regime of abstract debt and to the modern credit system.

The invention of national debt and the corresponding production of subjectivity expose the kernel of the capitalist form of alienation that Marx indicates in the term 'externalisation of the state'. The capitalist state simply *is* an institutionalised form of a more underlying, constitutive alienation, which determines the logical relation between economic 'abstractions', capital and labour-power. The externalisation of the state in the national

---

89   Marx, *Capital*, Vol. 1, 919. Translation modified.

debt is accompanied by its internalisation, in the sense that it shapes the nature of modern subjectivity. Being essentially grounded on indebting and standing for national debt as such, the modern state places every citizen in the position of the debtor, while the position of the creditor is assumed by the social institutions of capital: the central banks. At this point it becomes most evident that the emergence of the modern state is inevitably accompanied by the genesis of an extra-state power, which pertains to financial institutions and which is essentially authoritarian.[90]

The equivalent of the placement of the citizen in the position of the debtor is the transformation of the subject into a quantifiable and exploitable subjectivity, which is indebted *in advance* and is also produced as such. In this way Marx rejects the fantasmatic projection of some hypothetical subject of *jouissance* before the subject of abstract debt. His rationalisation of the political-economic myth shows that the capitalist demystification and quantification of the premodern religious debt creates a more efficient abstract universality – national debt – which leaves no subject outside its reach, thereby introducing a new 'Holy Spirit', that is, a social link grounded on the negative spiral of productive indebting, out of which rises the spectrality and apparent autonomy of capital.

To repeat, what is at stake in Marx's rationalised variant of primitive accumulation is the problem of constitutive alienation, on the level of which the production of capitalist subjectivity can be observed.[91] Abstract debt and abstract labour thereby become two inseparable aspects of the subject. And because the structure of the capitalist mode of production is internally doubled, the critical appropriation and rationalisation of the notion of primitive accumulation indeed shows features that are strictly homologous to the Freudian notion of originary repression, where the production of constitutively alienated subjectivity is no less central. Even if Marx and Freud might have taken the notion of origin literally, they still drew attention to a structural and temporal paradox, which undermines the linear representation of history thanks to the notion of retroactive causality. Consequently, the prehistorical origin in question turns out to be more a

---

90   See notably J. Vogl, *Der Souveränitätseffekt*, Berlin and Zürich: Diaphanes, 2015, where the central topic is the history of central banks and the form of power that they exercise over modern nations and nation-states.

91   See Read, *Micro-Politics of Capital*, 36, 153, where the author analyses the two aspects of primitive accumulation, the accumulation of wealth and the accumulation of subjectivity (the production of the industrial reserve army).

prehistory *within* the present, retroactively projected onto the past and operating within the present condition as a constant refoundation of the capitalist relations of production.[92] Behind the apparent quest for historical origin, Marx and Freud raise the logical and materialist question of the cause, which brought the indebted subject and the subject of the unconscious into being.

The paradoxical relation between accumulation and production, which supports the structure and the efficiency of capitalism, might indeed make this mode of production a vicious circle, from which no escape seems to be possible. At the same time this paradox is also the reason of its structural disclosure and permanent instability, which announce the opposite appearance, the imminent breakdown of the system. The conceptual couple of the fetish and the symptom, shared by critique of political economy and psychoanalysis, addresses precisely these two opposite appearances of capitalism.

---

92   Or as Jason Read has put it in the very subtitle of his *Micro-Politics of Capital*: a prehistory of the present.

CHAPTER 3

The Fetish and the Symptom

AGAINST PSYCHOANALYTIC GENERALISATIONS

Psychoanalysts often refer to Marx in order to discover in his critique of commodity fetishism the attempt to theorise capitalism as a form of perversion. Such readings, convincing as they may sound, nonetheless contain several risks. They can, for instance, immediately turn into a fascination with the presumably polymorphic nature and adaptability of capitalism, while overlooking the problem of negativity that persists in both Marx's and Freud's discussions of fetishism. Such readings can add up to a direct fetishisation of perversion. One can then hear that perversion manages to overcome the deadlocks of *jouissance*, to articulate a solution in which the subject assumes the position of the object, thereby becoming the support of the Other's *jouissance*. One of the differences between neurosis and perversion lies in the fact that for the neurotic, *jouissance* is strictly speaking impossible, immediately linked as it is to castration. Lack plays the central role in the economy of neurotic desire. One can say that psychoanalysis discovered neurosis as a social symptom, a particular expression of cultural discontent and an inevitable collateral damage of capitalism. An example would be the epidemic of war-neuroses that Freud discussed in relation to the First World War, and the entire argument of *Civilisation and Its Discontents*, in which the main focus is precisely on the proliferation of new mental illnesses under the exploitative regime of capitalist cultures.

While in neurosis the object of *jouissance* necessarily causes the subjective split, perversion is considered as overcoming this situation by inverting the role of the subject and of the object, as Lacan's formula of the perverse fantasy indicates: $(a \Diamond \$)$. This inversion presents the subject as the one who possesses knowledge of the Other's *jouissance*, precisely for offering him or herself as *the* object. We can find such a position notably in masochism, where the importance of commodity fetishism can hardly be ignored and where the masochist contract directly mocks the law, as Deleuze has pointed

out in his brilliant analysis of Sacher-Masoch.[1] Concretely, what masochism does is to caricaturise the law of exchange where it may seem that the
voluntary victim let him- or herself be sexually exploited and consumed by
the master. The masochist would then appear as the ideal subject of capitalism, someone who willingly offers himself to the exploitative tendencies of
the system. The moment of mockery consists in the fact that the masochist
contract nevertheless determines the terms and conditions of the sexual
relationship, thereby depriving the master of the position that he still has,
for instance, in sadism, where *jouissance* is imposed on the subject (hence
Lacan's reduction of the superego to the injunction to enjoy). In the masochist contract, however, the role of the master is restricted: he is placed in
the position of the labouring subject and its law is turned into a means of
jouissance. We should therefore bear in mind here that the perverse inversion of the subject-object relation does not imply that the masochist subject,
when it assumes the position of the object, becomes an actual subject of
jouissance and thereby realises the (ideological) fantasy of the subject-
supposed-to-enjoy. By occupying the position of the object, the perverse
subject becomes the cause of the Other's split, as is the case in the masochist
caricature of the contract, which undermines the very consistency and
presumable neutrality of the law. The situation is nevertheless more complex
and I shall return to this problem again in the final section of this book.

Capitalism seems to comply with this perverse scenario. Does not the
subject of the capitalist mode of production, labour-power, assume precisely
the position of commodity, whose function is to produce surplus-value, this
Marxian name for the *jouissance* of the system? This inversion, through
commodification, could be a possible departure for the psychoanalytic reading of capitalism as perversion. However, Marx's determination of the place of
labour-power in the production process shows that this perverse appearance
is grounded on the mystification of the inconsistency of the commodity
universe. The perversion of capitalism, this time in a strictly metaphorical
sense, lies in the fact that the system *imposes* the perverse position on the
subject and with this move masks the symptomatic status of labour-power.
The abstraction, contained in every act of exchange, makes labour-power
appear as any other object, from which surplus-value can be extracted, once it
is thrown on the market. And if there is a relation between capitalism and
perversion, then this relation should be sought in the already mentioned
imposition of the object-position, which means that every subject is confronted

1   G. Deleuze, *Présentation de Sacher-Masoch*, Paris: Minuit, 1967, 107.

with the imperative to become the support of the Other's *jouissance* and hence the object of exploitation. The exploitation of labour is precisely this – turning labour into a commodity, imposing on every subject the position of the object-source of value. Capitalism is *not* perversion, but it *demands* perversion from its subjects. In other words, capitalism demands that the subjects *enjoy* exploitation and thereby abandon their position as subjects.

Going back to psychoanalysis, the perverse solution of the deadlock of *jouissance* is supposed to be a problem for psychoanalysis, since it cannot be subjected to analysis or critique. Perversion entails a rejection of psycho-analysis, in the face of which analysts can only acknowledge the irreducible singularity of its mode of enjoyment. Such a position has unpleasant politi-cal implication. It immediately suggests that capitalism entails a generalisation of the perverse *jouissance* at the level of the social link, an insurmountable horizon, in which a thousand perversions may blossom, while the general social framework remains unchangeable: the closed world of commodity form, whose polymorphous nature enables the processing, integration and neutralisation of all forms of antagonism. The capitalist subject mocks castration, declares it an anachronism and a remainder of the phallocentric universe that the postmodern has overcome once and for all. Castration, and consequently psychoanalysis, is considered to be merely one of those famous grand narratives, whose end needs to be acknowledged. In the end, this position conceives capitalism as a vicious circle, from which it is impos-sible to break out.

Before passing to the function of fetishism in Marx and Freud's critical projects, we should mention that the interpretation of capitalism as gener-alised perversion has only a minimal grounding in Lacan, for instance in the following ambiguous remark, where one cannot avoid suspecting that it was implicitly responding to Deleuze and Guattari's *Anti-Oedipus*:

> What distinguishes the capitalist discourse is this – *Verwerfung*, rejection from all the fields of symbolic, with all the consequences that I have already mentioned. Rejection of what? Of castration. Every order, every discourse that aligns itself with capitalism leaves aside what we will simply call the matters of love.[2]

Lacan makes an interesting turn in relation to the popularised versions of Freudo-Marxism, according to which cultural mechanisms neutralise the

---

2   J. Lacan, *Je parle aux murs*, Paris: Seuil, 2011, 96.

emancipatory potential of sexuality. Unlike the partisans of the sexual revolution, who see in oppressed sexuality a positive (energetic) substance, Lacan insists that capitalism is grounded precisely on the opposite, on the foreclosure of negativity. Capitalism rejects the paradigm of negativity, castration: the symbolic operation that constitutes the subject as split and decentralised. Through this foreclosure capitalism determines other discourses that can emerge in the capitalist universe. Psychoanalysis can prosper under these conditions only by adopting the demands of the market: reintegration of individuals, adaptation, strengthening of ego, reduction of 'disorders', strategies that in the end support the capitalist fantasy of an uncastrated subject, which would respond to the capitalist imposition of perverse position. Capitalism only tolerates a psychoanalysis that has abolished the central Freudian-Marxian lesson: alienation as constitutive for the production of subjectivity and for the production of *jouissance*. The notorious 'neuroticisation of desire', so heavily attacked in *Anti-Oedipus,* in fact prevents psychoanalysis from being integrated into the ideological framework of capitalism. Unlike perversion or psychosis, neurosis essentially is a subjective form of protest against the capitalist injunction to enjoy exploitation.

The return of negativity, in the guise of castration, can serve as a minimal localisation of the political dimension of psychoanalysis, although we should not forget that this return obtained in Freud a *mythical* narration, Oedipus, while its *logical* form followed under Lacan's theorisation of the signifier and its subsequent homological development in parallel with Marx's science of value. Freud's sexual aetiology of neuroses nevertheless establishes the correct connection between sexuality and negativity, and even the notorious polymorphous perversion of infantile sexuality, of which Freud first spoke in his *Three Essays* (1905), cannot mean the foreclosure of negativity and the assertion of the purely vitalist and productive potentials of sexuality. The point that Freud addresses through this ambiguous and rather unfortunate expression aims at the discovery that all choices of the sexual object gravitate around a void, where one would expect to find a normative model. It is at this point that Lacan's formula 'There is no sexual relation' intervenes. After polymorphous perversion has obtained its vitalist meaning, we need to be constantly reminded that the scandal of psychoanalysis lies in the fact that it understands sexuality through the absence of a corresponding natural need. Capitalism does not want to know anything about the inexistence of the sexual relation and strives to make sexuality inseparable from sex, which would be the commodified image of sexuality. The immediate conclusion would be that commodification simply *is* the rejection of castration.

Lacan's association of capitalism with the operation of foreclosure is nevertheless ambiguous. The term opens up another alternative, in which capitalism appears as a generalised psychosis, since Lacan's aforementioned quote combines the psychotic *Verwerfung*, foreclosure, with the fetishist *Verleugnung*, disavowal. While the focus on disavowal implies that the capitalistic social link is constituted on a mechanism, which allows the subject to avoid the intertwining of castration and sexuality, foreclosure attributes to capitalism a more radical confrontation with negativity. Generalised perversion could still be compatible with Marx's dialectic of fetishism from commodities to capital, while the second perspective assumes the position that the capitalist operations abolish the double character of production (production of lack and production of surplus). In this perspective, Joyce's writing becomes the privileged reference, through which Lacan addresses the problem of 'psychotisation' of language, the dissolution of its consistency and the domination of production over subjectivation, the realisation of the autonomy of the signifier, and finally another form of the rejection of psychoanalysis. Based on this dramatic perspective, several prominent psychoanalysts have introduced the notion of the 'real unconscious'[3] in order to describe this presumably psychotic development. As already mentioned, the association of capitalism with the foreclosure of castration – rather than its imposition – leads to an implicit polemic with Deleuze and Guattari, for whom castration is enforced onto the subject by the existing regime of production (capitalism, when it comes to social economy, and psychoanalysis, when it comes to libidinal economy). Lacan inverts the schizo-analytic perspective: if capitalism indeed strives to reject castration, it is essentially Anti-Oedipal. Marx's analysis of the way capitalism mystifies and distorts social antagonisms is clearly an important ally in this critical inversion.

In returning to Marx and Freud's critique of fetishism, I want to start from the assumption that both psychoanalytic generalisations repeat the

---

3   See C. Soler, *Lacan, l'inconscient réinventé*, Paris: Presses Universitaires de France, 2009, and J. A. Miller, 'L'envers de Lacan', in: *La Cause freudienne*, 2007, Vol. 67. Both authors suggest that Lacan moves from the accent on transference, where the unconscious still appears to be inscribed in the social link, to the so-called real unconscious, where only the production of *jouissance*, without any trace of negativity, is at work. We can hear the echo of the problematic of financial capital, where the creation of value out of value and the absolute autonomy of financial capital come to dominate all other forms of production.

foreclosure of negativity and end up fetishising *jouissance* and the real, making the perverse or the psychotic subject appear as the incarnation of the subject of *jouissance*. In this respect, I do not find it necessarily correct to see a radical discontinuity between the structuralist Lacan of the fifties and the sixties and the quasi post-structuralist Lacan of the seventies. Lacan's teaching should be approached more like a parallax that starts from discussing the unconscious and the autonomy of the signifier exclusively from the perspective of the *logic* of the signifier and then progressively moves towards the *causality* of the signifier, thus finding itself on the flip-side of the autonomy in question. Generalised perversion and generalised psychosis abolish the embedding of psychoanalysis in the broader *philo-sophical* project of the critique of appearance, which has determined modern thought since Descartes. The crucial dimension of this modern orientation in philosophy concerns the introduction of alienation as a fundamental philosophical problem and as a privileged entry to the theory of the subject. It is not surprising that the three central philosophical refer-ences in Lacan's teaching are also the most radical thinkers of alienation: Descartes, whose methodological doubt provides the first immediate link-age of alienation with subjectivation and lays the epistemological foundations for Freud's differentiation of the subject of the unconscious from the subject of cognition; Hegel, who extended alienation to history and becoming; and finally Marx, whose materialist turn exposes the strict equivalence between alienation and structure, thereby opening up the hori-zon in which psychoanalysis will address the intertwining of both aspects of the autonomy of the signifier.

The two psychoanalytic generalisations associate capitalism with pathologies that are most often considered non-analysable and represent two cases of the dissolution of the social link. The perverse subject may possess a solution regarding *jouissance*, but this solution is strictly private. The social link is suspended because the subject is supposed to stand in an immediate relation to the object of *jouissance* or offers itself as *the* object of the systemic enjoyment. The difference between the economic and the sexual fetish seems clear. The money fetish may be the privileged embodi-ment of value, but it is also the support of exchange. The sexual fetish, by contrast, excludes the economy of exchange and bends the libidinal econ-omy back onto itself. Foreclosure of castration then means as much as foreclosure of exchange, since there is no exchange without difference, which is for structuralism, psychoanalysis and critique of political econ-omy the 'royal path' to negativity.

However, things get complicated even in perversion. Despite this 'privatisation of the object', it would be exaggerated to claim that perversion stands outside the social link. The schoolbook examples of perversion, sadism and masochism, constantly demonstrate a social dimension in their fantasmatic scenarios. This is most evident in masochism, which presupposes a contract that determines the relation between the master and the slave. Even the aforementioned masochist mockery of the law does not suspend its symbolic power. We merely need to imagine a scenario in which the master would cease playing the role according to the contract and transform into a sadist master, hence precisely in the subject assuming the position of the object-cause of *jouissance*. Then he would no longer serve the masochist but the Other. The sadist cannot be the ideal partner of the masochist, as Deleuze already cogently argued, because he takes the letter of the law seriously and makes of it an imperative of *jouissance*. By making the law an obscene entity that supports the *jouissance* of the system, he corrupts the masochist's mode of enjoyment. While masochism is grounded on the abstract and neutral character of the contract, just as the commodity exchange is according to economic liberalism, sadism departs from the concrete terrorism of the law. Thus, when it comes to capitalism, Marquis de Sade's catalogues of sexual fantasies communicate a more accurate critical truth concerning the subject's relation to *jouissance* than the literary works of Leopold von Sacher-Masoch, whose scenarios of sexual submission only apparently outline a subversive position of enjoyment.

In psychosis, presumably the second case of the dissolution of the social link, the subject's body is invaded by *jouissance*, as in the famous case of President Schreber.[4] But here, too, the dissolution should not be fetishised. All in all, the Schreber case is much more than a delirium, which would place the subject outside the social link. It is also an autobiography, which contains the subject's attempt to reconstruct the social relation. Daniel Paul Schreber wrote his memoirs in order to legally demonstrate his sanity (and he succeeded), thereby rejecting the mystification of psychosis as an antisocial delirium. Still, it is true that psychosis exhibits some sort of inversion of the 'privacy' at stake in perversion. While in the latter the limit of the social link lies in the object, the small other, in psychosis the same limit is

---

4   Commented on by both Freud (*Standard Edition*, Vol. 12, 9–82) and Lacan (*Écrits*, 445–88). For the best historical and theoretical account of the Schreber case, see E. Santner, *My Own Private Germany: Daniel Paul Schreber's Secret History of Modernity*, Princeton, NJ: Princeton University Press, 1996.

encountered in language, the big Other. The perverse localisation of *jouissance* in the object and the psychotic globalisation of *jouissance* in discourse destabilise the articulation that essentially grounds the social link, representation and production, the Other and the other.

No critique of capitalism can be grounded on these two generalisations, which explains why today so many European psychoanalysts politically associate themselves with classical liberalism or neo-conservatism (e.g., the alliance between École de la Cause freudienne and the *nouveaux philosophes*). Both readings – capitalism as generalised fetishist disavowal of negativity or as psychotic foreclosure – reduce the impact of the fact that Lacan's later *critique* of libidinal economy remains in immediate continuity with both the structuralist isolation of the autonomy of the signifier and with Marx's critical examination of the link between the autonomy of exchange-value, the alienation of labour-power and the production of surplus-value. Generalised perversion is grounded on reading Marx's notion of fetishism from the Freudian perspective, where it describes the subject's resistance to castration, a screen that separates the subject from its own lack-in-being. My guideline will be that there is a critical continuity between Marx and Freud: Freud's notion addresses more than mere sexual perversions and, consequently, Marx's notion covers more than the subjective misperception of commodities, values and other capitalist abstractions.

FETISHISM WITHOUT PERVERSION

The affinity of Marx and Freud's use of fetishism is grounded in the discontinuity that they both produce in the historical context, in which the notion was initially deployed.[5] The word originates from Portuguese *feitiço*, and from Latin *facticius*, which mean 'artificial', 'unnatural', 'fabricated', 'fake' and 'imitation'. From the very outset, fetishism seems to indicate a problematic dimension of appearance, not subjective misperception of reality, which would still remain in the context of cognition and in the opposition of truth and error, but objective appearance, which operates beyond this opposition. This is how it is finally used in Marx and Freud, who

---

5   I rely here on the excellent historical and theoretical overview in A. Iacono, *Le fétichisme. Histoire d'un concept*, Paris: Presses Universitaires de France, 1992. For a more detailed psychoanalytic discussion of the history of fetishism see P. L. Assoun, *Le fétichisme*, Paris: Presses Universitaires de France, 1994.

accomplish the move from the imaginary appearance to the symbolic semblance. However, this move presupposes a fundamental epistemological shift in the framework in which the notion of the fetish was introduced before the critique of political economy and psychoanalysis deployed its critical meaning. It is well known that the notion emerged from the ethnographic and the colonial context, in order to designate the difference between the European colonisers and the peoples of the colonised African and American territories. From the critical perspective, the pseudoscientific use of the fetish in colonial ideology provided the paradigmatic example of fetishisation. Marcel Mauss famously wrote that the notion of fetishism contains an 'immense misunderstanding between two cultures, the African and the European',[6] a misunderstanding that pinpoints the ideology of progress shared by colonialism, liberalism and the Enlightenment. The notion addressed notably the differences in religious practices, covering religions of the African and American peoples and the objects of their adoration. It first described the present difference between the European cultures of progress and the indigenous cultures of colonised territories but was later extended to describe the originary state of man. In the beginning there was fetishism.

The fetish appears as a border that delimits the rational from the irrational, true religion from superstition. In his book *Du culte des dieux fétiches*, Charles de Brosses introduces fetishism in order to describe a religion that precedes polytheism, the zero level of religious belief, where the symbolic dimension of worship is not yet present. De Brosses reduced fetishism to the imaginary relation to the object, where the subject worships the empirical objects directly and does not address any divine abstractions behind them. In other words, worshipped objects do not *represent* divinities; they *are* divinities. The symbolic relation of representation considered absent, the colonial ideology connects fetishism with ignorance regarding the 'irregular phenomena in nature'[7] – a response to an epistemic dilemma and an attempt to fill in the gap of the positive knowledge of nature. Fetishist belief does not include knowledge and therefore contrasts with the developed – symbolic – forms of religious belief, which already contain a corpus of knowledge, the highest point being, of course, the religion of revelation, which supposedly follows immediately from divine knowledge: absolute religion.

---

6   Quoted in Iacono, *Le fétichisme*, 116.
7   Ibid., 10.

In order to determine the critical break of Marx and Freud's conception of fetishism, the Italian philosopher Alfonso Iacono draws attention to the relation between the observer and the observed. The colonial context used fetishism in order to demonstrate the prehistoric status of the African and the American peoples, the state of quasi-natural man before the fall into history and its presumably perpetual progress towards the good. Thereby, the colonial ideology introduced a seemingly insurmountable division between the observer and the observed, the man of history and the man of nature, this good but ignorant savage. The colonial discourse places the observer in a metaposition over the observed.

Marx and Freud's transformation of fetishism into a critical notion intervenes precisely at this point. Fetishism can become a tool of critique only under the condition that the seemingly unproblematic division of interiority and exteriority be abolished. The operation is now inverted and fetishism is applied back to those societies from which it was projected on the 'primitive Other'. The terrain, where the importance of fetishisation in the social and the libidinal economy can be observed, is now the industrial societies. In *The Poverty of Philosophy* and in *The German Ideology*, Marx criticised the division between 'natural institutions' and 'artificial institutions', between 'divine laws' and 'human laws'. This critique consequently repeats de Brosses's use of fetishism, albeit under the presupposition of the universal validity of the notion and hence under the abolition of the metaposition that capitalist cultures had assumed. This repetition within the 'domestic' context produced the minimal difference, which transformed fetishism into a critical notion – precisely the axiom that there is no (cultural) metaposition.

As a consequence of this conceptual reinvention, the critique of political economy later demonstrated that there is no possibility of demarcating the language of commodities from the language of political economy. The prosopopoeia of commodities, which concludes the chapter on commodity fetishism in *Capital,* is possible only under the abolition of the fantasy of economic metalanguage, the defetishisation of economists as subjects of knowledge. When economists speak, they speak the language of commodities, which is conditioned by the very same autonomy of the signifier as human language. They unknowingly remain in the horizon of the fetishist appearance, which now designates more than it did in colonial ideology: not the prehistoric state of ignorance, imaginary illusion or cognitive error, but an objective misunderstanding generated by the autonomy of exchange. By abolishing the hypothesis of the economic metalanguage, fetishism as a critical notion includes the observer in the observed: Marx and Freud do not speak from a metaposition but assume the double role of critics and subjects of fetishism.

Freud repeated the same operation in relation to sexuality, thereby problematising the established and, until then, unchallenged division between normal and abnormal sexual goals, of 'natural' sexuality, anchored in the primacy of anatomical difference, and its 'unnatural', perverted, degenerated image, which aims at partial objects or goals that are antithetical to nature. Far from being the partisan of vulgar phallocentrism, Freud demonstrated that the apparent necessity and univocity of the phallic reference is constantly undermined, from within, by contingency. The phallus is the privileged semblance, which has little, if anything, in common with anatomy. What is most important in Freud's conception of sexuality is not so much that he rejects the opposition of the normal and the pathological but that he discovers a cut between sexuality and biology, its presumably natural and ultimate normativity, a minimal displacement, which constitutes human sexuality as essentially polymorphous and decentralised. In other words, the pluralism of forms stresses that sexuality is marked by equivocity and inadequacy. By distinguishing sexuality and anatomical sexual difference, it can be safely said that Freud problematised the very notion of nature. To repeat, psychoanalysis turns around the postulate that there is no sexual norm, hence no sexual metaposition, from which the sexual relation could be articulated. The extension of sexuality beyond the anatomical and procreative framework contains the basic psychoanalytic insight that sexuality cannot be traced back to a supposedly natural need and should instead be recognised as a material consequence of the causality of the signifier.

Another important shift concerns the relation between knowledge and fetishism. While the colonial use of fetishism is undoubtedly rooted in the simple opposition between knowledge and ignorance, Marx and Freud introduced a new form of knowledge, which reaches beyond the cognitive framework of the ideological use of fetishism: knowledge that does not know itself, to repeat Lacan's reformulation of the concept of the unconscious. Even if it would be exaggerated to search for the discovery of the unconscious in Marx, the form of unknown knowledge is at least indicated in his apparently marginal remark, which resumes the fetishist projection, 'they do not know it, nevertheless they do it': the colonialist ideologues did not know that the knowledge they produced of the 'primitive Other' reflected their own relation to commodities, money and capital, or as Iacono writes:

> The European ideology of the eighteenth century tried to reduce all the space occupied by contemporary 'savages' to a simple reflection of the past. It imposed *its* history by presenting it as a universal one. The way, in which the Western observer penetrates the universe of the other, is thus determined by an idea of history and time, which, by including this universe in its own, simultaneously *excludes*.[8]

The central operation of fetishism is this internally doubled operation of *inclusive exclusion* and *exclusive inclusion,* the only place from which it is possible to assume the fantasmatic metaposition. Marx was the first to localise a case of fetishism, commodity fetishism, in its actual cultural environment, and he determined the projection that supports the capitalist social link, the subversion of the relations between men through the relations between things, the fetishisation of objects rather than the fetishisation of subjects (even if the latter is not abolished in capitalism).

Very early on, Lacan noticed the logical value of Marx's critique of fetishism, which enables psychoanalysis to think fetishism *without* perversion and to overcome the predominantly biological signification that the notion obtained in Freud. Marx's critique of fetishism anticipates nothing less than the notion of the signifier. To repeat the entire passage in question:

> If we place the interhuman relation at the root of everything we finally merely reduce the fact of fetishisation of human objects onto some interhuman misunderstanding, which presupposes a reference to meaning as such . . . In short, it is highly surprising that the doctrine that describes itself as Marxist argues for the thesis that takes human subjectivity as its first given but not human praxis. Contrary to this, it seems to me that we merely need to open the first volume of *Capital* in order to become aware of the fact that Marx's first step in the analysis of the fetish character of the commodity consists in the fact that he approaches the problem on the level of the signifier as such, even if the term is not pronounced. The relations between values are given first as relations between signifiers and the entire subjectivity, in

---

8   Ibid., 64.

the concrete case of the subjectivity of fetishisation, is inscribed in this dialectic of the signifier. There is absolutely no doubt about this.[9]

Marx's anticipation of the signifier consequently implies a more radical theory of the subject from the later Marxist hypostasis of class-consciousness, which is presumably embedded in a historical process of overcoming alienation. According to Michael Heinrich,[10] the history of Marxism is marked by two false conclusions: the conclusion from class position to class-consciousness, and further from class-consciousness to its a priori revolutionary character. The conclusion concerning the revolutionary character of the proletariat is not erroneous in itself, since the correct placing of the proletariat as the privileged social embodiment of the structural contradictions of capitalism already disturbs the established fetishist appearance and opens up the minimal space for political organisation and revolutionary politics. What is problematic in this conclusion is that Marxism in its worldview tendency deduces the revolutionary character from a quasi-positivist epistemology and a false theory of the subject, which make this subversive potential seem strictly univocal: a matter of positive knowledge or consciousness. This univocity consequently reintroduces the teleological understanding of history that the mature Marx abolished in favour of a more radical conception of alienation, necessitated by nothing other than the autonomy of value. Both conclusions that Heinrich criticises in worldview Marxism draw from the pre-critical Marx, for whom alienation still signifies a reflexive and presumably reversible relation – alienation of the generic human essence that precedes it – while for the critical Marx alienation signifies the production of subjectivity that is irreducible and heterogeneous to consciousness.

Marx's trajectory from idealist humanism to historical materialism reveals that alienation could be attributed a positive meaning. Being inseparable from structure, it no longer stands for the loss of some originary fullness in being but for a productive process endowed with a transformative potential. Freud made the same point in his minimalist epistemological discussion of the revolutionary sciences (physics, biology, psychoanalysis). In its decentralising effects, the modern scientific revolution is a form of alienation, which suspends the domination of human narcissism in premodern forms of knowledge. The epistemological and political triumph

---

9   Lacan, *Le désir et son interprétation*, 371.
10 Heinrich, *Kritik der politischen Ökonomie*, 198.

of capitalism, however, consists in the fact that it succeeded in healing the narcissistic wounds while also introducing a new form of alienation (commodity form) that no less draws from scientific sources.

The same mistake as in the Marxist fetishisation of the labourer can be repeated in the fetishisation of the capitalist, by reducing the existing forms of exploitation to the supposedly conscious knowledge of the capitalist class. In contradistinction to such a simplification, Marx repeatedly insisted that the capitalist is more than a man with bad intentions; he is the person-ification of capital. The fetishisation of the capitalist nevertheless persists and stands at the very core of the modern power relations:

> Now, it is extraordinary that ever since there have been economists nobody, up till now, has . . . ever made this remark that wealth is the property of the wealthy . . . The wealthy have property. They buy, they buy everything, in short, well, they buy a lot. But I would like you to meditate on this fact, which is that they do not pay for it . . . And why does one let oneself be bought by the wealthy? Because what they give you stems from their essence of wealth. Buy from the wealthy, from a developed nation, you believe – and this is what the meaning of the wealth of nations is – that you are simply going to share in the level of a rich nation.[11]

Lacan's seemingly superficial remark targets one of the central and most persis-tent illusions that the advocates of neoliberalism and the ideology of progress incessantly repeat, that in some undetermined future all social differences and antagonisms will be abolished and a stable and full-functioning social relation will emerge from the present social inequalities. Behind this fairy tale scenario, the actually existing power relations are reproduced, which makes of progress the central hypothesis of the modern master.[12]

The rich buy everything, or more generally, the only goal of capital is to valorise itself. This structural tendency generates the fetishist appearance of self-engendering value, which causes the 'desire for participation' in the presupposed essence of wealth. In order for this obscenity of capitalism to be socially implemented with success, it must be accompanied by an ideo-logical fiction, precisely the idea of a permanent and unstoppable progress with no foundations whatsoever in economic, political or logical reality but

---

11   Lacan, *The Other Side of Psychoanalysis*, 82–3.
12   'Development is confused with the development of mastery' (Lacan, *Encore*, 56).

which the self-proclaimed economic experts persistently substantiate with statistical data, economic mathematics and political reforms throughout history.[13] Behind all the appearance of democratic change and progress in equality, wealth remains the property of the wealthy, despite all the efforts other nations make to establish a participatory relation to it. The more the wealthy buy everything, the more they are fetishised and the deeper the gap between the rich and the poor, from which capitalism successfully extracts surplus-value. What really works (in both meanings of the word) and is the privileged source of wealth in capitalism is the structural non-relation. No other system in history was more successful in turning social inequalities and structural contradictions into the privileged source of value, of course under the condition that this 'exploitation' of non-relation is covered with the familiar layers of appearances (abstract notions of freedom and equality).[14]

The fetishisation of the wealthy is linked to the repetition of the act of buying, through which the capitalist became the modern master. But because this buying occurs under the tendency to self-valorisation, it contains the already mentioned renunciation of *jouissance*. What matters is the repetition of the act, which persists beyond what others project on the capitalist and which generates his supposed essence:

> Why is it that once he has become rich he can buy everything without paying for it? Because he will have nothing to do with *jouissance*. That is not what

---

13   Revising his prognosis, Francis Fukuyama recently published an online essay on the occasion of the twenty-fifth anniversiry of the fall of the Berlin Wall, in which he admits that the end of history may indeed not have occured with the collapse of Soviet communism. But the current historical sequence is merely some sort of delay, which nevertheless testifies that the symbiosis of liberal capitalism and democracy – another hypothesis of the master, which is built on shaky ground – has no real competition and is certain to prevail on the global level at some vague point in the future. See Francis Fukuyama, 'At the "End of History" Still Stands Democracy', available at: online.wsj.com (last access: 13 November 2014).

14   'What is the fundamental "discovery" of capitalism? That non-relation is profitable, that it is the ultimate source of growth and profit . . . Adam Smith's "capital" idea starts out from positing a social non-relation as a fundamental state also on another level: as elements of social order individuals are driven by egotistic drives and pursuit of their self-interest. But out of these purely egotistic pursuits grows a society of an optimal general welfare and justice.' A. Zupančič, 'The Sexual is Political?' in: Tomšič and Zevnik (Eds), *Jacques Lacan: Between Psychoanalysis and Politics*, 95.

he repeats. He repeats his purchase. He buys everything again or, rather, whatever turns up, he buys.[15]

The essence of the capitalist is not in some hidden treasure, *agalma,* nor in some presupposed knowledge of the relations that constitute the market but in the senseless repetition of buying, through which he appropriates the surplus-product, contained in every produced commodity, surplus labour. The social imposition of generalised indebtedness is clearly not excluded from this picture; it is its hidden support and flip side. Lacan exposes the nature of fetishisation by making a play on words with property. The fetishist mistake derives from the fact that it treats wealth as intrinsic to private property, which in the given case serves as the visibility and the empirical demonstration of wealth as a property of the wealthy. One buys from the wealthy, or one allows oneself to be bought by them because one believes that by being turned into their private property one will become consubstantial with their essence of wealth. One believes in the continuity between the visible and the invisible wealth, that behind the 'immense collection of commodities' the wealthy appropriate there is a deeper essence of wealth. In doing so, one believes that the wealth is transmissible, contagious, that the economic relations with a wealthy nation will give access to their secret. In this process, those who are bought obtain precisely the opposite, they end up with pure loss: 'However, in the process, what you lose is your knowledge, which gave you your status. The wealthy acquire this knowledge on top of everything else. It's simply that, precisely, they don't pay for it.'[16] The truth of fetishisation is revealed in the transference of knowledge in the most literal sense of the term. The fetishised subject, in the given case a wealthy nation, is supposed to possess knowledge that supports the production of wealth.

An entire segment of classical political economy is dedicated precisely to this question: what knowledge supports the economic growth? The introduction of *homo oeconomicus,* whose presupposed knowledge of the laws of the market is associated with the no less presupposed knowledge of its private interests, most firmly places the economic debate on the epistemic terrain. But the truth of fetishisation is that the transference pushes the subject into domination and inequality, e.g., economic dependency on a wealthy nation, just as the selling and buying of labour-power goes hand

---

15   Lacan, *The Other Side of Psychoanalysis,* 82.
16   Ibid.

in hand with the dependency of labour on capital. The poorer nation thereby becomes the passive recipient of economic and political dictates. The loss of knowledge, through its projection in the wealthy Other, which is supposed to know for the subject, summarises this dependency and immediately turns out to be logically equivalent to the loss of value in the labour process. When the wealthy nation buys everything in line – in the end this buying never remains limited to commodities but always comprises the infrastructure, banks, enterprises and so on, until the wealthy nation ends up determining the economic system of an entire country – it gains knowledge (the means of production) and surplus-value (the object of production) free of charge.

It is true that the apparently evident and banal conclusion, according to which wealth is a property of the wealthy – and not, for instance, a posi-tive quality of some abstract economic subjects – never occurred to political economy. The reason for this is evidently in the fact that political economy never thought of associating the source of wealth with the inex-istence of social relation and with the social inequalities that make this inexistence manifest. However, this association did occur to Marx, who also described the specific type of reflection that makes this property appear as a generic essence, while also liberating the creative potential of structural contradictions:

> The mysterious character of the commodity-form consists therefore simply in the fact that the commodity reflects the social character of labour as objective characteristics of men's own labour as the objective characteristics of the products of labour themselves, as the socio-natural properties of these things. Hence it also reflects the social relation of the producers to the sum total of labour as an externally existing relation between objects. With this quid pro quo the products of labour become commodities, sensual supra-sensual or social things.[17]

What matters here is the inversion that the seemingly innocent and banal act of exchange (quid pro quo) transforms the products of labour, the empirical objects or use-values, into commodities, exchange-values, defined as sensual suprasensual things. This last description is of central importance because it questions the simple distinction of the sensual and the suprasensual, the material object of labour and the immaterial system

---

17   Marx, *Capital*, Vol. 1, 164–5. Translation modified.

of differences and social relations. The critical materialist orientation uncovers their overlapping, equivocity and indistinctness, the intrusion of one realm into another, which questions the very idea of materiality. The order of predicates is crucial here. Marx does not speak of the suprasensual character of the sensual, because this would suggest that the sensual contains a more true suprasensual aspect, a hidden *agalma*, the valuable kernel behind the banal empirical shell. This is according to Marx the standpoint of classical political economists, for whom value, the suprasensual, is a positive quality of sensual commodities. Such placement makes wealth appear as an immense collection of commodities – the appearance that introduces the first volume of *Capital* and is immediately rejected – but not as a property of the wealthy, where an essential inequality and structural non-relation would enter the picture.[18] From the viewpoint of commodity fetishism, all commodities appear as suprasensual sensual, empiric objects endowed with an occult power to engender value. This suprasensual character of the sensual intensifies in the developed forms of capitalist abstractions (general equivalent and fictitious capital). Of course, Marx's move consists in showing that the actual efficiency of these objects becomes evident only after the perspective has been turned around and the formal determination of the subjective attitude to commodities, money and capital has been accounted for. Fetishism remains caught in a 'religious' standpoint, suprasensual sensual, while the critical materialist turn assumes a logical position, sensual suprasensual. Only as sensual suprasensual objects can commodities be said to be social or discursive – and not metaphysical – objects, which support the isolation of the actual subject of value. Again, from the viewpoint of fetishism, the subject of value is value itself, a vital subject, which accounts for the apparently automatic and autonomous increase of value. From the viewpoint of critique, the subject of value is a rejected negativity, which remains heterogeneous to the apparent vitalism of values.[19]

---

18   Let us recall Marx's remark from his discussion of primitive accumulation that the national debt, the capitalist abstract debt, is the only wealth that belongs to everyone. In other words, if wealth is an immense collection of commodities, then the national debt is an immense collection of labour-power, to which every individual is reducible as a subject.

19   A similar fetishist standpoint determines the worldview Marxism, for which the proletarian class-consciousness, another suprasensual, is hidden (alienated) in the sensual process of labour, rather than in the gap between the abstract regime of exchange-values and the concrete regime of use-value.

The move from the suprasensual sensual to the sensual suprasensual contains a shift in the conception of materiality. The fetishisation of commodities reveals behind the apparent political-economic materialism a deeply rooted idealism and even spiritualism because it treats value as *causa sui* and capitalist abstractions as living forces. To this *spiritualised* materialism Marx opposes the materiality (sensuality) of structural and logical relations (suprasensual): it is not objects but structures that are autonomous and hence endowed with causality. In order to rigorously determine the materiality in question, Marx first rejects the possibility of reading the sensual suprasensual through the physiological metaphor of perception (e.g., seeing the unseeble). This would not amount to a materialist critique of objective appearance:

> In the same way the impression made by a thing on the optic nerve is perceived not as a subjective excitation of the optic nerve but as the objective form of a thing outside the eye. In the act of seeing, of course, light is really transmitted from one thing, the external object, to another thing, the eye. It is a physical relation between physical things. As against this, the commodity-form, and the value-relation of the products of labour within which it appears, have absolutely no connection with the physical nature of the commodity and the thingly [*dinglich*] relations arising out of this. It is nothing but the definite social relation between men themselves which assumes here, for them, the fantastic form of a relation between things. In order, therefore, to find an analogy we must take flight into the misty realm of the religious world.[20]

The mirror reflection oversimplifies the torsion within the commodity form, because it still points towards a symmetrical relation.[21] The secret of commodity form comes down to the minimal shift in reflection, which seemingly departs from a symmetry between object relations and human relations but actually contains an additional distortion. The imaginary mirror reflection is internally broken because it contains a symbolic abstraction (quid pro quo), exchange-value or signifier, which are both cases of non-identity: value is nothing but a relation to another value, and signifier a

---

20   Marx, *Capital*, Vol. 1, 165. Translation modified.

21   One can hear the echo of the famous Marxian metaphor of camera obscura from *The German Ideology*, only that in *Capital* the accent on non-reflexivity and on distortion as a necessarily structural feature is decisively pushed into the foreground.

relation to another signifier. Consequently, the commodity is non-identical as well. This non-identity manifests in its double character, use-value and exchange-value, and comprises two relations: the sensual relation of commodity to human need and the suprasensual relation of commodity to another commodity. The social link seems to be constituted on the second level, but it does not leave the first one outside. To recall again Marx's point from the *Grundrisse*, the production of commodities *is* the production of needs. There is no unproblematic relation to commodities.

Marx's entry into the logic of the signifier consists in his definition of fetishism: the inversion of relations between men in the relations between things. This inversion presupposes the shift from the imaginary to the symbolic, the primacy of the abstract but no less material act of exchange, that the above passage addresses through the shift from the physiological metaphor of vision to the misty realms of religion. That the imaginary reflection contains an additional deformation, a symbolic *torsion* within the imaginary *reflection*, which can be accounted for only through the autonomy of value (quid pro quo) did not go unnoticed in Iacono's discussion of fetishism:

> There are two moments in the inversion: the first moment concerns the process of restitution of the image of social characters of human labour; the second moment concerns the fact that this restituted image is modified in relation to the reality that it reflects. It is very important to mark the distinction between both moments, in order to avoid the simplification and misunderstanding, which very often make the inversion simply coincide with alienation.[22]

Marx's comparison very clearly stresses the necessity of distinguishing between constituted alienation, which signifies an imaginary projection exemplified by the model of vision and by the projection of human essence in God (Feuerbach), and constitutive alienation, which comes down to the non-identity of value and signifier. This does not mean that Marx simply equates the relations between things and the relations between men, since such a move would again imply a reflexive turn. Marx claims that in order to think the connection between the production of value and the social non-relation we first must reject the idea that the relation between conscious individuals is exported into the kingdom of objects. Instead he insists that behind the constituted alienation, where social relations assume the

---

22   Iacono, *Le fétichisme*, 83.

fantasmatic form of relations between commodities, there is a more fundamental constitutive alienation, which distorts every immediate relation
between men. In the end, commodity fetishism is the 'immediate' capitalist
form of social relation. In feudalism, fetishisation would assume a different
form, for instance the fetishisation of the king's body.[23] A materialist reading
of alienation moves not from the religious-metaphysical sphere to its anthro-
pological-empirical background (in this respect, Freud's reduction of
religion to obsessive neurosis and the explanation of divinities as projections
of human desires echoes Feuerbach rather than Marx) but from the foreground of human and commodity relations, to the misty realms of religion.

Why do religious abstractions explain constitutive alienation? What in
religion allows us to think alienation as a productive process resulting in a
specific form of subjectivity? Precisely the recognition of the autonomy of
these abstractions: 'There the products of the human brain appear as independent figures endowed with a life of their own, which enter into relations
both with each another and with the human race.'[24] The statement is ambiguous because Marx again refers to the dialectical appearance, which always
includes an illusory dimension. The religious mistake consists in the false
understanding of the autonomy in question: it conceives it in terms of positive entities (objects) and not in terms of logical relations. Abstract
silhouettes (*Gestalten*) are not spectralities that would need to be brought
down to a solid ground of human reason. Marx is neither a humanist reduc-
tionist (empirical materialist) nor an exorcist or ghost buster (speculative
idealist). His critique of political economy is a *hantologie*,[25] an attempt to
isolate the logic that generates the fetishist appearance, where the logical
autonomy of value assumes the form of objects and positive qualities. This
critical and materialist move is in perfect accordance with the way modern
science treats natural appearances.

Unlike empirical materialism, which remains centred on immediate
sensuality and consciousness, religion takes the autonomy of value, hence
the autonomy of logical relations, seriously, thereby offering an essential
dialectical-materialist lesson. According to Marx, religious abstractions
and commodities should be thought in a homological way: 'So it is in the

---

23   See E. H. Kantorowicz, *The King's Two Bodies: A Study in Medieval Political Theology*, Princeton: Princeton University Press, 1957.
24   Marx, *Capital*, Vol. 1, 165.
25   J. Derrida, *Spectres de Marx*, Paris: Galilée, 1993, 31.

world of commodities with the products of men's hands.'[26] In the capitalist universe, we are dealing with the same logical autonomy and with the same mystification of this autonomy. As exchange-values, commodities become more than mere human products because they represent a discursive consequence marked by non-identity, labour-power, thereby making of labour, too, a sensual suprasensual process. Commodities thus display the autonomy of value, and in this respect Marx makes a minimal yet crucial correction of the fetishist theory of value, for which, again, the same autonomy appears as a positive and objective quality of capitalist abstractions.

After having situated the importance of religion, Marx finally introduces the notion of fetishism: 'I call this the fetishism which attaches itself to the products of labour so soon as they are produced as commodities, and is therefore inseparable from the production of commodities.'[27] Production of commodities *is* production of the fetishist appearance. The fetishist relation is inseparable from the structure of production, and different structures ground different fetishisations. In the last instance, fetishisation and exploitation are two interdependent components of every hitherto existing social relation.

Marx's move from the subjective to the objective appearance points in the direction of what Lacan later called the semblant. In order to show the point of the autonomy of the signifier, Lacan starts from the objective semblance in nature, like reflections on the water surface, rainbows or an animal's protective colours, and so on. This objective semblance remains imaginary and is not to be mistaken with the signifier, which also creates the appearance of imitating reality: communication, the adequate relation between words and things, meaning and univocal relation to the signified. However, the semblance in nature imitates merely through reflection, while the signifier imitates through differentiation. Recall the Hegelian statement that already served the early Lacan and that defines the word as the murder of the Thing. This surely does not suggest that the signifier abolishes some presupposed immediate relation to the Thing but that it becomes the privileged mode of its presence. The Hegelian reference, well-pointed as it may seem, nevertheless remains in the frame of the signifying function of speech and of the relation between the signifier and the signified and does not exhaust the consequences of its absolute autonomy.

The emergence of the signifier denaturalises the semblance in nature by introducing into nature something that its semblances do not possess,

26   Marx, *Capital*, Vol. 1, 165.
27   Ibid.

difference: 'The semblance, in which the discourse is identical to itself . . . is the semblance in nature'.[28] To put it in the most banal way, the semblance in nature does not point to another semblance but to another thing. It deceives through the imitation of an empirical quality. In this imitation, it remains identical with itself, and so its autonomy and objectivity are merely apparent. In relation to this multiplicity of natural semblances, the signifier turns out to be semblance 'as such', the Semblance, which subordinates and transforms all natural semblances. These now become, for the speaking being, indistinguishable from the Semblance. Unlike natural semblance, the discursive semblance is pure difference, S_1, the master-signifier, which signifies the non-identity of every signifier with itself. In relation to the denaturation of the semblance, which follows from the intervention of the signifier, Lacan even speaks of the 'accumulation of the signifiers',[29] primitive accumulation that concerns the emergence of language, the birth of the master-signifier, through which the things are 'murdered' and the semblances in nature are transformed into signifiers. The natural reflections become 'the prose of the world' and the 'language of things' that Foucault accentuates in the theory of signs,[30] through which the Renaissance rediscovered Plato's linguistic myth. The second example, which could illustrate the transformation of natural semblances, even if only in a limited range, is Galileo's metaphor of the book of nature written in geometrical language: according to Galileo, the mathematical signifier is already operative in nature, in the movement of astronomical bodies, this paradigmatic case of natural semblance, which seduced ancient and medieval science to geocentrism and the spherical conception of the universe. In opposition to this quest for the continuity between the natural and the discursive semblance, between semblances and Semblance, identity and difference, Lacan marks the discontinuity that the 'primitive accumulation' introduces into the semblance – a process that progressively gives birth to the autonomy of difference, this systematic break, which in the end reveals that nature, as such, is an 'immense collection' of semblances.

The aim of Lacan's hypothesis of the primitive accumulation of semblances is to show that the signifier introduces a constitutive alienation, which contains a break with alienation in nature (in the sense of mirror reflection) and is also irreducible to the capitalist forms of

28 Lacan, *D'un discourse qui ne serait pas du semblant*, 16.
29 Ibid., 16–17.
30 M. Foucault, *Les mots et les choses*, Paris: Gallimard, 1966, 32ff.

alienation. Returning at this point to Marx, if his critique of fetishism would not move from the physiology of vision to the materialist lessons of religion, the inversion would simply repeat his pre-critical and human- ist reading of alienation and thereby overlook the break between alienation as an imaginary reflection and alienation as a structural oper- ation. The point is to show that human relations exist in the way in which they are distorted. There are no human relations without distortion.

However, the metaphor of the mirror is not necessarily limited to the reflexive model of alienation. In this regard, the notion of the mirror stage that Lacan introduced in his early work is as essential for highlight- ing the constitutive character of alienation as his later notion of the signifier. The mirror stage, this originary 'drama' that gives birth to the human ego through the child's recognition in the mirror image, already contains a split. The recognition of the external image is not so much the recognition of its identity with the inner stream of consciousness but moreover the first objective encounter of the split that separates me from myself through my own image. The recognition of identity always- already contains a recognition of difference, the identity of the identity and difference, to put it in Hegelian language. The imaginary contains a constitutive alienation, the production of the split ego, and a constituted alienation, the production of the asymmetrical relation between the subject and the other. The unity of the ego is established through the encounter of the externality of my own image, the projection of the bodily surface, which stands opposite to my gaze as an enclosed totality. However, this constitution of the ego excludes the split from which this projection was possible in the first place. When Iacono writes that the reconstructed image remains within deformation, this means that the inversion of reflection, the attempt to read the reflection backwards is already productive: it gives birth to the fantasy of unity and identity, immediacy and authenticity. To repeat, the reconstruction of the alien- ated entity produces a new fetishisation, which should be traced back to the structural relations that produced it.

THE ORGAN AND THE ANIMAL

The notion of the fetish wraps up Marx's correction of the political- economic misperception of the autonomy of value. Rather than conceiving this autonomy in a substantialist sense, which makes of value a positive quality of commodities and eventually a vital force of capitalist abstractions, the critical turn departs from the autonomy of logical relations. Every act of exchange contains an abstraction, which always-already articulates a system of differences. Exchange-value follows the same laws as the signifier. Yet the critical analysis of the fetish exposes other complications that follow from the double character of commodity. It is necessary to differentiate two objects, the object of need, endowed with positive qualities and corresponding to empirical materiality, and the object that is produced within the autonomy of exchange-value, whose materiality is of entirely different order. At this point the fetish points towards the Lacanian object *a*:

> It is only when the status of that object that I call the object small *a* . . . has been acknowledged that we will we be able to give a meaning to the alleged impetus you attribute to the subject's revolutionary praxis of going beyond his alienated labour. In what way can one go beyond the alienation of his labour? It is as though you wanted to go beyond the alienation of discourse. All I can see as transcending that alienation is the object sustaining its value, what Marx, in a homonym singularly anticipatory of psychoanalysis, called the fetish, it being understood that psychoanalysis reveals its biological signification.[31]

This does not mean that the fetish is identical with the object *a*. The fetish is rather an attempt to fixate the logical object in an empirical object and to conceal the gap that separates the two orders of reality. The problematic of castration, but also of alienation, which the fetish is supposed to foreclose from the symbolic, gravitates around this gap. In the critical context, the fetish becomes a hieroglyph of alienation, which conceals the link between alienation, production of surplus-object and production of subjectivity. Labour and speech are two processes from which alienation cannot be eliminated, for the simple reason that these are the actions of constitutive alienation, as Hegel has already noticed.[32]

---

31   Lacan, *Television*, 111. Translation modified.

32   'Speech and work are outer expressions in which the individual no longer keeps and possesses himself within himself, but lets the inner get completely outside of him, leaving it to the mercy of something other than himself.' G. W. F. Hegel, *Phenomenology of Spirit*, Oxford: Oxford University Press, 1977, 187. The entire work of Marx and Lacan could be considered an immense footnote and precision on this Hegelian passage.

Yet how does Marx's critical use of the fetish go together with the biological signification that Freud ended up privileging? If Marx's critique anticipates psychoanalysis, then Freud's idea of biology is more extravagant than it seems. Through the notion of the fetish, Freud explores the colonisation of the anatomical and biological body by discursive abstraction. A return to the famous metapsychological writing on fetishism is called for at this point. It was there that Freud defined fetishism through a specific symbolic operation, which he called *Verleugnung*. The word means disavowal and represents a modality of negation. In *Verleugnung* we find the reference to *Lüge*, lie, which makes of the fetishist disavowal a procedure that presents castration as something untrue. The literal meaning of *Verleugnung* would be falsification, but a falsification that does not demonstrate anything. Instead, the fetishist tendency strives to replace the association of subjectivity and negativity with the fantasy of an uncastrated subject, *jouissance* without lack and so on. This defence mechanism, characteristic for perversion, stands in-between neurotic repression and psychotic foreclosure. Negation places the conflict in the mental apparatus, preserving the border between external reality and psychic reality, while foreclosure situates the same conflict outside and thus abolishes the border between both orders of reality. In comparison to both procedures, disavowal operates at the very limit between the inside and the outside.

Freud provides two definitions of *Verleugnung*. According to the first, disavowal concerns a representation (*Vorstellung*), unlike repression, which targets the affect that the representation causes in the subject. This feature makes of repression a defence from internal impulses, while disavowal is directed against the demands of reality, striving for their neutralisation. Yet the withdrawal it accomplishes does not have the radical character of foreclosure, in which the exterior is modified according to psychic reality, making the subject appear delirious. According to Freud's second definition, disavowal aims at perception (*Wahrnehmung*), which again contains the reference to truth (*Wahrheit*) and whose literal meaning is 'taking for true', recognition of truth. Fetishism is resistance against an already manifest verification. *Wahrnehmung*, the persistence of truth in experience, awakens a counter-tendency, which demands 'a very energetic action' in order 'to maintain the disavowal'.[33] Again we come across the demand for labour, which is supposed to construct a non-conflictual reality, as in dreams and worldviews.

---

33   Freud, *Standard Edition*, Vol. 21, 154.

How then does biological signification enter the picture? In the case of fetishism that caught Freud's attention, the perception concerns the absence of penis on the female body, and more generally, the reduction of sexual difference to the binary opposition of presence and absence, completeness and incompleteness. The fetishised object – a part of the body or any material object that can prolong human anatomy – becomes a substitute-penis, a prosthetic organ of *jouissance*, whereby Freud remarks the following:

> When now I announce that the fetish is a substitute for the penis, I shall certainly create disappointment; so I hasten to add that it is not a substitute for any chance penis, but for a particular and quite special penis that had been extremely important in early childhood but had later been lost. That is to say, it should normally have been given up, but the fetish is precisely designed to preserve it from extinction. To put it more plainly: the fetish is a substitute for the woman's (the mother's) penis that the little boy once believed in and – for reasons familiar to us – does not want to give up.[34]

Sexual fetishism is restricted to the male subject. Without preserving the hypothesis of the woman's penis the subject would have to confront his own castration, the possibility of losing what he understands as the privileged organ of *jouissance*. In its biological signification, fetishism thus stands for the unconscious belief in the non-castration of the woman, or more generally, a belief in some sort of sexual monism, according to which there is only one organ of *jouissance*, the penis, and consequently only one signifier of *jouissance*, the phallus. The imaginary (the body, penis) and the symbolic (the signifier, phallus) are supposed to overlap without any remainder. For now let us leave aside the problematic status of this biological reduction, the identification of the phallus with the penis, which is already a fetishist lapsus. What matters is the insight that the subject's belief in a female penis functions as a screen for another belief that concerns the subject's own relation to castration. Freud discovers that fetishism involves a belief in the non-universality of castration. Through the hypothesis of the non-castrated Other, the phallic Woman, the fetishist postulates his own non-castration and avoids the link between truth and negativity. By making of the woman a non-castrated exception, he simultaneously exempts himself from castration. We can notice in passing that Lacan formalises this fetishist belief in his masculine formulas of sexuation, in which the universality of the phallic

---

34   Ibid., 152–3.

function is supported by the phallic exception, some sort of meta-phallus impossible to castrate.

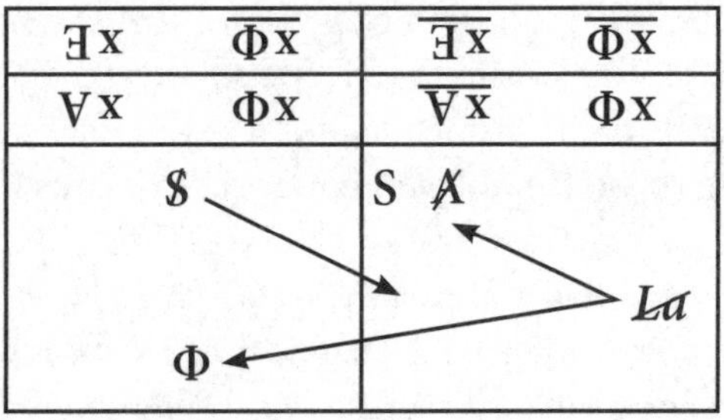

Image 1. The Formulas of Sexuation

The masculine formulas (left) contain Freud's myth of the primordial father, the uncastrated bearer of castration, who can be castrated only by being murdered. The point of this translation is that, beyond biology and the amateur ethnology of Freud's reconstructions of cultural prehistory, it uncovers the structure of the fetishist disavowal, where the subject is split between the verification of castration, the encounter with sexual difference, which takes the form of misunderstanding that the woman is lacking the organ of *jouissance*, and the falsification of castration, since the fetish substitutes the supposedly missing organ. If we move to the lower level of Lacan's formulas, which concern the relation of the subject to the object of *jouissance*, we find the fetishist relation symbolised by the vector that goes from the barred subject to the object *a* on the feminine side. The fetish 'completes' the feminine subject and in the end reduces the woman to an object. The subject cannot enjoy in the body of the other, he can only 'play' with the organ of *jouissance* embodied by the fetish.[35]

Still, for Freud, the function of the fetish is more ambiguous. It is true that on the one hand it is declared to substitute the penis, which seems to be in accordance with the phallocentric reading in the vulgar anatomical sense. On the other hand, the phallus is also and above all a *hieroglyph of castration*, and in this respect it signifies the radical absence of the organ of *jouissance*.

---

35   'As is emphasized admirably by the kind of Kantian that Sade was, one can only enjoy a part of the Other's body, for the simple reason that one has never seen a body completely wrap itself around the Other's body, to the point of surrounding and phagocytizing it. That is why we must confine ourselves to simply giving it a little squeeze, like that, taking a forearm or anything else' (Lacan, *Encore*, 23).

The phallus is a dethroning of the penis as the privileged organ of *jouissance*, showing that the metonymisation of *jouissance* cannot be avoided and that the penis is merely one organ among others. Put differently, the penis already is a prosthetic phallus.

Freud's discussion of the fetishist case concludes with this radical ambiguity of the fetish. The observation of a woman's body in the same move verifies and falsifies, preserves and abolishes the hypothesis of the feminine phallus:

> It is not true that, after the child has made his observation of the woman, he has preserved unaltered his belief that women have a phallus. He has retained that belief, but he has also given it up . . . Yes, in his mind the woman *has* got a penis, in spite of everything; but this penis is no longer the same as it was before. Something else has taken its place, has been appointed its substitute, as it were, and now inherits the interest, which was formerly directed to its predecessor. But this interest suffers an extraordinary increase as well, because the horror of castration has set up a memorial to itself in the creation of this substitute.[36]

The hypothesis in fact emerges together with the child's first confrontation with sexual difference. In this observation, the subject obtains the insight that he is always-already castrated, i.e., that his being depends and emerges from difference that defines the signifier. The observation is surely empirical but it is also inscribed into structure, just as commodity fetishism is not merely a way to experience the objects of value but inevitably follows from the double character of the commodity. Being a *memorial of castration*, the fetish designates the opposite of the organ of *jouissance*, the materialisation of a radical absence, which consequently implies that the perverse subject is anything but uncastrated. Castration is neither neutralised nor overcome; on the contrary, the fetish is its negative, a *negation of negativity*. Castration may be abolished in the empirical object, which is turned into a prosthetic organ, but it is sustained in the signifier.

The ambiguity of Freud's biological signification goes even further. What is the feminine phallus? It is not an actual but a hypothetical organ, which differs from the male penis and which never existed. The fetish masks a negativity that reaches beyond the anatomical and biological context, not the inexistence of something that could potentially exist but

---

36   Freud, *Standard Edition*, Vol. 21, 154.

something whose existence is strictly speaking impossible: an Organ of *jouissance* that would abolish the negativity in the field of sexuality and establish a sexual relation. There is no Organ of *jouissance* but there is a signifier of *jouissance*, and this signifier covers the interdependency between *jouissance* and castration. The difference between the masculine and the feminine penis should therefore obtain its full symbolic weight: 'If the fetish is given as a substitute, a placeholder of something else it is not a substitute of something that is but of something that is not'.[37] Again, not of something that does not exist only on the feminine body but of something that does not exist on the speaking body as such. What the subject deals with is *jouissance without the Organ, jouissance* caused by the signifier.

The fetish merely appears to substitute something that could potentially or actually exist. Its main function is to reject castration from the symbolic, but this move always backfires and the fetish turns from a prosthetic organ into a monument of castration, thereby enunciating something essential about the subject of the signifier. Freud translated this lesson in the universality of castration: there is no uncastrated subject and perversion is, in this respect, no metaposition either. Unlike Deleuze, who saw in masochism a subversive subjective position, psychoanalysis detects the true subversive potential in neurosis, where *jouissance* is directly exposed as impossible to sustain. Freud thus spoke of neurosis as the negative of perversion, and Lacan as a failed perversion. The neurotic might appear a loser in the eyes of the pervert, but his position in fact reveals the limit of fetishism. The neurotic repression contains an assumption of castration and reveals in neurosis a particular protest against the structurally imposed perversion. Recall that for Freud the neurotics are *the* embodiments of cultural discontent, *Unbehagen in der Kultur*, cultural products, which are not unrelated to the various traumatic effects of capitalism.

In the fetishist masquerade, the subject encounters his own castration in the feminine Other in the form of absence of the Organ of *jouissance*. The observation of the woman's body dupes the child with the appearance that there is something missing. Freud, too, might have been duped by the same appearance, but the reduction of the biological signification to logical mechanisms in the background reveals that his brief text contains a more general truth, a truth that explains what psychoanalysis understands by castration: not the absence of some potential presence but the impossibility to establish a relation between the surplus and the lack, the production of

---

37   Wajcman, *Collection*, 36.

jouissance and the production of subjectivity, the impossibility to enjoy *sans entraves,* without negativity and alienation. If Freud needs to be corrected, then it is in the following way: *anatomy is fantasy* (and not destiny). Once the confusion between the phallus and the penis is abolished, the conclusion is at hand that there is a multiplicity of prosthetic organs, but there is *one* signifier of *jouissance,* the phallus, albeit with no adequate organic reference, and there is one *jouissance,* the one caused by the signifier in the speaking body. The whole problem therefore comes down to the fact that the signifier of *jouissance* has no corresponding organ on the living body: it can designate several bodily regions or pieces of flesh as the privileged support of *jouissance.* This multiplicity merely reveals that there cannot be any *adaequatio* between the anatomical body and the libidinal body. Or differently put, an adequate relation can be forced only under the condition that one fetishises the penis as The Organ. That all fetish objects are merely prosthetic substitutes of the penis is a wrong conclusion, since the penis is no less a prosthetic organ. Hence, Lacan will correct Freud: the phallus is neither an organ nor an object but the Signifier, which designates the capacity of the signifier (the autonomy of the system of differences) to cause *jouissance* and to bring a (split) subject into being. As a signifier, the phallus signifies both *jouissance* and its lack.

At this point, it becomes clearer in what respect Marx's homonym anticipates psychoanalysis. The best lesson for understanding the ambiguous status of the phallus between the biological and the linguistic can be found in the first edition of *Capital,* where the discussion of the general equivalent contains an excellent point that Marx unfortunately omitted from the second edition:

> It is as if, alongside and external to lions, tigers, rabbits, and all other actual animals, which form when grouped together the various kinds, species, subspecies, families, etc. of the animal kingdom, there existed in addition *the animal,* the individual incarnation of the entire animal kingdom. Such a particular which contains within itself all really present species of the same entity is a *universal* (like *animal, god,* etc.).[38]

In order to exemplify the structure of the commodity universe, Marx's comparison outlines two situations: one in which we have the abstract set

---

38   K. Marx, 'The Commodity', (Capital 1867), available at: marxists.org (last access: 16 November 2014).

'Animal' comprising all particular animals and another in which this set contains itself as a particular embodiment. Unlike the animal kingdom, the commodity world is indeed structured like Russell's paradox of a set containing itself as an element. The Animal is first presented as an abstract universality, contained in every animal, and then as a concrete abstract universality (sensual suprasensual thing), an element of the animal kingdom and its limit. Because the universality of the commodity world can be held in hands, money is the privileged object of fetishism. The space of values is curved, and this internal torsion supports the apparition of generality in the form of particularity. Fetishisation of the general equivalent becomes a particular case of fetishism and a universal model.

The general equivalent actually abolishes the classical understanding of the relation between the universal and the particular, being both a *concrete universality* and an *abstract particularity*. The couple formed by desire and drive perfectly responds to this double aspect. As an abstract particularity, the general equivalent endows commodities with the power to cause desire, making them more than objects that satisfy human needs in an unproblematic way. As a concrete universality, it becomes the object of the drive because it embodies the value of *jouissance*. As abstract particularity, money embodies the autonomy of the chain of commodities and of the metonymic movement that directs desire from one particular object to another, making it chase its object of satisfaction that appears to be lacking. The failure of desire consists in the impossibility of its passing from abstract particularity to concrete universality, which would solely provide its satisfaction, and thereby its abolition, for on the side of concrete universality, we encounter the drive, which addresses the object immediately, that is, through the mediation of money, while in desire the mediation is doubled because it remains stuck on the relation between commodities and Commodity.

The general equivalent raises the same logical and topological problem as the phallus in the universe of signifiers.[39] The Phallus is the Animal, the general equivalent of *jouissance*. Even if Freud believed he had found in the unconscious hypothesis of the feminine phallus a justification for its biological signification, the phallus brings the causality of the signifier to the point. Pursuing its biological signification, psychoanalysts might insist that the feminine phallus is equivalent to the body as such and not to the masculine penis. Due to this differentiation, they introduce the distinction between *having* and *being* a phallus, which supposedly translates sexual

---

39   See J. J. Goux, *Freud, Marx. Économie et symbolique*, Paris: Seuil, 1973, 73ff.

difference. Lacan's claim that the phallus stands for the entirety of the signifying effects, as always, complicated the matter.⁴⁰ Freud's mistake was that
his later work sought to 'rationalise' his earlier insight, which placed the
cause of *jouissance* entirely on the side of the signifier. The primacy of the
signifier clarifies the *Three Essays on the Theory of Sexuality*, which turn
around the fact that there is no such thing as normative sexuality and that
every body region can become an organ of *jouissance*:

> The part played by the erotogenic zones is immediately obvious in the case
> of those perversions which assign a sexual significance to the oral and anal
> orifices. These behave in every respect like a portion of the sexual apparatus.
> In hysteria these parts of the body and the neighbouring tracts of mucous
> membrane become the seat of new sensations and of changes in innerva-
> tion – indeed, of processes that can be compared to erection – in just the
> same way as do the actual genitalia under the excitations of the normal
> sexual processes . . . in scopophilia and exhibitionism the eye corresponds
> to an erotogenic zone; while in the case of those components of the sexual
> instinct which involve pain and cruelty the same role is assumed by the
> skin – the skin, which in particular parts of the body has become differenti-
> ated into sense organs or modified into mucous membrane, and is thus the
> erotogenic zone *par excellence*.⁴¹

Freud describes here precisely the attribution of the value of *jouissance* or
sexual significance to a body part, which integrates it in the libidinal economy,
transforming anatomy into a component of the sexual apparatus. As soon as
the signifier is envisaged as an apparatus of *jouissance*, biology and anatomy
become problematic, just as use-value became problematic and colonised
with abstraction in Marx's account of the commodity form. What matters,
again, is that every erogenous zone can behave as an organ of *jouissance* under
the condition that an intervention of the signifier has occurred. In the last
instance, the bodily surface is the site of the causality of the signifier, which

---

40   'In Freudian doctrine, the phallus is not a fantasy, if we are to view fantasy
as an imaginary effect. Nor is it as such an object . . . Still less is it the organ – penis
or clitoris – that it symbolizes. And it is no accident that Freud adopted as a reference
the simulacrum it represented to the Ancients. For the phallus is . . . the signifier that
is destined to designate the signifying effects [*effets de signifié*] as a whole, insofar as
the signifier conditions them by its presence as signifier' (Lacan, *Écrits*, 579,
translation modified).

41   Freud, *Standard Edition*, Vol. 7, 169.

separates the body from itself, the skin being the border, where the anatomical and the libidinal body become equivocal.

Let us at this point return to Lacan's formulas of sexuation (Image 1). In relation to the feminine position, Lacan raises the question of the Other *jouissance*, a *jouissance* that would be beyond the fetishism of the object, but this Other *jouissance* remains without a signifier. Rather than abolishing fetishism, the feminine position contains a displacement from the small other to the big Other, from the fetishism of the object to the fetishism of the signifier. This move enables us to expose the truth of fetishism: castration, the split that constitutes the subject. The controversial inexistence of *the* Woman that Lacan professes alongside the elaboration of the formulas of sexuation addresses this problem. 'The Woman does not exist' means first and foremost that 'The Subject does not exist', that the subject designates an empty place of radical split, which can be assumed by multiple figures. In Freud, this position is assumed by the hysteric and in Marx by the proletarian.

The unveiling of castration splits the phallic function, whose universality is affirmed without exception (the negation of the meta-phallic exception). The immediate consequence of the abolition of exception is that the phallic function no longer totalises the field of *jouissance*. For this reason, Lacan's second formula of feminine sexuation states that *not all* subject falls under the phallic function.[42] Does this mean that the feminine position abolishes the general equivalent? No, since it already affirmed its universality by undermining the exception, which supported the masculine fetishism. The lower feminine formula of sexuation simply states that the point where the universality of the general equivalent breaks is the subject itself. The feminine position thereby unveils in the apparently closed and homogeneous commodity universe unexchangeable negativity and points towards the logical and the actual opposition of the fetish: the symptom. It is not unusual that the function of the symptom, the rejection of universal fetishisation and the emphasis on the unexchangeable, are most evident in hysteria, which played such an important role in the invention of psychoanalysis. But here, too, Marx's critique contains anticipation.

---

42   'Not all' means here both 'not every' subject and 'not entire' subject. This equivocity of Lacan's concept of 'non all' again addresses the fact that the same structural antagonism traverses both the constitution of social structures and the constitution of the subject, the social outside and the subjective inside.

The Symptom Between Truth and Jouissance

How did Marx then invent the critical signification of the symptom? In 1966, Lacan frames this invention in the following way:

> It is difficult not to see that, even before the advent of psychoanalysis, a dimension that might be called that of the symptom was introduced, which was articulated on the basis of the fact that it represents the return of truth as such in the gap of a certain knowledge. I am not referring to the classical problem of error, but rather to a concrete manifestation that must be appreciated 'clinically', in which we find not a failure of representation but a truth of another reference than the one, whether a representation or not, whose fine order it manages to disturb. In this sense, one can say that this dimension is highly differentiated in Marx's critique, even if it is not made explicit there.[43]

The intertwining of the epistemological and the political problematic becomes most evident here. The symptom is the return of truth *as such* in the gap of *certain* knowledge. It manifests the incompatibility and conflict-uality of truth and knowledge, pointing beyond the field of positive science which supports, for instance, the medical notion of the symptom. The truth of cognition remains factual and comes in pair with error. Speaking truth, by contrast, disrupts the regime of knowledge by introducing an enuncia-tion that goes beyond the enunciated and uncovers the detachment of the signifier from its seemingly adequate relation to the signified. Consequently, the autonomy of the signifier implies another regime of truth, and this is what Lacan describes as the 'truth as such' – the conflictual rather than the factual truth. This conflictual truth corrupts a specific type of knowledge, which strives to constitute the 'beautiful order', an ordering knowledge of science, but also of certain philosophies, religion and political economy. This regime of knowledge necessarily excludes the conflictual dimension of truth and affirms the doctrine of truth-value, adequacy, facticity or conven-tion. In this epistemological conflict, we could envisage a particular expression of what Althusser called 'class struggle in theory',[44] which

---

43   Lacan, *Écrits*, 194. Translation modified.

44   L. Althusser, *Lenin and Philosophy and Other Essays*, London: New Left Books, 1971, 18. Althusser uses this description only for philosophy, but one could extend it to the entire field of knowledge and to modern science in particular.

manifests here through the struggle for a doctrine of truth and knowledge that does not subscribe to the positivistic ideal of scientificity. Herein lies the epistemological and political novelty of psychoanalysis: 'Analysis came to announce to us that there is a knowledge that does not know itself, a knowledge that is supported by the signifier as such.'[45] Both 'truth as such' and 'knowledge that does not know itself' are rooted in the 'signifier as such': pure and autonomous difference. Marx's critique pursues the same line. His invention of the symptom is contained in his correction of the labour theory of value, which equally consists in introducing the triplet formed by the signifier *as such* (exchange-value), truth *as such* (labour-power) and knowledge *as such* (abstract labour, which 'does not think, calculate or judge', as Freud would have put it) – three figures of negativity, which move from the appearance of market rationality to the contradictions in the capitalist mode of production. To these three figures, Marx and Freud added the fourth, the surplus-object.

Lacan's definition of the symptom points back to its Freudian theorisation as a compromise formation, which combines the demands of reality and the demand for satisfaction, to which the unconscious tendency comes down to. The return of the repressed evokes the paradoxical structure of repression that Freud highlighted in his metapsychology. While initially the psychic conflict appeared to him as a conflict between two heterogeneous instances, his later developments theorised repression in a complex topological and temporal relation, in which repression and the return of the repressed condition one another in a vicious circle of repulsion and attraction. With this, Freud moved from the primacy of the instances to the primacy of the relation, which constitutes the repressing and the repressed instance. For Freud, the symptom codifies the demand for satisfaction and the demand for censorship, but the actual conflict is between the insatiable imperative of the unconscious tendency, which uses reality in order to reach its goal – the reality principle is the extension of the pleasure principle – and the subject of the unconscious, or as Lacan rephrases it, between a certain knowledge (representation) and truth as such (the gap between

---

Contrasting the empiricist and the mathematical reading of scientific modernity would be another systematic expression of this theoretical class struggle. In this respect, Koyré's reading of the history of science, which played an important role in Lacan's reading of Marx, would be exemplary.

45   Lacan, *Encore*, 88.

representation and production). In the symptom, the subject comes to protest against the imperative of *jouissance*.

The claim that 'truth has no other form than that of the symptom' will be later described as the 'Marxian turn in the history of truth',[46] a turn that envisages in fetishism the rejection of conflictual truth from reality. The fetishist disavowal contains a passion of ignorance, which reveals that positive sciences and governing ideologies do not want to know anything of the relation between truth and negativity. The foreclosure of negativity that Lacan detected in the capitalist discourse allows only an abstract truth of the subject and of society. Marx named this abstract truth, when he criticised the fundamental concepts of classical political economy, the four building blocks of the capitalist worldview. Opposed to the fetishist passion of ignorance stands the passion of truth, which uncovers the antagonism between truth and knowledge and which unites unsurpassable thinkers,[47] thinkers that can be criticised, rejected, subverted but not simply left behind. Marx and Freud founded their sciences on the dialectical contradiction between truth and knowledge, which remains inscribed in the constitution of the subject and in the non-teleological movement of history. The fact that the passion of truth aims at the split in the regime of knowledge and consequently differentiates two dimensions of truth shows that this procedure is not simply equivalent to the philosophical love for truth, which still strives to establish a stable relation between truth and knowledge.

Historically, but also logically, psychoanalysis begins with aetiology, a theory of causality, which is supposed to explain the emergence of traumatic neurosis and which leaves its materialist mark on psychoanalysis. Freud, in strong opposition to the scientific and cultural spirit of his time, linked sexuality and neurosis and proposed a theory of causality that ranked the signifier in the category of material cause:

> Unlike a sign – or smoke which is never found in the absence of fire, a
> fire that smoke indicates with the possible call to put it out – a symptom

---

46   J. Lacan, *Le Séminaire, livre XIV, La logique du fantasme*, unpublished, 10. 5. 1967.

47   'It is rather fashionable these days to "go beyond" the classical philosophers . . . neither Socrates nor Descartes, nor Marx, nor Freud, can be "gone beyond", insofar as they carried out their research with the passion to unveil that has an object: truth' (Lacan, *Écrits*, 157).

can only be interpreted in the signifying order. A signifier has meaning only through its relation to another signifier. The truth of symptoms resides in this articulation. Symptoms remained somewhat vague when they were understood as representing some irruption of truth. In fact they are truth, being made of the same wood from which truth is made, if we posit materialistically that truth is what is instated on the basis of the signifying chain.[48]

The sign still represents something for someone, but in doing so it does not cause anything. The medical notion of the symptom perfectly fits in this register of representation. The signifier, however, represents the subject for another signifier. This autonomous relation is what brings the subject into being, or, in other words, in its absolute autonomy the signifier is the privileged sign of the subject. While the medical notion of the symptom does not presuppose any subject, its critical signification does. Exactly the same move from the sign to the signifier guides Marx's analysis of the commodity form: reduced to its use-value, the commodity is no more than the sign of a physiological or psychological need (rooted in the stomach or in fantasy, to recall Marx's formulation), while as exchange-value it is the sign of labour-power, a sign of alienation and negativity that traverses the commodity universe.

The invention of the symptom demands a double reform: a critical doctrine of truth and a materialist theory of the subject, since the truth of cognition and the reduction of the subject to consciousness perpetuate idealism. The Marxian and the Freudian notion of the symptom thus combines two dimensions: (1) the epistemological, according to which the symptom reveals an antagonism between knowledge and truth; and (2) the political, for which the symptom stands for the introduction of negativity into politics and reveals the foundation of social links in a structural non-relation.

In its epistemological value, the symptom subverts the regime of interpretation. It calls for an interpretation that is neither analytical in the sense that it reconstructs a series of objective historical facts, which produced the symptom, nor hermeneutic, which would uncover its semantic and meaningful dimension. The critical interpretation of the symptom can only be dialectical-logical. In this way, the symptom ceases to be an enigma that points to some hidden depth or invisible background and is recognised as

---

48   Ibid., 234–5.

an interpretation of structural contradictions. As Lacan insisted, the truth as symptom already speaks.

The epistemological value of the symptom highlights the exceptional status of psychoanalysis and of the critique of political economy in the modern scientific universe. The reform of the subject and of truth is necessary because science rejects these two central negativities: 'Science is an ideology of the repression of the subject'; 'Science does not want to know anything about the truth as cause. You may recognise therein my formulation of *Verwerfung*'.[49] Science thus performs the *same* operation on the *same* negativities as capitalism, which offers a particular insight into their structural compatibility. In relation to these two scientific rejections, psychoanalysis and the critique of political economy are an epistemologically and politically organised symptom, which reintroduces class struggle back into theory, to remain with Althusser's theses a bit further.

In one of the discussions of this problematic, Lacan indicates that the problem of primitive accumulation has its respondent in the register of knowledge. By grounding itself on the foreclosure of negativity, science inaugurates an endless process in the accumulation of knowledge, a structure on which capitalism grounds its infinite circulation (M – C – M'), in which negativity is still represented, albeit in its abstract equality with other commodities, and its fetishist form (M – M'), where negativity is most evidently rejected. The privileged name that marks the break that inaugurates the accumulative regime of knowledge is none other than Descartes:

> I would call the state of knowledge before Descartes pre-accumulative. With Descartes knowledge, scientific knowledge is constituted on the mode of production of knowledge. Just as an essential stage of our structure that one calls social but is in fact metaphysical, and which is called capitalism, is accumulation of capital, the relation of the Cartesian subject to this being, which is affirmed in it, is founded on the accumulation of knowledge. After Descartes knowledge is what serves to make knowledge grow. And this is an entirely different question than that of the truth.[50]

---

49   Lacan, *Autres écrits*, 437, and *Écrits*, 742.

50   J. Lacan, *Le Séminaire, livre XII, Problèmes cruciaux pour la psychanalyse*, unpublished, 9. 6. 1965.

The constitution of this accumulative regime presupposes the scientific repression of the subject. This repression resides in the way Descartes solves the problem of alienation, which he encounters in methodical doubt. How is the structure of the Cartesian *cogito* associated with the subject of the unconscious and to labour-power? According to Lacan's reading, Descartes's deduction of the *cogito* comprises two complementary procedures: the construction of the subject of cognition, which will lead Descartes from *cogito* to *res cogitans* as a basis for grounding metaphysics and science; and the flip side of this process, which reveals the gap between thinking and being in the statement: 'I think therefore I am'. Lacan exposes this gap by distinguishing the enunciation and the enunciated within the apparently immediate, unified and self-evident conclusion. The distinction shows that the subject of enunciation does not entirely overlap with the subject of the enunciated and that the prosopopoeia of *cogito* rejects alienation, the non-identity of thinking and being, on which rests the thinking substance. Hence Lacan's correction of the *cogito*: 'I think: "therefore I am"'. The 'therefore I am' is the content of 'I think' – consequently the 'I that thinks' is not identical with the 'I that is'. In order to think itself as identity of thinking and being, the 'I' needs to be split: non-identity is the repressed truth of the *cogito's* identity.[51]

With the rootedness of identity in the rejection of alienation in the mind, Lacan declares this rejection to be the necessary condition for the inauguration of the accumulative regime of knowledge, which distinguishes the modern *episteme* from the ancient and the medieval regime of knowledge. The modernity of Descartes lies in the fact that he did not enter philosophical and scientific discourse simply through knowledge but more importantly through alienation. This was the true novelty of Descartes's philosophical gesture: the suspension of love for knowledge with methodical doubt, in which the subject of cognition confronts its own negativity. The hypothesis of a benevolent, truthful and non-deceiving God, in which Lacan detects the hypothesis of the subject supposed to know, is a fetishist response to the encounter with alienation and a form of the repression of the subject. The subject supposed to know inaugurates a new type of fetishisation of knowledge, which replaces its premodern fetishisation through *philia* (love). Had Descartes remained with the subject of alienation, he

---

51   For a detailed discussion of the link between *cogito* and the unconscious, see M. Dolar, 'Cogito as the Subject of the Unconscious', in: S. Žižek (Ed.), *Cogito and the Unconscious*, Durham, NC: Duke University Press, 1998, 11–37.

would probably not have inaugurated the accumulative regime of knowledge, because alienation reopens the gap in knowledge and sabotages its seemingly unproblematic growth. Only under the condition of the repression of the subject do knowledge and value appear to grow automatically, without thinking, judging and calculating involved. For as soon as knowledge starts to think, judge and calculate, in other words, as soon as an enunciation of truth emerges in its regime, the subject reappears in knowledge: the subject of the signifier is something scientific knowledge does not want to know about, which is why Freud's contemporaries dismissed his aetiology of neuroses as 'scientific fairy-tale'.[52] Descartes might have encountered the subject of alienation, but due to its foreclosure he failed to invent the symptom. Marx's invention, by contrast, is the flip side of the Cartesian project, its repetition at the opposite end, from the perspective of the negativity that he rediscovers in the given social reality.

Freud's *Wo Es war soll Ich werden* equally repeats the Cartesian project by turning it on its head. Despite various readings of the imperative, Lacan constantly insisted that the *Ich* in question is not the thinking substance or the 'strong' narcissistic ego but the decentralised subject of the unconscious. 'Where it was there I shall come into being' is an imperative that orientates psychoanalysis back to constitutive alienation. Freud's formula accentuates that the transformation of the subject through alienation, a transformation that is the logical counterpart of reintegration, adaptation and normalisation, departs from an unconscious formation that embodies the insurmountable gap between the subject and consciousness, as well as between truth and knowledge. Far from calling for the abolition of alienation and the recentralisation of psychic life, the Freudian imperative demands that a subject be encountered in the unconscious formations, which seem to be without a subject. Only through this encounter can the symptom become more than an anomaly that would need to be abolished in order to sustain the functioning of the existing order.

The crucial critical and materialist point of psychoanalysis and the critique of political economy is thus that they both reach back to the repressed negative foundations of the modern *episteme* and can, for this reason, be constituted only as sciences of negativity. They abolish the amnesia that the positive and exact sciences imposed upon themselves, or as Lacan concisely puts it, 'the fact is that science, if one looks at it closely, has

---

52   S. Freud, *Briefe an Wilhelm Fliess*, Frankfurt am Main: Fischer Verlag, 1999, 193.

no memory. Once constituted, it forgets the circuitous path by which it came into being, otherwise stated, it forgets a dimension of truth that psychoanalysis seriously puts to work.[53] The same claim evidently holds even more of Marx's critique, which makes the labour of negativity the privileged object of his critical science and the necessary foundation of politics.

The declaration of the symptom as being Marx's invention continues Lacan's polemic with the Marxist worldview and with its reductive identification of the proletarian with an empirical subject. The doctrine, according to which the social symptom is a return of the subject as such in the field of economic science, additionally exposes the insufficiency of orthodox Marxism:

> In writing that 'Marx's theory is omnipotent because it is true', Lenin says nothing of the enormity of the question his speech raises: If one assumes the truth of materialism in its two guises – dialectic and history, which are in fact one and the same – to be mute, how could theorizing this increase its power? To answer with proletarian consciousness and the action of Marxist politics seems insufficient to me.[54]

Lacan does not question the pertinence of Lenin's statement. Instead the quarrel concerns the nature of truth and the place of subjectivity in Marx. If this truth is scientific, then it is reducible to knowledge; no invention of the symptom took place, and scientific socialism is merely a variant of the *politics of cognition*, just as political economy in capitalist societies. In worldview Marxism, the symptom and class-consciousness are mutually exclusive. If, on the contrary, Marx addresses the repressed truth that supports and traverses capitalistic and scientific modernity, then *Capital* does not contain a positive science but instead highlights the mistake that a critical theory of capitalism should avoid. While in capitalism the scientific discourse is mobilised in order to support the fetishist foreclosure of negativity, Marxist politics should ground a new form of scientificity on the return of negativity. One of the main goals of the critique of political economy is to show that classical political economy repeats the two constitutive operations of modern science and that the actual utopian endeavour lies in the attempt to provide a scientific foundation to the economic subject and to the notion of private interest.

---

53   Lacan, *Écrits*, 738.
54   Ibid.

Further, in referring to both Lenin and Lukács, Lacan does not simply suggest that class-consciousness and revolutionary action are false answers but that they are insufficient because the subject of value and the truth as cause both imply a radical decentralisation of history, which undermines the idea of the progress of consciousness. This critical point is best summarised in the *Communist Manifesto*, in which history is not defined as the History of Class Struggle, which would still refer to a transhistoric One, but as a history of struggles, a *history of negativity*. The multiplicity of struggles leaves no doubt that class struggle is not historically invariant, nor is the capitalist class struggle a simple continuation of previous struggles but their resolution. Consequently, class struggle as the name for the real of history cannot support its centralisation, as it unmasks teleological movement as fiction. That the unmasking of the inexistence of History does not anticipate the postmodernist cliché of the end of grand narratives becomes most evident in the change of the class struggle from feudalism to capitalism, which contains a kind of crystallisation and radicalisation, as only in capitalism the class struggle assumes the form of the conflict between two classes:

> Our epoch, the epoch of the bourgeoisie, possesses, however, this distinct feature: it has simplified the class antagonisms. Society as a whole is more and more splitting up into two great hostile camps, into two great classes directly facing each other: Bourgeoisie and Proletariat.[55]

It may seem unusual that Marx sees in capitalism a simplification of class struggle, since commodity fetishism is its perfect distortion and repression. In addition, this simplification does not mean that capitalism has revealed some essential truth of previous struggles: quite the contrary, class struggle has no positive existence and cannot be thought independently of its historical deformations, which are bound to different social relations and their fetishisation. The class struggle may distort appearances and the ideological constructions that foreclose its truth, but it is itself equally distorted by the fetishist semblance. The entire consistency of class struggle is contained in this twofold distortion, and in this respect it assumes the same status as the unconscious. It stands for the very distortion of history, which, through its symptomatic formations, reveals the dysfunction of the social link.[56] To

---

55   Marx, *Selected Writings*, 246.
56   I rely here on M. Dolar, *Prozopopeja*, Ljubljana: Analecta 2006, 85.

extend Lacan's claim: the unconscious and class struggle both assume a pre-ontological status. Once introduced, no attempt in ontology can avoid their implications for the science of being. Also, after Marx and Freud, no radical politics can ignore the function of the symptom, which brings together the proletarian and the subject of the unconscious.

In his later teaching, Lacan extended Marx's invention of the symptom from the question of truth to the problem of *jouissance*, which became the crucial problem of psychoanalysis. In this shift, Lacan noted a possible difference between Marx and Freud:

> I define the symptom as the way everyone enjoys in the unconscious as far the unconscious determines it. The origin of the notion of the symptom should not be sought in Hippocrates but in Marx, in the link he first makes between capitalism and what? The good old days, what we call feudalism. Capitalism is considered to have all in all beneficial effects because its advantage consists in the fact that it reduces the proletarian to nothing, thanks to which he realises the essence of man, after he is deprived of everything and becomes the messiah of the future. This is the way Marx analyses the symptom. Of course he lines up other symptoms but the relation of this with a belief in man is undeniable. If we stop making man the bearer of a future ideal, if we determine him in every case with the particularity of his unconscious and with the way in which he enjoys in it, the symptom stays where Marx has placed it, but assumes a different meaning. No longer a social symptom, but a particular symptom.[57]

Talking of the displacement from the social symptom to the particular symptom makes the later Lacan sound postmodern, negating every possibility of the universal, and the main obstacle to this universalism is precisely *jouissance*, which points back to the irreducible singularity of the unconscious. However, is this really what Lacan argues? Does he not argue, on the contrary, that only the abolition of the faith in man and in the teleological understanding of history reveals the actual place where Marx situated the proletarian and Freud the subject of the unconscious? Lacan adopted the differentiation between two figures of Marx. The humanist Marx does not conceal his belief in man, and for him the proletarian is still the bearer of a political ideal that envisages social relations

---

57   J. Lacan, 'Séminaire du 18 fevrier 1975', in: *Ornicar?*, 4, Paris: Le Graphe, 1975, 105–6.

without alienation. However, the mature Marx grounded his critique of political economy precisely on the shift that unites the social symptom and the particular symptom. The proletariat is a particular type of the universal, a singular universal, which stands opposite to the abstract and false universalism of the general equivalent and the commodity form. The truth represented by the symptom exposes the materiality of alienation, which also highlights the way everyone enjoys in the unconscious, as far as the production of *jouissance* is determined by the autonomy of the signifier, in the given historical moment, the articulation of labour-power and surplus-value. For this reason, the proletariat cannot be simply identified with the essence of man but is a marker of the fact that capitalism merely imposes an abstract social truth. This is the point of Marx's analysis of the capitalist transformation of labour that Lacan's critique of the humanist Marx neglects to mention. The critique of political economy presupposes the death of man and not the belief in man, and in this respect Foucault, too, was wrong to limit Marx's critique to the nineteenth-century *episteme*.[58] On the contrary, Marx's critique logically anticipates the structuralist project, which strived to bring about the repetition of the modern scientific revolution in the field of language, thinking and society.

The invention of the symptom is possible only after capitalism has changed the regime of social abstractions, which introduced a new form of class struggle. In other words, the invention of the symptom is possible only in the regime of abstract freedom and equality. In *Capital*, Marx reveals a specific deadlock in this universalism, which again addresses the tension between the fetishist appearance and the symptomatic truth:

> The wage-form thus extinguishes every trace of the division of the working day into necessary labour and surplus labour, into paid labour and unpaid labour. All labour appears as paid labour. Under the *corvée* system it is different. There the labour of the serf for himself, and his compulsory labour for the lord of the land, are demarcated very clearly both in space and time. In slave labour, even the part of the working day in which the slave is only replacing the value of his own means of subsistence, in which he therefore actually works for himself alone, appears as labour for his master. All his labour appears as unpaid labour. In wage-labour, on the contrary, even surplus labour, or unpaid labour, appears as paid, In the one

---

58   Foucault, *Les mots et les choses*, 274.

case, the property-relation conceals the slave's labour for himself; in the other case the money-relation conceals the uncompensated labour of the wage labourer.[59]

Neither the ancient slave nor the feudal serf can appear as a social symptom because such appearance demands the abstract universality of the commodity form. Commodity fetishism subordinates all social relations to the economic contract, which departs from freedom and equality, whose abstract range and character is determined by property (the buying and selling of labour-power) and the pursuit of private interest (profit, means of subsistence). This foundation of politics on abstractions that are articulated through exchange replaces the past fetishisations of social relations, the foundation of politics on transference, or the politics of *philia* (love).

The foundation of the social link on *philia* as the paradigm of relation is most explicit in Aristotle, where the hypothesis of the social relation is grounded on friendship, which supports three possible constitutions, monarchy, aristocracy and timocracy, while the lack of *philia* gives ground for three social perversions: tyranny, oligarchy and democracy. In a famous passage, Aristotle compares these constitutions, respectively, to man's love for his children, man's love for his wife, and finally brotherly love. In this description, the slave appears at the point where Aristotle seems to encounter the social symptom. Defined as a living tool, the slave cannot be the subject of *philia*, he cannot be loved, nor can he love in return. Aristotle's definition is supported by the idea that the slave's body and his being overlap. The slave *qua* tool does not *have* a body; he *is* the body, and precisely by not owning his body, he can belong to others, who are foremost masters of their own bodies. Aristotle articulates the kernel of the fetishisation of the slave, but his discussion is countered by the obvious fact that the slave is also a being of *logos*, a speaking and therefore rational being. Consequently, if *philia* is universal, the slave should be loved as well:

> There is no friendship nor justice towards lifeless things. But neither is there friendship towards a horse or an ox, nor to a slave *qua* slave. For there is nothing in common to the two parties; the slave is a living tool and the tool a lifeless slave. *Qua* slave then, one cannot be friends with him. But *qua* man one can; for there seems to be some justice between any man and any other

---

59   Marx, *Capital*, Vol. 1, 680.

who can share in a system of law or be a party to an agreement; therefore there can also be friendship with him in so far as he is a man.[60]

As a living tool, the slave stands outside the social relation, while as a speaking being he is within the pseudo-contractual system that makes him a slave. But because the slave does not embody the way in which *each* individual is constituted as a subject, he cannot appear as a social symptom. The contradiction in Aristotle's discussion concerns the specificity of ancient fetishism, which culminates in the argumentative effort to naturalise slavery.

The difference between the slave and the proletarian first appears in Roman law, where the proletariat is defined as the class whose social contribution consists entirely and exclusively of their body, in the reproduction of their class, thereby creating offspring, future Roman citizens, who will do military service, or give birth to new proletarians. They produce a new population, which will colonise the conquered territories and help spread the empire. From here, Marx will adopt his definition of the modern proletariat as an industrial reserve army, in both meanings of the term: reserve army and unemployed population.[61] However, this already implies an important shift because the Roman proletariat makes its social contribution in a different sense. Since it hardly possesses any property and cannot be taxed as other Roman citizens, its social contribution is identified with its body and its capacity to produce other bodies. The proletarian's body no longer overlaps with its being, so the fetishisation changes. But he, too, cannot become a social symptom for the very same reason as the slave.

At the other end of history, commodity fetishism abolishes the foundation of social relations on the fetishisation of persons. The industrial capitalist does not fetishise the labourer as a producer of value but the product as the embodiment of surplus-value. For this reason, we would need to correct the claim that Marx fetishises the proletariat. In fact he de-fetishises commodity, which then reveals the double status of labour-power in the commodity universe. In any case, the necessary condition for Marx's invention of the symptom lies in the rootedness of fetishisation exclusively in the abstract universality of the general equivalent. Only in

---

60   *Eth. Nic.* 1161b 1–7. See *The Complete Works of Aristotle*, 1835.
61   Fredric Jameson therefore described *Capital* as a work on unemployment. See F. Jameson, *Representing Capital*, London: Verso, 2010, 2.

capitalism do we encounter the conditions for the articulation of universal-ism and of the social symptom, which makes the proletarian appear as a free subject.[62]

Finally, Lacan's discussion of Marx's invention of the symptom empha-sises that the symptom introduces an epistemological break with medicine. In its understanding of the notion, medicine still departs from what it recognises as the normal functioning of the body. The symptom would signal the corruption of equilibrium, which supports the preservation and the survival of an organism. In his tendency towards a scientific foundation of the unconscious, Freud adopted this model for explaining the function-ing of the mental apparatus. But already the first symptom he dealt with sabotaged this attempt. In an early discussion of hysteria, Freud makes the following observation:

> I, on the contrary, assert that the lesion in hysterical paralyses must be completely independent of the anatomy of the nervous system, since *in its paralyses and other manifestations hysteria behaves as though anatomy did not exist, or as though it had no knowledge of it.*[63]

The symptom rejects scientific knowledge, and hysteria does not want to know anything about anatomy. The discovery of the unconscious amounts to the introduction of 'enjoying substance', as Lacan puts it, a substance irreducible to *res extensa* and to *res cogitans*, the empirical materiality of the body and the subject of cognition, which is everything that the scientific discourse can admit, without encountering its own inconsistency. The hysteric symptom, by contrast, is objectivity and materiality that entirely depends on the causality of the signifier. When Freud reads the symptom in

---

62   'For the transformation of money into capital, therefore, the owner of money must meet in the market the free labourer, free in the double sense, that as a free man he can dispose of his labour-power as his own commodity, and that, on the other hand he has no other commodity for sale, i.e., he is rid of them, he is free of all the objects needed for the realisation of his labour-power' (Marx, *Capital*, Vol. 1, 272–3, translation modified). We find here all the key abstractions that support the invention of the symptom: the transformation of money into capital, the free individual, i.e., the abstract legal subject, *homo legalis*, who is also the economic man, *homo oeconomicus*, and finally labour-power, which results from the transformation of the market into a market of labour. In this economic encounter, both parties are presumed to form a just and symmetric relation, with no disturbance involved.

63   Freud, *Standard Edition*, Vol. 1, 169 (Freud's emphasis).

relation to symbolism, he necessarily encounters its social value. The hysteric is no less a social symptom, and Freud's later insisting that there is something like a cultural discontent implies that the particular symptom cannot be detached from the social structures and that, strictly speaking, there is no such thing as private symptom, no symptom that would not be supported by the same structure as the social link.

Medicine uses the symptom in order to produce knowledge that comprises both diagnostics and the prognostics. The symptom enables the detection of the illness and its future prevention. For Marx and Freud, the symptom has a merely diagnostic import, because it no longer refers to the production of knowledge but to the unveiling of the truth of the actually existing social relations. More precisely, the symptom for both addresses an underlying inexistence:

> Inexistence is the very consistency of the symptom since this expression, which appeared with Marx, obtained its value. In the principle of the symptom is the inexistence of truth, which the symptom presupposes, despite marking its place. The symptom attaches itself to a truth that no longer works. We can therefore say that none of you are foreign to this form of answer, just as no one else is who exists in the modern age.[64]

Lacan's theory of discourses, which finally systematises the homology between Marx and Freud, proposes a formal and a critical tool to think the material consequences of this inexistence and examines the various aspects of discursive change from a structural point of view. The theory of discourses is indeed a structuralist theory of revolution, which unites the epistemological and the political signification of the term and thereby contains an effort to think together the structural and the historical dynamic.

---

64   J. Lacan, *Le Séminaire, livre XIX, . . . ou pire*, Paris: Éditions du Seuil, 2011, 52.

CHAPTER 4

What Is the Capitalist Discourse?

MARX AND THE THEORY OF DISCOURSES

Marx's analysis of the commodity form and its anticipation of the autonomy of the signifier gives way to a materialist reorientation of ontology
that questions the two Parmenidian axioms that initiated philosophy:
the sameness of thinking and being and the univocity of being. Following
this line, Alfred Sohn-Rethel famously suggested that modern ontological categories are correlative to capitalist abstractions, and he went
even so far as to condition the historic emergence of systematic thinking – philosophy and mathematics – with the economic exchange and
the introduction of the general equivalent.[1] Whether we subscribe to
Sohn-Rethel's thesis or not, the commodity form most certainly touches
a fundamental speculative question concerning the ontological status of
discursive production – capitalist as well as technological, mathematical and linguistic objects – and the way structural relations complicate
the presumed sameness of thinking and being. The Lacanian-Marxist
take on the problematic would perform an additional turn in Sohn-
Rethel's perspective: not simply reducing ontological categories to
economic abstractions but circumscribing the ontological theses that
are implicitly articulated in the theories and actions of political economy. The model for such an undertaking is again Marx's critique of
fetishism, which most openly exposes the ontological and even the
onto-theological aspiration of economic theories. The rootedness of
economic knowledge in the fantasy of self-engendering value leaves the
structural relations unthematised, removing their immanent deadlocks
from the picture. For this reason, political economy is a pseudoscience,
standing closer to alchemy and astrology rather than chemistry and

---

1   See, for instance, A. Sohn-Rethel, *Geistige und körperliche Arbeit*, Frankfurt
am Main: Suhrkamp Verlag, 1973, 96–7.

astronomy.[2] A theory of relations of production, however, not only reintroduces the rejected problematic of the structural non-relation, which
drives the capitalist mode of production, but in the same move proposes
a critical epistemology and a materialist ontology of discursive
consequences.

Let us recall the minimal common ground of the critique of political
economy and that of psychoanalysis. Marx and Freud both insisted that
the symbolic networks operate beyond consciousness and are endowed
with causality, the power to work back on conscious subjects. Their
autonomy involves two main consequences: a subject, whose being
comes down to non-identity and loss, and a surplus-object, whose being
is marked by intensification or increase. The immediate result is an
underlying asymmetry between the lack-in-being and the surplus-in-
being. This is the critical point of departure for the Freudian and the
Marxian displacement of the ontological problematic. Once the
discourse is theorised in a materialist way – as autonomous and effective – being turns out to be marked by instability and contradiction,
split between decrease and increase. It is not surprising that Marx and
Freud find in the energetic notion of entropy the crucial scientific reference in order to theorise this structural imbalance.

Lacan pursued this line throughout his teaching. The subject's
dependency on the signifier marks being with metonymy, in which the
emergence of the subject exchanges with its disappearance in the chain
of differences. Once the philosophical question of being is reformu-
lated, 'the gap of the unconscious may be said to be *pre-ontological*'[3] in
the double sense that it determines the subject's mode of being and that
it becomes a precondition of ontology, once the autonomy of the signifier has become the object of inquiry in at least three revolutionary
human sciences (the critique of political economy, psychoanalysis and
structural linguistics).

The production of the surplus-object addresses the flip side of this
subjective drama. Through its analysis, Marx questions another philosophical classicism, the ancient division between *praxis,* the activity of
free men aiming at perfection and self-realisation, and *poiesis,* the activity
of slaves constrained by natural laws and material conditions, hence

---

2   'So far no chemist has ever discovered exchange-value either in a pearl or a
diamond' (Marx, *Capital*, Vol. 1, 177).

3   Lacan, *The Four Fundamental Concepts of Psychoanalysis*, 29.

action rooted in freedom and action out of necessity. The true accomplishment of Marx's critique consists in the abolition of this distinction.[4] Their contiguity affects the highest form of human production, *theoria*, the production of concepts and knowledge.

Marx's critique of *theoria* turns around the *equivocity* of commodities which is stated in nearly all the introductory lines in the first chapter of *Capital*:

> A commodity is, *first of all*, an external object . . . *Initially* the commodity appeared to us as an object with a dual character, possessing both use-value and exchange-value . . . they only *appear* as commodities, or have the form of commodities, in so far as they possess a double form, i.e., natural form and value form . . . A commodity appears *at first sight* an extremely obvious, trivial thing. But its analysis brings out that it is a very strange thing, abounding in metaphysical subtleties and theological niceties.[5]

Marx inverts the classical metaphysical strategy, say Aristotle, who departs from the equivocity of being in order to establish its univocity through the system of categories. Commodity, by contrast, appears univocal, but the split between use-value (empirical materiality) and exchange-value (discursive materiality) reveals that the production is internally doubled. The lesson of the double character of commodity reaches beyond the framework of the capitalist problematic and echoes the ancient scandal of sophistry, whose rhetorical techniques demonstrated language is not merely a 'house of being'[6] but a particular *factory* that produces within being more being. The shared discovery of Marx and Freud, however, consists in the fact that this production also contains *more than being*, objects that are irreducible to the opposition of being and non-being, precisely surplus-value and surplus-*jouissance*.

The shift to discursive production retrospectively uncovered the double historical foundation of ontology, pitting Heraclitus against Parmenides, movement against rest, materialism against idealism. The crucial aspect of this opposition concerned the claim that the signifier is an essential part of the question of being. Lacan's later quarrel with philosophy was therefore focused around the '*jouissance* of being', the inclusion of production in the

---

4   E. Balibar, *Marx's Philosophy*, London: Verso, 2007, 40–1.
5   Marx, *Capital*, Vol. 1, 125, 131, 138, 163 (my emphasis).
6   M. Heidegger, *Wegmarken*, Frankfurt: Klostermann, 2004, 333.

register of ontological inquiries. As already noted, this *Materialismusstreit* echoes in the historical foundations of ontology:

> I fail to see in what sense I am stooping to the ideals of materialism . . . when I identify the reason for the being of signifierness in *jouissance*, *jouissance* of the body. But, you see, a body hasn't seemed materialistic enough since Democritus . . . In fact, the atom is simply an element of flying signifierness . . . it is extremely difficult to make it work out right when one retains only what makes the element an element, namely, the fact that it is unique, whereas one should introduce the other a little bit, namely, difference.[7]

Democritus was the first one to problematise the univocity of matter. The introduction of the atom, this 'radical real', as Lacan claimed on another occasion, distinguishes the materiality of composed bodies and the materiality of the elements, which should be conceived not through their uniqueness but through their relation. The first orientation remains caught in vulgar materialism, where the materiality of atoms remains unquestioned and empirical, while the introduction of difference and metonymy ('flying signifierness') grounds an orientation that theorises the materiality of structural relations and exposes the equivocity of matter: the very same equivocity that returns through the examination of the linguistic structure and the causality of the signifier. In equivocity, meaning and *jouissance* overlap, and through this overlapping the autonomy of discursive production undermines the philosophical hypothesis of the univocity of being. No surprise then that, at the background of this materialist orientation, Lacan recalled the initial tension in philosophy:

> The fact that thought moves in the direction of a science only by being attributed to thinking – in other words, the fact that being is presumed to think – is what founds the philosophical tradition starting from Parmenides. Parmenides was wrong and Heraclitus was right. That is clinched by the fact that, in fragment 93, Heraclitus enunciates . . . 'he neither avows nor hides, he signifies' – putting back in its place the discourse of the powerful – . . . 'the prince' – in other words, the powerful – 'who prophesizes in Delphi'.[8]

---

7   Lacan, *Encore*, 67.
8   Ibid., 103. Translation modified.

The Parmenidian founding axiom of ontology matters less than the Heraclitian Prince, the master, and even the master's discourse (the identification of ontology with the master's discourse is a constant in Lacan's later teaching), which departs from the non-identity and the equivocity of the signifier. The Parmenidian axiom, however, contains a double identity, besides that of thinking and being also the self-identity of thinking: the thinking of thinking that is, according to Aristotle, actualised in metaphysics. Modernity transformed this transparency of thinking into the subject of cognition, and into *homo oeconomicus*, the identity of private interest with the positive knowledge of this interest.

Marx's rejection of the political-economic fantasies of social homeostasis and market providence significantly directed Lacan's attempt to formalise the contradictions of the autonomy of the signifier. They both start from the inversion of the spontaneous philosophy of political economy, best summarised in the controversial Thatcher axiom: 'There is no such thing as society'. The statement targets Marx's discovery that social reality is traversed by class struggles and that consequently society is essentially grounded on the inexistence of social relation. Liberalism and neoliberalism, however, claim that there is *only* social relation, precisely the social relation that Marx summarises in the four cornerstones of the capitalist worldview. 'There is the social relation' is the unpronounced corollary of the neoliberal slogan 'There is no such thing as society'.[9]

Lacan's theory of discourses is thus an attempt to formalise the inexistence of social relation and its material consequences. The term 'discourse' underwent a significant development throughout Lacan's teaching. At first synonymous to speech, it later quite openly translated Marx's 'mode of production'. Recall that the homology of surplus-value and surplus-*jouissance* determined two heterogeneous but interrelated axes in the

---

9 In the field of *scientia sexualis*, to use Foucault's expression, we encounter a similar claim regarding sexuality. Is the cultural and scientific resistance against psychoanalysis not a resistance against the conception of sexuality without an underlying and normative sexual relation? The claim 'There is sexual relation' perfectly matches the attempts to reduce sexuality to biology, a reductionism that is shared by scientific positivism and religious dogmatism. It is amusing to observe how religion grounds its objections to same-sex marriages and to redefinitions of the family on biological determinism and the vulgar materialism of the univocity of sex and gender, hence precisely on the postulate of a positive existence of sexual relation, albeit without sexuality – for sexuality is anything but reproduction.

autonomy of the signifier: (1) the axis of representation, comprising the relation between the signifiers and the subject and recapitulated in Lacan's definition of the signifier ('the signifier is what represents a subject to another signifier'); and (2) the axis of production, addressing the relation between the signifiers and the object and elaborated through a structural reading of Marx's deduction of surplus-value.

The structure comes down to a parallax: from the position of the surplus-object it appears that values and signifiers interact without any reference to the subject. The contemporary fascination with the absolute autonomy of fictitious capital and the psychoanalytic thesis on the 'autism of *jouissance*' or the 'generalised perversion' privilege this position. From the position of the subject, however, signifiers seem to be evacuated of *jouissance*, and the subject appears to be deprived of the surplus-product. With this parallax in mind, we can observe that Marx's critique of political economy assumes neither the position of the subject, which still marked his humanist accounts of alienation, nor the position of the object, from which political economy articulates its fetishist theories of value. Critique assumes the impossible position of the parallax, which is expressed in the coexistence of the corrected labour theory of value and the dialectic of fetishism.

We should again recall that, during his earlier teaching, Lacan privileged the antagonistic relation between the signifier and *jouissance*, in which the former entails a 'mortification' of the latter. The parallax of representation and production, formalised in the theory of discourses, finally resolves the question: how do both processes intertwine? They stand in a topological relation of simultaneous continuity and rupture, which additionally contextualises the discrepancy between appearance and structural relations that Marx traced throughout his critical work. The break in question is resumed in the following diagram of the social link:

Image 2. The Discursive Relations

The square indicates the relations that are operative in both processes and can be decomposed into two triangles, the triangle of representation (left) and the triangle of production (right).[10] Based on the logic of the signifier, the four elements of the social link are named the master-signifier (S_1), knowledge or the battery of signifiers (S_2), the subject of representation ($\$$) and the object of production (a). As we know, the elements are embedded in circulation, which enables the deduction of three other structures on the background of the general logic and topology of the signifier.

For the four discursive places, Lacan proposed different nominations, which can be provisionally called Marxian and Freudian, depending on the notions deployed in their nomination. The first and most recurrent nomination is proposed in *Radiophonie* and in *Seminar XVII*, and repeated three years later in *Seminar XX*:

Agent	Labour
-------	-------
Truth	Product

This nomination openly addresses Marx's correction of the labour theory of value and the invention of the social symptom, the proletarian, which assumes the position of truth, the same place where Lacan situates the subject of the unconscious. The relations in the discursive square (Image 2) are no less important because they indicate that truth is the place of a constitutive split, the realisation of the autonomy of differences.

Seminar XVII proposes yet another nomination, which aims at the lessons of Freud's labour theory of the unconscious:

Desire	Other
-------	------
Truth	Loss

On this second nomination, Lacan reminds his audience that it dates back to the time when he defined the subject's desire as desire of the Other. Alienation

---

10   Here the formalisation visualises the inexistence of the social relation. The connection between formalisation and inexistence can again be traced back to Marx's *Capital*, which already attempts a formalisation of the capitalist discourse in the relation between the two heterogeneous circulations: C – M – C (Marx's version of the axis of representation) and M – C – M' (Marx's version of the axis of production).

is now openly identified with the structure of the social link, and in regard to the four discourses that follow from the rotation of elements (Image 3) it also shows four possible faces, depending on which element occupies the position of truth. In the master's discourse, alienation concerns the subject/ labour-power, represented between two signifiers/values and mobilised in order to work for the satisfaction of the 'unconscious capitalist'. In the university discourse, alienation concerns the master-signifier, revealing that it is pure difference to another signifier but also an empty and insatiable imperative of production. In the hysteric discourse, alienation assumes the form of the object a, which now unveils its metonymic status and can be recognised as the element around which the insatiability of demand is articulated. Finally, in the analytic discourse, alienation assumes the form of the unconscious, knowledge that does not know itself but is nevertheless put to work in the production process. With this shift, the analytic discourse stands at the opposite end of the master's discourse and is even its inversion. Its critical value consists in the fact that it determines the root of the given relations of domination and initiates the production of a new master-signifier, which could potentially ground a new social link. This logic is not foreign to Marx, whose critique of political economy equally turned around the production of a new political master-signifier, which would announce the possibility of a social order, in which the foundation of social links on the imperatives of capital and the private interests of the capitalist class would be abolished. Was Marx an analyst of the proletariat?

A crucial factor for Lacan's systematic inclusion of production in the already elaborated logic of representation was May '68. While for some observers these events demonstrated that structuralism encountered its limits in the notion of the event,[11] Lacan proposed a conception of discourse that stands for a 'structure that walks in the streets', rejecting the opposition between the structure and the event. Structure is less about stable and necessary relations than about contingency and contradiction, and the privileged name for this structural articulation of contradiction is no other than revolution, albeit in the epistemological meaning of the term: circular movement, which contains an immanent distortion.[12] Hence Lacan's

---

11   Such was, for instance, Foucault's claim in a famous interview with Alessandro Fontana and Pasquale Pasquino from 1976. See Foucault, *Dits et écrits*, 2, 144–5.

12   The model of such revolution is Kepler's mathematisation of elliptical movement that Lacan refers to on several occasions, most systematically in 'L'étourdit' (*Autres écrits*, 421–2).

reservation towards revolutionary enthusiasm, which in his view marginal-
ises the structural aspect of revolution and its unpredictable or unwanted
outcome (like in the case of the Soviet Union that Lacan refers to in his
confrontation with the revolutionary students). The theory of discourses
will evolve around the discursive shift, with which Lacan strived to account
for the disruptive nature of May '68 and even more so for the failure of its
agents to accomplish a transition towards the communist social order. This
and nothing else was what Lacan aimed at when he compared the students
with hysterics who demand a new master: a new master-signifier, which
would replace the structuration of social links around the imperatives of
capital.

The structural disclosure supports the deduction of three discourses,
which depart from the logic of the signifier, now called the master's
discourse:

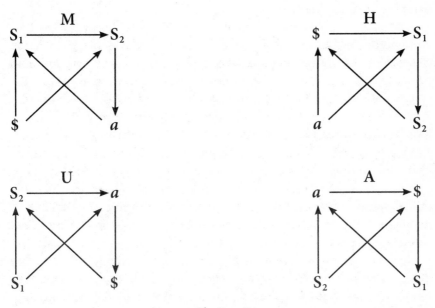

Image 3. The Four Discourses

The vectors that connect the elements and their places indicate that the
discourse is internally broken (Lacan's notion of non-all describes this
disclosure). All discourses are grounded on a 'weak logic', which leaves
room for 'imperfections'[13] actualised in the form of – epistemological,

---

13   See Lacan, *The Other Side of Psychoanalysis*, 207.

political, traumatic and other – events. The discursive logic consequently provides a *minimum of consistency* by constituting the subjective and social reality while simultaneously introducing in this reality a *maximum of instability* that manifests through the formation of symptoms, crises or revolutions. It is no coincidence that the link between this weak logic and the social uprisings, consistency and instability was addressed at one of the symbolic sites of the student movement in France: University Paris VIII. The street and the university become two privileged sites where the action of structures can be observed. The theory of discourses proposes a redefinition of structuralism in a moment when it is already declared defeated or even buried. Structuralism now designates more than a mere science of language. It stands for a science of the structural real, extending the notion of structure from linguistics to other sciences and continuing to pursue a repetition of the modern scientific revolution in the field of 'human objects' (language, labour, thinking).

The master's discourse – the logic of the signifier – provides the four elements that compose a social link and determines the topological relation between representation and production as well as the order according to which the elements relate to each other. The discursive shift reveals the compatibility between different discourses, depending on which articulation of elements follows from which shift. The quarter turn supports direct passage from the master's discourse to two other formations, the hysteric and the university. This immediacy signals that both transformations, far from overcoming the master's discourse, provide its developments: a 'regression' or radicalisation in the university discourse, in which the master-signifier assumes the position of truth, and 'progress' or destabilisation in the hysteric's discourse, in which the truth concerning the produced surplus-object is revealed. Departing from the function of the symptom, the hysteric's discourse questions the master and thereby reveals the truth of the relations of production. The vectors between the discursive elements, however, show that the hysteric's discourse preserves the same relation between the master-signifier and surplus-object as the master's discourse. What it alters is the product, which is now knowledge. The revolutionary discourse comprises a hysteric dimension, as far as it produces knowledge – theory of value – which places the truth of the 'wealth of nations' in the extraction of surplus labour from labour-power. The right side of the formula, the master-signifier above knowledge, suggests that Marx's questioning of the capitalist in the name and from the position of the proletarian produces knowledge of the capitalist mode of production. Finally, the discursive circulation shows that the knowledge produced in the confrontation between capital and labour-power joins the proletarian – it is the *labour* theory of value and represents the epistemological ground of revolu.tionary or emancipatory politics. Was Marx a hysteric?

Another exemplification of the relation between the master's and the hysteric's discourse lies in the transformation of the epistemological status of hysteria through psychoanalysis. Before becoming the subject of the 'talking cure' hysteria was considered a limit of medical knowledge and was treated with obscure techniques, such as hypnosis, hydrotherapy and electroshocks. Simultaneously, the enigma of the hysterical symptom, its ambiguous status between the physiological and the psychological, gave rise to an entire industry of knowledge. Freud's predecessors, from Charcot to Breuer laboured to solve the hysterical enigma. In his contributions to the *Studies on Hysteria*, Breuer for instance produced a theory of the so-called hypnoid states and speculated on the physiological aspects of hysteria, bashfully avoiding the sexual aetiology and the theory of symbolisation proposed by Freud. The *Studies* themselves remain an important historical document of two thoroughly incompatible approaches to hysteria, the declining pseudoscientific hypnotism and the emerging psychoanalysis. While for hypnotism the hysteric symptom remained ignorant and numb, Freud addressed it as a discursive formation, endowed with the power of speech, and a form of knowledge that may not know itself but still assumes the articulated form of signifiers. Freud thereby demonstrated two ways of producing the fourth discourse: by departing from the hysteric discourse (the patient's speech) or the university discourse (the critique of knowledge, in this case of Breuer); or by directly inverting the master's discourse (hypnotism), starting from the repressed moment of Breuer's analysis of Anna O. (Bertha Pappenheim), the transference, in which the analyst is reduced to the object of desire. Lacan consequently defined psychoanalysis as the *envers* of the master's discourse: the analytic discourse is the only one that produces the complete inversion of the relations of domination, thus standing both inside and outside, on the border of the dominating mode of production.

There is another compatibility between Marx and the theory of discourses. In the discourses we can discern four possible forms of fetishisation that are, in one way or another, linked to labour. In the master's discourse, the dominating appearance is that the master does the labour. Marx addresses this appearance through the critique of commodity fetishism that obfuscates the relation between value and labour-power. The dominating appearance is that capital automatically creates value, and this structural appearance echoes in the false identification of money with the master-signifier, which repeats the fetishist 'money labours'. In the hysteric discourse, it appears that labour comes from the subject. Let us take again the relation between Breuer and his patient. The process of treatment amounted in the production of knowledge, but it was Breuer and not Anna O. who produced it: the patient addressed Breuer as the subject supposed to know, and his theory of hypnoid states was the response to this 'interpellation'. In the university discourse, knowledge appears as the labourer, but the actual labour is accomplished by surplus-value, which in Marx's analysis of technology appears in its true form, unpaid surplus labour, and in Lacan's critique of the university as the student. Finally, in the analytic discourse it seems that labour is done by the surplus-object, now embodied by the analyst, but the actual labour (free association) takes place in the patient's unconscious, while the analyst's task is to disrupt the speech at critical points, when the associative production amounts to a master-signifier, which determines the analysand's relation to *jouissance*.

The theory of discourses is not meant to provide a timeless theory of social links without relation to the present moment, nor is it alien to the historical development of capitalism. When Lacan presented it to the revolutionary students of Paris VIII, he claimed that his theory aims to situate the target of their revolts, the logical and the structural opponent. However, the development of his theory contains a complication, since Lacan proposed three different formalisations of capitalism. The homology of surplus-value and surplus-*jouissance* identifies it with the master's discourse, but already one year later Lacan declares the master's discourse to be the oldest, precisely because it stands for the logic of the signifier, for which it would be absurd to claim that it is historically conditioned by capitalism. The social dimension of the master's discourse is no longer discussed exclusively through the relation between the capitalist and the proletarian but between the ancient master and the slave, in reference to Plato's *Menon*, and between the feudal lord and the serf, through Hegel's *Phenomenology of Spirit*. Lacan traces the historical metamorphoses of the master figure, which ends in its capitalist liberation from concrete embodiments and which is intensified by the foundation of social links on the fetishisation of things rather than on the fetishisation of persons. This liberation of the master, the flip side of what Marx's discussion of technology called the liberation of labour from its content – including the labourer – implies a ground-breaking discursive shift, which introduces the modern form of domination, the university discourse, in which the master is decentralised and brought to the highest point of abstraction. The old master's discourse, which can still be associated with the early stages of industrial revolution, seems to describe the 'old spirit of capitalism', while the scientific progress and the developed forms of capitalism imply an anonymous and headless master.

From the Master's Discourse to the University Discourse

When Lacan attempted to theorise the consequences of May '68, he started with the university reform, with which de Gaulle's government responded to the demands of the students. Here a symptom of a more general function of knowledge in capitalism could be detected, its mobilisation as a means of fabrication of the capitalist form of subjectivity, as the formula of the university discourse indicates. Lacan took the alliance of workers and students seriously, claiming that the student's task within the system consists in progressively assuming the position of the 'subject of science'. However, in the capitalist universe, this subject knows only the commodity form, which turns it into a quantifiable and measurable labour-power.

Given this production, it seems logical that the revolutionary students identified with the proletariat. Lacan, however, corrected their intuition: 'If they search on that side, they may find that with my little schemas they can find a way of justifying that the student is not displaced in feeling a brother, as they say, not of the proletariat but of the lumpenproletariat.'[14] The students thus form a heterogeneous, passive and disorganised group, not the position of the subject of value but that of the object, which still needs to become the labourer (see Image 3). In their revolts, they were not aware of the actual role they play in the reproduction of capitalism: 'And the first to collaborate with this, right here at Vincennes, are you, for you fulfil the role of helots of this regime. You don't know what that means either? The regime is putting you on display. It says: "Look at them enjoying!"'[15] Lacan again draws the attention to the objectification of students (the vector $S_2 \rightarrow a$), whereby he highlights the function of surplus-*jouissance* that pertains to the object *a*. Combining the Marxist and the psychoanalytic perspective, we can conclude that the student is both the social embodiment of

---

14   Ibid., 190.
15   Ibid., 208.

surplus-*jouissance* and of surplus labour. But why is he now compared to the helot? In ancient Greece, helots were a particular social class that consisted of subjugated populations of the territories occupied by Spartans.[16] Their actual social situation was very much comparable to slaves, with the exception that they were not bought and sold. Once conquered, they were forced into labour for the free citizens of Sparta and could be mistreated and killed without persecution, precisely because they were not considered property, unlike the slaves. With this characterisation, Lacan makes a rather unusual move, because he implicitly draws an analogy between the ancient helots and the capitalist lumpenproletariat, both of them being the wretched of the world, social outcasts, which can be mistreated because they are considered to be subjects of *jouissance*, objects, which are forced to carry out surplus labour. The students are comparable to the helot and the lumpenproletariat, as far as they are also fetishised as subjects of *jouissance*, but this is where the parallel ends. For unlike the other two historical figures of the subject of *jouissance*, the students are obliged to engage in a formative process, to work on themselves in order to become the subject of value and enter the 'market of knowledge'.[17] In this formative process, Lacan envisages the main link between capitalism and the university, and more generally between capitalism and science.

In autumn 1968, the experimental university centre, soon thereafter named University Paris VIII, was created in Vincennes, the unconventional character of which was a *novum* in continental Europe. Its experimental side consisted in interdisciplinary programmes, but the actual novelty was the credit-point system, which adopted the Anglo-American model of the valorisation of knowledge. The French expression for credit points, *unité de valeur*, unit of value, stands at the centre of Lacan's attempt to tackle the shift that structured the old continental university, whose model was the Humboldt University in Berlin, in accordance with the capitalist market: 'The credit-point, the little piece of paper that they want to issue you, is precisely this. It is the sign of what knowledge will progressively become in this market that one calls the University.'[18] The transformation of the university into an enterprise certainly signals the commodification of knowledge, but this is not the

---

16   In the historical contextualisation of the helot I rely on *Encyclopaedia Brittanica* (online version).

17   Lacan, *D'un Autre à l'autre*, 39.

18   Ibid., 42.

object of Lacan's concern. Behind it stands a more fundamental shift in the relation between knowledge and power, which dates further back into history. As already said, Lacan's formula of the university discourse envisages the structural compatibility of capitalism and science, the foundation of capitalist power relations – what Foucault called power-knowledge – on the social implementation of the modern *episteme*, which amounts to the production of capitalist subjectivity. Lacan's placement of the subject in the position of the product signifies both the scientific isolation of labour-power in natural bodies and the consequent quantification of subjectivity, as well as the political-economic fabrication of *homo oeconomicus,* no less a product of the social implementation of a knowledge rooted in the imperatives of capital. In the end, the truth of the political-economic hypostasis of private interest and social egoism[19] is the abstract interest of capital, the tendency towards permanent self-valorisation. There is, strictly speaking, no private interest; behind every apparent private interest of individuals lies the structural imperative of capital itself.

Subsequent developments have revealed an additional aspect of this total integration of the education system into the reproduction of capitalism. The privatisation of universities amounted to the proliferation of student loans, which immediately turned the education process into production of indebted subjects. From this perspective, the university has become the microcosm of the more general capitalist tendency to ground economy on indebting. The Italian post-workerist philosopher Maurizio Lazzarato recently argued that in financial capitalism the relation between the creditor and the debtor replaced the old antagonistic relation between the capitalist and the labourer.[20] Though this may seem to be the case, one cannot overlook that both are already at work in Marx's reinterpretation of primitive accumulation. Marx shows that appropriation through dispossession, which creates on the one side the owners of capital and on the other side the owners of labour-power, and the historical genesis

---

19 'It is not from the benevolence of the butcher, the brewer, or the baker that we expect our dinner, but from their regard to their own interest. We address ourselves, not to their humanity, but to their self-love, and never talk to them of our own necessities but of their advantages.' A. Smith, *An Inquiry into the Nature and the Causes of the Wealth of Nations,* London: Penguin Books, 1999, 119. Smith places in the very core of social relations that which Freud would call 'human narcissism'.

20 M. Lazzarato, *Gouverner par la dette,* Paris: Les Prairies ordinaires, 2014, 11.

of national debts, which transforms entire populations into indebted nations, are two interdependent faces of the same process, which injects the asymmetry between capital and labour-power in the inequality between the creditor and the debtor, and *vice versa*.

Lacan's discussion of the students' status recalls the central thesis of the political-economic tale of primitive accumulation, according to which the indebted subject is born out of *jouissance*: those who labour stand in debt, which signals their past excessive enjoyment. The formula of the university discourse, too, associates the birth of this indebted and labouring subject with surplus-*jouissance*. What needs to be added here is that the extraction of the subject (labour-power) from *jouissance* presupposes an epistemic intervention, the ordering knowledge. To quote once more the passage where Lacan brings up this point:

> Something changed in the master's discourse at a certain point in history. We are not going to break our backs finding out if it was because of Luther, or Calvin, or some unknown traffic of ships around Genoa, or in the Mediterranean Sea, or anywhere else, for the important point is that on a certain day surplus-*jouissance* became calculable, could be counted, totalized. This is where what is called the accumulation of capital begins.[21]

Primitive accumulation is a logical event that unites three important aspects. First is the already mentioned shift in the relation between power and knowledge. The efficiency of capitalism is grounded on the permanent scientific revolution and innovation (accumulative regime of knowledge) and no longer exclusively on raw power relations like feudalism or slave-holder societies. As an immediate consequence of this shift, the social implementation of modern scientific knowledge rationalises the surplus-object – which antiquity and Christianity still mystified – precisely by making it calculable and countable. This, too, is the achievement of the modern credit system, through which the capitalist social link is grounded on the creation of profit out of indebting. Because of this social transformation, the prosopopoeia of the regime and its advocates could indeed be 'capital owes you nothing',[22] together with the implicit conclusion, 'but you owe yourself to capital', since everyone, as labour-power, assumes the

---

21   Lacan, *The Other Side of Psychoanalysis*, 177.
22   D. Hoens, 'A Subject Staging Its Own Disappearance: A Lacanian Approach to Phantasm and Politics', unpublished paper.

position of the debtor. This is the point of the third aspect of primitive accumulation, the birth of the capitalist subjectivity out of the rationalisation of the surplus-object. As Lacan's formula indicates, the subject has to join knowledge (the vector $\$ \rightarrow S_2$), through which capital exercises its insatiable demands.

The reason why the student's position nonetheless importantly deviates from the ancient helot and the modern lumpenproletariat or, rather, represents their capitalist displacement lies in the specificity of object a. The object a should not be mistaken for other forms of surplus-object that Lacan discussed in the various stages of his teaching related to antiquity (*agalma*) and the middle ages (*das Ding*), since they presuppose entirely different social contexts. The mathematisation of surplus is accompanied by the foundation of social links on the fetishisation of the object. Marx made this point by saying that in capitalism the social relations between things replaced relations between men. To repeat, this does not mean that social relations became alienated and mediated through capitalist abstractions. It merely suggests that the fetishisation of objects absorbed the fetishisation of persons. Consequently, Lacan discusses *agalma* and *das Ding* exclusively in relation to the fetishisation of persons in the ancient and the feudal discourse of the master: Alcibiades's fetishisation of Socrates as the master of knowledge (*agalma*) addresses an object in Socrates, a treasure that makes him worthy of desire. The troubadour's fetishisation of the Lady or the serf's fetishisation of the King (*das Ding*) displays a different topological placement of the object. Now the surplus-object is transcendent, an unreachable and sublime entity, which makes of the Lady and the King social embodiments of the Thing. Yet in both cases the surplus is a positive quality, which stands outside the sphere of exchange. Object a, by contrast, is a surplus that emerges out of the system of exchange and becomes the more overwhelmingly present the more it is embedded in quantification and mass production. In capitalism, object a becomes the defining feature of every commodity on the market and makes the exchanged objects appear as vessels of surplus-value.

With the inauguration of the university discourse, the master becomes irreducible to concrete embodiments, inaccessible, invisible and abstract. Unlike the master's discourse, in which the alienated subject occupies the position of truth and is dependent on the master-signifier, in the university discourse the relation between the subject and the master, now transformed into labour-power and capital, is interrupted. The subject joins the apparatus of knowledge that represents it in the production process and is thereby disarmed of its ability to act:

> What is striking, and what no one seems to see, is that from that moment on, by virtue of the fact that the clouds of impotence have been aired, the master signifier only appears even more unassailable, precisely in its impossibility. Where is it? How can it be named? How can it be located – other than through its murderous effects, of course. Denounce imperialism? But how can this little mechanism be stopped?[23]

The university reveals the truth of the master, its headlessness and decentralisation. In other words, when the subject assumes the place of product, resistance to the master turns automatically into a constitutive component in power relations. This is the kernel of the non-relation between the creditor and the debtor, which, to refer again to Lazzarato, neutralises the antagonistic tension in the contradiction between capital and labour-power and introduces a more radicalised and 'abstract' regime of domination, through a multitude of small masters (S_2): bankers, bureaucrats, experts, academic networks, 'professional' politicians and so on, which all exercise the structural imperatives of capital.

Freudo-Marxism and the sexual revolution of the late 1960s and 1970s met this deadlock of decentralised power. Freeing sexuality from cultural censorship and oppression did seem to challenge the old cultural institutions, but it also opened up the terrain for new forms of exploitation and new institutions of repression, which assume the appearance of liberators. The liberal form of the 'repression of sexuality' is repression through commodification, where the antagonistic and non-relational aspect of sexuality (what psychoanalysis calls castration) is removed from the picture. Neoliberal ideologies have indeed adopted the political *parole* of the liberation movements: spontaneity, flexibility and 'multi-stability'. Neoliberalism no less departs from what Foucault criticised as the repressive hypothesis: the market and financial abstractions are said to be endowed with creative potentials, which need to be liberated by creating the political, economic, legal and finally subjective conditions under which the presumed rationality of the market can engender value. The necessary condition for liberating these hypothetical creative potentials is deregulation, austerity and restriction of historically obtained social rights. Spontaneity and vitalism – this is the general spirit of financial capitalism.

The inauguration of this 'new spirit' cannot mean, however, that we are dealing with an entirely new logic of capital but that capitalism has

---

23   Lacan, *The Other Side of Psychoanalysis*, 207.

succeeded to deploy the essence of the master, making the imperatives of capital more rooted in social and subjective reality and its spectral character omnipresent. This development has immediate consequences for labour, which is metonymised to the utmost and pushed into precarious conditions, as the distinction between employment and unemployment is abolished. Herein lies the continuity between the student and the proletarian, in the sense that the student has to engage in the process of self-proletarianisation. The revolutionary students of the 1960s identified with the labourers because they were aware that they shared the same *Unbehagen*, discontent in capitalism, as the labourers: 'The unease of the astudied is, however, not unrelated to the fact that they are nevertheless requested to constitute the subject of science with their own skin.'[24]

The infamous credit point lies at the heart of this process once again: its achievement is 'the reduction of all life to an element of value'.[25] Lacan illustrates this reduction with Pascal's wager, in which he recognises the main feature of modern morality, renunciation of *jouissance* and the emblematic insight into the spirit of capitalism, grounded precisely on the extraction of the surplus-object from this new moral ground. In his fragment on wager, Pascal engages in an imaginary dialogue with a libertine, who questions the existence of God. The wager thereby addresses a double problem: behind the question whether God's existence can be proven or not, there is a more fundamental dilemma: whether there is a God at all. The logical demonstration is counteracted by the logic of gambling and probability. Pascal writes: 'If you win you win everything, if you lose you lose nothing . . . here there is an infinity of infinitely happy life to be won'.[26] By renouncing the life in *jouissance*, the libertarian can gain life in surplus-*jouissance*. This is apitalism at its most speculative. No wonder that Lacan would see in Pascal the most accurate and abbreviated expression of the essence of capitalism. The modern master renounces *jouissance* in profit in order to create more *jouissance*, or, correctly, he demands renunciation from all in order to create profit for some. Marx came to the same conclusion: a 'bad' capitalist wastes his profit for his personal enjoyment or keeps it jealously for himself; he has a naïve understanding of *jouissance*, confusing it with pleasure in spending and consumption, while a 'good' capitalist knows that *jouissance* is

---

24 Ibid., 105.
25 Lacan, *D'un Autre à l'autre*, 18.
26 B. Pascal, *Pensées*, London: Penguin Books, 1995, 123.

irreducible to pleasure, and can only be extracted from risk management, indebting and speculation.

But there is more: what in Pascal seems to be a groundless, unfounded and contingent wager in fact concerns the function of science in the globalisation of capitalism:

> And it is thus that, for a science so well founded on the one hand, and so obviously triumphant on the other . . . things happen that land us on our feet again, and bring us into contact with what follows from the fact that the pure and simple command, that of the master, is substituted at the level of truth. Don't think that the master is always there. It's the command that remains, the categorical imperative, 'Keep on knowing'. There is no longer any need for anybody to be present. We have, as Pascal says, all embarked upon the discourse of science.[27]

In order to wager, no God is needed – the wager, as Pascal persistently repeats, is imperative. The libertine must wager, whether God exists or not. What does this have to do with science and capitalism? In order to wager, precisely science is needed, a science mobilised for the production of 'waste material', for permanent revolution of the means of production and, last but not least, for the mathematisation of probability, which would give insight into the presupposed rationality of the God of economists and thereby finally prove its positive existence. The libertine would then turn into a true believer. As a good political economist and a subject of private interest, the libertine will obey the imperative to wager, since he can gain infinitely more than he will lose. However, precisely at this point he is duped, for Pascal claims in another part of his fragment on wager that belief emerges from the repetition of senseless rituals. In order to become believers, we do not really need to believe, just as the libertine does not need to believe in order to wager. In fact, he only can wager as far as he does not believe, and through the repetition of wager in the moments of opposite temptation he will be progressively transformed into a religious subject, for religion has no substantial essence; it is an entirely superficial compulsion to repeat. Pascal here surprisingly joins Freud, for whom compulsory action in obsessive neurosis was the model of a religious ritual. The empty ritual finally reveals the true function of the master-signifier: it is the imperative within the compulsory force. But

---

27   Lacan, *The Other Side of Psychoanalysis*, 105–6.

its presence can also be revealed in the successful cohabitation of science and capitalism, as formalised in the university discourse. The imperative 'keep on knowing' that supports the regime of knowledge contains a double demand: organise knowledge in such a way that it will serve for the production of subjects of capitalism and contribute to the stabilisation of the economic Other. In short, produce knowledge that will serve the market and the reproduction of capitalism. That everyone embarked upon the discourse of science simply means that everyone has been turned into a quantified subjectivity.

Lacan emphasises that in the university discourse knowledge appears as 'all-knowledge', not because it would know all but because it is rooted in the foreclosure of negativity that supports its wholeness. University knowledge knows itself as knowledge and even claims to be nothing but knowledge: Stalinist bureaucracy but also capitalist I-cracy, the rule of self-interest and of the 'strong ego'. In Lacan's view, Western capitalism and Soviet communism developed two concurrent systems of power-knowledge, an apparatus of commanding knowledge, in which the Stalinist bureaucrat, the capitalist expert and today's Eurocrat, behind the appearance of neutrality, embody the master that Lacan illustrates with the reference to the transcendental ego, an ego that would be identical with itself, and more precisely, the signifier, which would be its own signified: 'The myth of the ideal I, of the I that masters, of the I whereby at least something is identical to itself, namely the speaker, is very precisely what the university discourse is unable to eliminate from the place in which its truth is found.'[28] The master is the truth of the apparently neutral subject of cognition, and it is all the more understandable why Marx and Freud founded their sciences on the rejection of the ideal of cognition. The truth revealed in the university discourse is not simply that the master is split but that it is reduced to the categorical imperative: 'enjoy', 'work', 'know', three variations of 'serve the system to which you owe your existence'.

THE FIFTH DISCOURSE?

The university discourse was not Lacan's final word on capitalism. A further development took place in 1972, when he determined the foreclosure of castration as the defining feature of capitalist discourse, and in a conference

---

28   Ibid., 63.

in Milan proposed its formula, which many consider an independent structure, the fifth discourse:

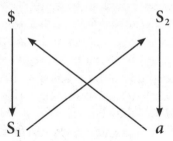

Image 4. The Capitalist Torsion

This development is rather surprising, given that the theory of discourses is grounded on a strict order that supports only four formations.[29] While other discourses depart from a quarter turn, which passes from the fundamental logic (the master's discourse) to other immediate structures and allows only four such turns, without altering the places and their mutual relations, capitalism seems to accomplish a turn that does not displace the elements but the structural places and thereby alters their mutual relations. It inverts the position of truth and agent, which makes the subject appear as an autonomous agent and the initiator of an infinite circulation, from which there is no breakout. The vectors show that the capitalist discourse is grounded on the foreclosure of the impossibility of totalisation that marks other discourses, an impossibility that is structurally determined by the fact that the signifiers constitute an open system of differences. The capitalist *torsion* of the master's discourse, however, claims to establish the missing relation between the subject and the object and even proposes the paradigmatic example of this relation: financial capital.

The immediate consequence of the torsion is the rejection of the split that marks the place of truth, which is, according to Marx and Freud, occupied by a subject, whose being is marked by inconsistency and metonymy because it depends on the system of differences (signifier and exchange-value). To this truth, capitalism opposes its own truth: the subject, here capital, contains a vital power, which supports its automatic

---

29   'If it seems justified to say that the chain, the sequence of letters of this algebra, must not be disturbed, then by performing this operation of a quarter turn we will obtain four structures, and no more, the first of which in some way gives you the starting point' (Ibid., 13).

growth. Lacan's formula anticipates the appearance of the absolute autonomy of financial capital in the epoch of financialisation, but it also specifies
its meaning: financialisation is the rejection of the contradiction between
capital and labour-power from the subjective and social reality and its
replacement by the immanent and seemingly productive split of capital.
Just as in the university discourse, the truth of the master becomes the
determining factor that structures and destabilises reality in the same
move. We can recognise in the proposed torsion of the master's discourse
a translation of Marx's abbreviated circulation (M – M'), in which money
directly engenders more money and value-representation coincides with
value-production.

The fantasy of the subject's self-sufficiency, completeness and vitality
thus echoes Marx's point regarding fetishism and for this reason *cannot*
represent an actual discursive formation but formalises the *appearance* that
traverses all stages in the fetishisation of capitalist abstractions. It is not a
fifth discourse – it is a fake discourse. Moreover, the rejected negativity
returns in the form of the crisis, which necessarily involves production of
surplus populations and demolition of what Milner called the 'waged bour-
geoisie',[30] whose social task is to mediate and neutralise the class-conflict
between the capitalists and the proletariat.[31]

If Lacan's fake 'fifth discourse' formalises anything, then it is the
following:

> As the dominant subject of this process, in which it alternately assumes and
> loses the form of money and the form of commodities, but preserves and
> expands itself through all these changes, value requires above all an inde-
> pendent form by means of which its identity with itself may be asserted.[32]

Marx describes fictitious capital as *übergreifendes Subjekt*, dominating and
self-exceeding subject. The fetishisation of capitalist abstractions contains its
own labour-theory of value, according to which capital *is* the true labouring
power, a subject that represents ($\$ \to S_1$) and engenders ($a \to \$$) itself. Both
meanings of *übergreifen* address the direct continuity of representation and

---

30   J. C. Milner, *Le salaire de l'idéal*, Paris: Seuil, 1997, 23–31.

31   'If, in the modern bourgeois society, every bourgeois tends to become
waged, the direct correspondence that Marx established between the proletariat and
the salariat is interrupted' (Ibid., 23).

32   Marx, *Capital*, Vol. 1, 255.

production in self-valorisation. But there is a more appropriate critical term for this operation, self-fetishisation, the ultimate obscenity of capitalism, which contaminates all levels of production and makes of the most banal commodities sublime incarnations of value. Capital is labour-power without a symptomatic social embodiment but therefore surrounded by a multitude of objects, through which the vital capitalist spectrality adopts and abolishes its sensual form. Capital here assumes another feature of the subject of the signifier, the alteration of appearance and disappearance, the *Fort-Da* movement that Freud described in *Beyond the Pleasure Principle*[33] and Lacan later analysed as the subject's staging of its metonymic becoming. But here the metonymisation of Subject-Capital is brought down to its presumed self-identity, which drives its transformation.

The same spectrality insists in the master's discourse. Not only is capital (S_1) pure difference, like the signifier, but also the appearance of self-valorisation immediately follows from the structural disclosure, which enables the joining of surplus-value to the initial value (the vector $a \rightarrow S_1$). The torsion of the master's discourse displaces this relation to the fantasmatic fusion of the subject and the object ($a \rightarrow \$$), thereby concealing the mutual heterogeneity of labour-power and surplus-value. What political economy does is translate the fetishist attitude in human actions into theoretical constructions, which identify the subject of politics in capital and subsume politics under the structural tendency of capital to self-valorisation. In Marx's critical scenario, however, the subject of politics is radically heterogeneous to the presumed vital forces of capital, and its social embodiment, the proletarian, is the necessary condition for reversing the relation between politics and economy and for detaching the subject of politics from its integration into commodity form.

The spectrality of capital and the political-economic belief it causes (the invisible hand of the market, the quasi-natural necessity of economic laws in liberalism, the absolute autonomy of fictitious capital in neoliberalism) not only denounces the circulation (M – M') as appearance but above all questions the epistemological status of economic knowledge. Political economists, these self-proclaimed scientists of value, treat capital as an autonomous subject and, in the same move, situate their own economic discipline as a subject supposed to know. The belief in economy is not only limited to economists but makes of everyone an amateur economist in the common belief that

---

33   See Freud, *Standard Edition*, Vol. 18, 14ff.

economic knowledge can not only analyse past events, retrospection, and the present state of the market, diagnostic, but also foretell the future of financial flows, prognostic. The presupposition is that economy is a rigorous and positive science of value, with privileged insight into the spirit of capitalism, and consequently that the rationality of the economy is the same as the rationality of financial markets. The ongoing crisis once again unmasked the rootedness of dominating political-economic ideologies in this speculative belief and denounced liberal and neoliberal economy as a pseudoscience.

Marx's analysis of fictitious capital nevertheless assumes a careful position in relation to the autonomy of capital. He does not denounce the structural appearance of self-valorisation as a pure and innocent performative fiction, as it has destabilising consequences, which manifest through the repetition of economic crises and make of capitalism as such an ongoing crisis (the 'permanent revolution' described by the *Communist Manifesto*). The movement of capital seems to overcome all dependency on labour, but the negativity is not eliminated from the system, as it returns in the form of systematic instability. The tendency of structural appearances to absolute autonomy is another description for crisis. The third volume of *Capital* situates this instability, subsequent to the progressive autonomisation of fetishist appearances, in the following way:

As interest-bearing capital, and particularly in its immediate form of interest-bearing money-capital . . . capital obtains its pure fetish form, $M - M'$ being the subject, a thing for sale. Firstly, by way of its continuing existence as money, a form, in which all capital's determinations are dissolved and its real elements are invisible. Money is in fact the very form in which the distinctions between commodities as different use-values are obliterated, and hence also the distinctions between the industrial capitals, which consist of these commodities and the conditions of their production; it is the form, in which value – and here capital – exists as autonomous exchange-value. In the reproduction process of capital, the money form is an evanescent moment, a moment of mere transition. On the money market, on the contrary, capital always exists in this form. Secondly, the surplus-value it creates, here again in this form of money, appears to accrue to it as such. Like the growth of trees, so the generation of money seems a property of capital in this form of money capital.[34]

---

34   K. Marx, *Capital*, Vol. 3, London: Penguin Books, 1993, 517.

Again, what Marx claims here is not that we have the good solid ground for the production of use-values and the bad progressive abstraction from commodity-production. The fetishist circle is closed and the most immediate production is always-already mediated by the capitalist abstractions, which display the same autonomy at the level of the commodity form and fictitious capital. The problem lies in false representation of the autonomy of exchange-value. Marx also writes: 'In $M - M'$ we have the irrational form of capital, the misrepresentation and objectification of the relations of production, in its highest power.'[35] The misrepresentation lies precisely in objectification, which makes the autonomy of structural relations appear in the form of an uncanny, self-engendering and absolutely autonomous Thing. Here it becomes obvious once again that the subject is in any case not misrepresented. The subject is foreclosed – this is the central point of Marx's critique of fetishism. Or, stated differently, the subject *is* misrepresented insofar as it is fictionalised as a positive vital force of capital and not as decentralised negativity that traverses the universe of capitalist abstractions and sabotages the seemingly self-generating mechanism of value. The relations of production are represented without any trace of negative production, such as of indebted subjects, surplus populations and so on.

The autonomy of exchange-value is the rational kernel from which the representation of social relations should depart. Yet the fetishist belief makes the irrational move of mistaking the autonomy of relations for the autonomy of the object. The abstraction from use-value eliminates the difference between commodities and commodity-producing commodity, the product and the producer. Capital, of course, can also become the producer, but then we are dealing with the structure of the university discourse, in which the product of appropriation of surplus-product is the indebted subject. It is impossible to assimilate the representation of the subject through the system of differences. This is why capital can never coincide entirely with the subject, abolish the negativity of labour-power and resolve the initial paradox of the commodity universe, according to which there is one commodity that differs from other commodities and in the end embodies the non-identity of commodities and values with themselves. This symptomatic commodity finally unveils the non-identity of capital: capital is neither a subject nor an object but an internally broken process.

The foreclosure of negativity strengthens the belief in the existence of the Other: through misrepresentation the market can appear as a positive entity,

---

35   Ibid., 516.

not merely the abstract Other of liberalism, the neutral and spontaneous rationality of Smith's invisible hand but also the capricious Other of neoliberalism, which demands cuts, saving, renunciation from its economic subjects. Financialisation intensifies the unconscious belief in the Other's positive existence and the God of the economists effectively replaces the God of philosophers as well as the God of religion. This change is the direct result of the capitalist inversion in the social function of fetishism, its transformation into the fetishism of the object, which allows only divinities according to the model of the God of economists. The circle of belief seems entirely closed. The more the market reality is unstable, the stronger the belief in the Other becomes, the more the fetishisation of capital appears as its self-fetishisation and the more vulgar political economy subordinates politics:

> For vulgar economics, which seeks to present capital as an independent source of wealth, of value creation, this form is of course a godsend, a form in which the source of profit is no longer recognizable and in which the result of the capitalist production process – separate from the process itself – obtains an autonomous existence.[36]

Again, the most problematic aspect of economic fetishism is not the assertion of discursive autonomy but the substantialisation of capital, the detachment of the autonomy of exchange-value from the negative it inevitably produces. Based on this appearance, we can again focus on the relations between the elements in Lacan's formula of the capitalist discourse, which allow the following reformulation:

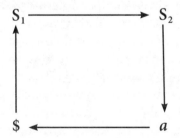

Image 5. The Capitalist Circle

This writing explains Lacan's remark that the master's discourse 'embraces everything, even what thinks of it as revolutionary . . . The master's

---

36   Ibid., 517.

discourse accomplishes its own revolution in the other sense of doing a complete circle.'[37] The permanent revolution sustained by the fetishisation of financial abstractions incessantly returns to its departure. No permutation of elements alters the structural relations. The exit from capitalism is experienced as a structural impossibility: 'Indeed this cannot go better. But the thing is that it goes too fast, that it consumes itself, it consumes itself so well that it wears itself out. The crisis, not of the master's discourse, but of the capitalist discourse, which is its substitute, is open.'[38] The self-fetishisation of capital *is* synonymous with crisis, but this crisis is merely a total distortion of class struggle. Eventually it produces a critical mass of surplus population, which reintroduces the class antagonisms into the picture. This is also one of the results in the ongoing crisis, in which the old antagonism between capital and labour-power re-emerged in the core of the creditor-debtor relation.

Lacan's formula of the capitalist discourse continues the line according to which capitalism essentially tends towards the foreclosure of castration. Its worldview strives to heal the subjective split by way of the fetishisation of the object, which would establish a univocal relation between the subject and *jouissance*. Of course, the foreclosure of castration does not imply that *jouissance* becomes accessible. On the contrary, the foreclosure radicalises the deadlock of *jouissance* and turns the superego into an insatiable demand for *jouissance*.

The imperative of *jouissance* throws additional light on the problem that Dostoyevsky addressed through the death of God. For Dostoyevsky, this death implies that everything is permitted, thereby proposing an imaginary and inherently religious understanding of its consequences. Together with the death of authority, the symbolic mandate of the law collapses, the barricade between the subject and *jouissance*, which makes the latter immediately accessible. Lacan repeatedly proposed to correct Dostoyevsky on this point with the lesson contained in the Freudian myth, according to which the symbolic law emerged from the killing of the primordial father. The Freudian conclusion directly reverses Dostoyevsky's assumption: the death of God does not abolish the law; it constitutes it and implies universal prohibition. If God is dead, then nothing is permitted. The death of the obscene father, this uncastrated bearer of castration, who limits his sons'

---

37   Lacan, *The Other Side of Psychoanalysis*, 99.

38   J. Lacan, 'Du discours psychanalytique', in: *Lacan in Italia 1953–1978*, Milan: La Salamandra, 1978, 48.

access to *jouissance*, does not bring liberation from prohibition. The dead father returns in the symbolic in the form of the superego. Freud's founding myth contains a rational kernel, according to which the abolition of the real obstacle constitutes the symbolic prohibition, and the signifier colonises the place that the father's death left empty. The imperative character of the signifier becomes the symbolic representative of the dead father. However, this Freudian conclusion remains within the paradigm of the contradiction between the signifier and *jouissance*, which marked Lacan's early developments, and fails to account for the genesis of capitalist morality, which grounds the production of *jouissance* on its renunciation. Renunciation does not disappear, neither in the regime of prohibition nor in the regime of permission. While Dostoyevsky's conclusion turned out to be too religious, Freud's remained too mythical. Lacan's second return to Freud finds in Marx the response that allows him to situate the real consequence of the death of God, which resides in the transformation of the relation between the signifier and *jouissance*. If God is dead, then *jouissance* is neither allowed nor prohibited but ordered and imposed. This imposition can be situated in every particular commodity and more generally in the commodity form as the privileged form of *jouissance* in capitalism. The death of God undermines the demarcation of prohibition from permission, and while the permission of *jouissance* still implies a possible defence (negation or disavowal), which prevents the intrusion of *jouissance* into the subject, the imperative abolishes this barrier. Castration is displaced from the symbolic law, which permits and prohibits, to the imperative of *jouissance*, which now imposes its own obscene law.

The capitalist foreclosure of castration and the transformation of *jouissance* into an imperative additionally situate Lacan's identification of the student with the helot. Lacan's prosopopoeia of the regime, 'Look at them enjoying', can be read as the flip side of the prosopopoeia of the capitalist superego. Jacques-Alain Miller has argued that this prosopopoeia reveals the impotence of the regime's gaze to produce shame and to be the bearer of castration.[39] But there is much more at stake in this metaphor than the impotence of the gaze. The gaze is rather the incarnation of the regime's power. It places the subject, in Lacan's concrete case the student, in the position of the object of the regime's *jouissance*, hence in the position of perversion. The subjects offer themselves to the regime's gaze and

---

39   J. A. Miller, 'On Shame', in: Clemens and Grigg, *Jacques Lacan and the Other Side of Psychoanalysis*, 14–15.

shamelessly exhibit *jouissance*, not knowing that the regime in the position they assume establishes the continuity between *jouissance* and labour. Once in the position of surplus-object, the students are themselves *studied* by the regime's gaze. Their demand for *jouissance* without castration – *Vivre sans temps mort, jouir sans entraves*, to recall the famous graffiti from 1968 – is the productive ground for the *jouissance* of the system. Life without boredom (dead time) and enjoyment without restriction (or without castration) inaugurate a new, more radical and invisible form of exploitation. Of course, the inevitable truth of creativity, mobility and flexibility of labour is the creativity, mobility and flexibility of the capitalist forms of domination.

Masochism gives the key to the capitalist foreclosure of castration. One of the main differences between masochism and its opposite, sadism, is in the articulation of *jouissance* with shame. Sade's bureaucratic descriptions of torture show that the sadist's aim is not to turn pain into pleasure but precisely to cause shame. Shame signals *jouissance* and emerges at the point when the victim becomes aware that her enjoyment has become visible. In Sade, shame is the sign of castration. It therefore makes sense to describe Sade as the one who suspended the commodification of *jouissance*,[40] and thereby reintroduced negativity into enjoyment. Sade could draw a limit to fetishist *jouissance* because his position remained in the grey zone between the ancien régime of the lord and the serf and the new regime of the capitalist and the labourer. Shame confronts the subject with its own status as a commodity-producing commodity, hence as a producer of the *jouissance* of the system, whereby we can again recall that Lacan declares the superego to be the imperative of *jouissance* in reference to Sade. In this respect, sadism remains an essential component of the capitalist *dispositif*, a component that nevertheless addresses the truth of the conversion of the prohibition of *jouissance* into its injunction.

At the same time, masochism is not only a perversion, in which commodity fetishism plays a significant role, but also the perversion that is essentially defined by the absence of shame, the neutralisation of the castrating power of the master's gaze. While in Sade's scenarios the distribution of the roles seems univocal, masochism blurs the fact that behind its contract a subversion of domination took place. The subject, who can enjoy in the position of the object, is the only true master, while the apparent executor is merely a prop, a subject for whom the contract presupposes *not to enjoy*. The contract demands a castrated master, deprived of the power to

---

40 See Milner, *Le triple du plaisir*, 89.

cause shame; it prevents him from causing pain, which would exceed a certain limit. The role of the contract in masochism shows why there cannot be any sexual relation between the sadist and the masochist. In sadism, the involuntarily character of *jouissance* is crucial, the victim finds in torture more than she expects, she encounters the negativity of castration in the intertwining of pain and *jouissance*, while masochism neutralises the possibility of deviation from fantasmatic *jouissance* in pain into the real pain of *jouissance*. Sadism reveals the truth of *jouissance, das Unbehagen im Genießen*, discontent in enjoyment, whereas masochism avoids the moment of this discontent by taking unpleasure as an immediate source of pleasure, thereby establishing the alliance between sexuality and the rejection of castration through the commodity form.

In this respect, the masochist would indeed be the perfect subject of capitalism, someone who would enjoy being a commodity among others, while assuming the role of surplus labour, the position of the object that willingly satisfies the systemic demands. The capitalist regime demands from everyone to become ideal masochists and the actual message of the superego's injunction is: 'enjoy your suffering, enjoy capitalism'.

Conclusion: Politics and Modernity

In his reading of Lacan, Jean-Claude Milner proposed a brief but provocative reading of what he calls Lacan's 'anti-politics', an orientation that he carefully distinguishes from simple rejection of politics or political indifference. From the perspective of Freud's cultural pessimism and Lacan's ambiguous position towards revolutionary movements, 'politics . . . turns out to be radically unsynchronised with the modern universe . . . Is it a coincidence that, if speaking about the state, democracy, domination or freedom, politics speaks Greek and Latin (as far as it speaks at all; in most cases it mutters)?'[1] For Milner, modernity means first and foremost scientific modernity, the great revolution in knowledge initiated by seventeenth- and eighteenth-century physics and progressively extended to other fields, including the critique of political economy, psychoanalysis and structuralism, which mobilised its political weight: after the decentralisation of the universe in physics and the decentralisation of life in biology followed the trichotomous decentralisation of history, thinking and language. Milner here rephrases Freud, for whom the scientific revolution is understood correctly only by extending its operations and consequences from the natural sciences to the human sciences, the final revolutionary stage. Freud saw the main achievement of this historical development as the direct undermining of human narcissism and the goal of scientific modernity in the instauration of an epistemological and political condition, for which he proposed the enigmatic description 'dictatorship of reason'. All this is directly opposed to what is at stake in capitalism, the dictatorship of irrational beliefs and the restoration of human narcissism, the self-love and self-interest that Adam Smith and other political economists took for the foundation of social relations. The lack of synchronicity between politics and modernity comes down to the implementation of

---

1   Milner, *L'oeuvre claire*, 151.

economic fictions in politics and the enthroning of economy as some sort of new 'queen of sciences'. Capitalism constructs an economic-theocratic order, which entirely absorbs politics and science. In this scenario, critical orientations like Marx's and Freud's indeed engage in what Althusser called 'class struggle in theory', which evolves around the fact that, after the God of religion and the God of philosophers have been pronounced dead, what remains is the God of economists. The abolition of the economic theocracy is the necessary condition for the synchronisation of politics with the modern universe.

Capitalist democracies claim for themselves the title of political inheritors and responses to the modern scientific revolution. But Marx already drew attention to the fact that the political signifiers of the French Revolution – freedom, equality and fraternity – were transformed by property and private interest. These political-economic signifiers rejected the idea of fraternity and restricted the revolutionary character of freedom and equality through the narcissism of the private. Fraternity, however, strives to found the social link on a form of *philia* that Marx had also been aiming at when he described the communist society as an association of free subjects: freed of the narcissism of private interests, which are, in the last instance, determined by the imperatives of capital. Of course, Marx did not create the illusion that the features of the communist social order could be foretold. What is certain is that such a political project demands 'rigorous workers', to use Lacan's expression from his founding act of École freudienne de Paris.

In an infinite universe, where nature no longer speaks Aristotelian and scholastic language but adopts the language of geometry and mathematics, as Galileo wrote, politics continues to use dead languages, which root it in the old topology of political space. Both languages also serve as metaphors for the general space of thinking. Aristotle and the scholastics are inevitably associated with the closed cosmological model, the system of spheres that knows no outside, while the language of mathematics immediately connotes the modern infinite universe. To this reading one could easily object that the main problem of modern politics is not so much tied to dead languages but to the fact that politics is compromisingly intertwined with a highly problematic living language: commodity language, the language of economic liberalism and neoliberalism, which precisely is modern and no less autonomous as the language of mathematics.

From a Marxist perspective, the problem is then not in a hypothetical pre-modernity of politics but rather in the fact that there is no structure of political emancipation or, as Lacan has put it, no discourse of which the proletarian, this universal subjective position in modernity, could make a social link. Political language was absorbed into the abstract language of economic categories, which consequently led to the reduction of subversive social movements first to democratic and later to identitarian politics. An even more dramatic failure marked the revolutionary attempts to build a free and egalitarian communist society, in which politics exercised structural and real violence under the pretence of abolishing capitalist social relations and reintroducing presumably immediate relations between men, which it eventually did in the form of immediate relations of domination and a state-sanctioned system of terror. Back in the democratic context, identitarian politics pursued the proliferation of minoritarian identities and moved towards the problematic of representation (e.g., gender quotas), which successfully neutralised the language of revolutionary politics. The subject of identitarian politics no less rejects the actual subject of revolutionary politics, which is constitutively pre-identitarian, non-individual and non-psychological, hence irreducible to particular identities or identifications. In the end, identity politics proposes its own version of a narcissistic subject.

For the non-identical subject of the unconscious, Freud and Lacan argued that it could be discovered only under the conditions and within the horizon of the modern scientific revolution. This means that the subject of modern politics *is* the subject of modern science, and while politics grounded on the economic and legal abstractions repeats the capitalist rejection of this negative subjectivity, communist politics would have to start from the practical mobilisation and organisation of the subject that Marx isolated in his science of value. Lacan's reading of Marx insists that his critique comes down to the effort of such theoretical isolation, a materialist theory of the subject, which provides a new orientation of political practice. While capitalism considers the subject to be nothing more than a narcissistic animal, Marxism and psychoanalysis reveal that the subject of revolutionary politics is an alienated animal, which, in its most intimate interior, includes its other. This inclusion is the main feature of a non-narcissistic love and consequently of a social link that is not rooted in self-love.

Anti-politics comes down to an attempt to go against the politics of capital and the 'democratic' politics of human narcissism. Recall Lacan's declaration that the aim of psychoanalysis is the 'exit from the capitalist discourse . . . for everyone.'[2] Indeed, Lacan's take on politics is, despite all the

2   Lacan, *Autres écrits*, 520.

appearances, not that foreign to Deleuze and Guattari's *Anti-Oedipus*. One of the crucial tasks of their versions of the critique of libidinal economy is the liberation of desire from commodity form, the unique formal envelope of thinking in modernity, by means of which capitalist abstractions colonise the mental apparatus and determine unconscious mechanisms. Lacan's quarrel with the authors of *Anti-Oedipus* and with the revolutionary students, who sought their political inspiration in Reich and Marcuse, turned around the signification of this liberation, which comes down to the theory of the subject. Does a radical political program of liberation necessitate the disso-lution of the link between subjectivity and negativity? Should one not, rather, determine the subject of politics by following Marx's example when he recognised in the proletariat the symptomatic and negative point, from which the capitalist mode of production can be undermined and, more importantly, the impersonal and non-narcissistic foundation of politics can be extracted? A materialist theory of the subject, such as that proposed by structural psychoanalysis and the critique of political economy, is the logical response to the capitalist rejection of negativity.

The main political and epistemological contribution of the critique of political economy is worth recalling here. Marx introduced two corrections of classical political economy, which served as the general points of departure in his mature work. The first correction concerns the autonomy of value that political economists mistakenly understood in terms of vital force or positive quality of commodity, money and capital. In other words, they conceived the autonomy in question as an external object. This is what Marx calls fetishism. For the critique of political economy, however, the autonomy in question should be envisaged not as some positive substance but in terms of logic. Marx's second correction concerns the labour theory of value. Unlike the English economists, who saw in labour a source of value, Marx's surprisingly banal yet far-reaching differentiation between labour-process and labour-power (use-value and exchange-value) unveils a structural paradox, which is, as such, the driving force of the capitalist mode of production. Labour-power materialises the structural gap, which is contained in the commodity form and which becomes the actual source of value. Marx indeed proposes some-thing that one could call a *non-relational theory of value*: the fact that there is no such thing as social relation is indeed profitable (for some).

Lacan's reading takes a step further by recognising in labour-power the distorted version of the subject of modern science. For both Marx and Lacan, the negative, which, again, means the non-narcissistic subject, is the necessary singular point on which political universalism should build. The capitalist appropriation of the subject cannot ground any real political universalism because it places the subject in the position of the object. Transformed into labour-power, the subject is turned into one among many things that constitute the 'immense collection of commodities' (Marx). The subject becomes 'human capital'. This *Aufhebung* of the subject in the object is necessarily accompanied by the production of fetishist scenarios and pseudoscientific economic hypotheses, which place capital in the position of the exclusive subject of politics. The tendency of capital to self-valorisation neutralises every attempt to ground politics on anything other than private interest, not the private interest of some hypothetical *homo oeconomicus* but of capital. From this perspective, Milner's thesis of the premodern nature of contemporary politics might turn out to be more Marxist than it seems, under the condition that the same reproach can be addressed to capitalism. Capitalism then needs to be thought of as the restoration of pre-modernity within modernity, a counter-revolution that neutralises the emancipatory political potential of scientific revolution.

For Freud, pre-modernity meant to remain in worldviews rather than adopting the revolutionary lessons of modern science. By filling the gaps in reality, worldviews strive to construct a closed world, marked by totality, finitude and centralisation, while the modern universe seems to contain nothing but contingency, infinity and instability, three features that go against the rootedness of human narcissism in thinking. Capitalism seems to have embraced all of them. Not only did it present itself as the paradigm of modernity (we still hear that modernity essentially means capitalist modernity: industrial and post-industrial revolution, which precisely conditions the social process with scientific progress), but also capitalist reality appears as infinite, disclosed and unstable as the universe of modern science. If modern science abolished the ancient division of the superlu-nary and the sublunary world, capitalism willingly adopted the scientific thesis: there is, indeed, only one world, the global market, which brings 'the stars down to Earth', rejecting the divide of social reality between a 'super-lunary' feudal and religious master and the 'sublunary' serf. Capitalism and science go equally well together when it comes to the permanent revolution of the means of production, which makes the modernity of capitalism unquestionable. But this modernity ceases at the critical point of the subject.

In order to account for the existence of the subject, capitalism produces a system of economic, political and juridical fictions, which strive to conceal the politically subversive and destabilising non-identity that constitutes the subject, and more importantly, which strive to disavow the impossibility of the integral commodification of the subject. Of course, the instability of capitalism is structural, to the extent that every economic crisis reveals the normal functioning of capitalism. However, the core of the crisis is not so much the incapacity of capitalist fetishisations to regulate the instability of financial capital and the impossibility to provide prospective insight into the 'spirit of capitalism' but the production of global surplus populations, which personify the return of the rejected negativity. The crisis itself is internally doubled and equivocal, it contains a crisis within the crisis, in which the social masses articulate their rejection of the commodity form as the sole realistic political universalism offered by capitalism.

Let us here recall Koyré's interpretation of the modern scientific revolution and its Lacanian extension to psychoanalysis. Modernity stands for two ground-breaking effects: (1) the abolition of the cosmological division on the higher sphere of eternal mathematical truths and the lower sphere of generation and corruption, where the use of mathematics made little sense for the old *episteme*; (2) the abolition of the hypothesis of the soul, which is replaced by a new hypothesis, that of the subject. Unlike the metaphysical soul, which presupposes the premodern cosmologies, the modern subject implies a different topology of thinking, which questions the primacy of the centralised ego. The shared modernity of the critique of political economy and psychoanalysis consists in the fact that their materialist theory of the subject went against the reduction of subjectivity to consciousness or to private interest. From the Marxian and Freudian perspectives, to say false consciousness is to pronounce a pleonasm, since there is no other consciousness than false consciousness.

In its materialist orientation, psychoanalysis stands in immediate continuity with Saussure's discovery of the autonomy of the signifier, which provided the first modern, non-Aristotelian theory of language, and with Marx's departure from the autonomy of exchange-value, which developed the first defetishised economic theory. All three sciences provide rigorous demystifications of thinking, language and value, hence of social relations and of subjectivity. Both autonomies in question provide insight into the structural conditions of capitalism, but in order for capitalism to emerge the commodification of the subject and the mathematisation of the surplus-object need to take place. The ambiguity of capitalism resides in this process, in respect to both ground-breaking consequences of modern science. On the one hand, it does seem to pursue the scientific move by quantifying both the subject and the object, but on the other hand it restores the soul through the feigned hypotheses of commodity fetishism. The capitalist fetishisation fills reality with spectral entities and enthrones capital as the vital soul of the world, the highest sphere of the closed capitalist world, from which, as we are told, there is no exit, unless we want to finish in a new barbarism. In this respect, capitalism reinstalled the division in the superlunary sphere, now inhabited by the capitalist abstractions subjected to mathematisation, which would, ideally, provide their future predictability, and the sublunary sphere, where a contingent and non-mathematical interplay of particular interests and political manipulations takes place. The highest sphere (financial capital) continues to move all other spheres of human production.

One revolutionary feature of modern science, to recall Koyré's main thesis, lies in the fact that its use of mathematics no longer sustains the phenomena and is not centralised on the way reality appears to the human observer. This move abolishes the three cornerstones of the ancient *episteme:* totality, harmony and regularity, which are not incidentally the three main features that the liberal and neoliberal political economies attribute to the laws of the market (self-regulation and economic homeostasis). Financial mathematics distorts the structural instabilities and inequalities in capitalism and conceals that the capitalist fetishisations cannot bridge the gap between the conglomerate of economic fantasies and political subjectivity that capitalism inevitably reproduces. In opposition to these scenarios, Marx's and Lacan's methods and concepts offer a critical tool, which corrupts the ongoing fetishisation of economy as a subject supposed to know. In the last instance, predominant economic knowledge contains a conglomerate of irrational beliefs and a systematic strategy to repress the fact that the creation of wealth requires the reproduction of premodern relations of domination and subjection.

Finally, what does the combination 'Marx *and* Lacan' stand for? Lacan next to Marx questions the optimistic and humanist readings, according to which Marx's critique aims to break out of symbolic determinations, negativity and alienation. Marx next to Lacan questions the pessimistic and apolitical readings, according to which Lacan's reformulation of the structuralist project supposedly amounts to the recognition of the 'universal madness' and autism of *jouissance*, which dissolve the social links, and to the affirmation of the discursive a priori, which determines human actions and presumably reveals the illusionary features of every attempt in radical politics. The shared logical and political project of psychoanalysis and Marxism is to determine the terrain in which the subject is constituted and to detach this subject from its commodified form that capitalism imposes on everyone through direct forms of domination as well as through the hyper-fetishisation of financial abstractions.

Marx and Lacan thus highlight two aspects of modernity that still call for political realisation and that map the terrain of political and theoretical struggles for the exit from capitalism. One is the necessity to mobilise the subversive dimension of modern science that Freud so persistently accentuated. Here, the theoretical struggle for the extension of scientificity takes place, a struggle that Koyré exemplified in his insistence on the Platonist nature of the modern scientific revolution: Plato against Aristotle, Descartes against Bacon, revolutionary science versus the combination of positivism and quantification. To repeat one last time, for Marx, science could and should amount to the liberation of the labourer from labour, which means the liberation of the subject from the commodity form. For Freud, science could and should suspend human narcissism, which means detaching the subject from the ego and politics from private interest. Science is one of the central terrains of political struggle precisely because it became the main tool of capitalism against the realisation of political modernity. A materialist reading of modern science necessarily includes the question of its subject, as Lacan's critical appropriation of epistemological questions constantly demonstrates. The second unrealised aspect of modernity is directly related to the first one and concerns the actualisation of the third term that drove the French Revolution, *fraternité*, the enigmatic signifier of communism, which is only possible under the condition that a materialist theory of the subject replaces idealist theories, through which the capitalist economy managed to take politics and the entirety of social reality as its hostage. Only then will politics be consistently in sync with modern science and inhabit the same universe.

Index

Bold indicates image.